Healing Racism:
Education's Role

For Inez & Paul,
much warmth,
strength & love,
Nathan Rutstein

Healing Racism:
Education's Role

Edited by
Nathan Rutstein
Michael Morgan

Design by Chester Makoski, Jr.

ISBN: 0-9633007-3-3

Library of Congress Card Number: 96-60133

Acknowledgements

Without Carroll Robbins' meticulous copy editing and formatting suggestions, this book would not have taken its present shape. We also deeply appreciate his patience, good common sense and gentle manner in guiding us through the development of *Healing Racism: Education's Role.*

TABLE OF CONTENTS

Introduction IX

1 Racism as a Disease 1
by John Woodall

2 Children as Sacred Beings 39
by Robert Atkinson and Patricia Locke

3 Racism and Anxiety: Talk to Kids about Unity 59
by Anita Remignanti

4 Creating Racial Harmony in the Learning Center 77
by Bernie Streets

5 Why and How the History of Racism Should be Taught in Schools 105
by Tod Rutstein

6 School and the Child of Color 133
by LeNise Jackson-Gaertner

7 Taking a Close Look at Self-Esteem, and How to Strengthen It in Children of Color 147
by Bernie Streets

8 Why Many Students of Color Have Trouble Learning in Schools 177
by Nathan Rutstein

9 Advice for Teachers on Racism and Oneness 187
by Barbara Hacker

10 Prejudice-free Schools: A Vision of the Future 205
by Donald Streets

11 Healing Racism: Education's Role 225
by Brian Aull, Barbara Hacker, Robert Postlewaite, Nathan Rutstein and Tod Rutstein

12 Institutes for the Healing of Racism in Primary and Secondary Schools 249
by Paul Herron

13 Institutes for the Healing of Racism on University Campuses 261
by Denise Gifford

14 May This Circle Be Unbroken: Race and the Teaching of English 279
by Michael Morgan

15 Cooperative Learning and Racial Harmony: Working Together with a Difference 309
by Lynn Kirk

16 The School of Education's Role in Healing Racism 335
by Nathan Rutstein

Appendix 345

About the Contributors 355

Introduction

Because we are in the midst of a great social transformation, teachers and educators from kindergarten to college are being asked to perform duties with which their professional predecessors didn't have to bother. This is causing considerable tension and frustration, even disillusionment, within the educational community, mainly because most teachers and educators haven't been trained to carry out these duties.

Yet, it is our belief, and the belief of the contributors to this book, that the work has to be done. One of the duties which we believe to be the responsibility of every educator in this nation is the elimination of prejudice, not only because our schools and classrooms are the logical places to help in the struggle to heal the disease of racism, but for practical reasons. More and more racial flare-ups are being reported at all levels of the formal educational spectrum, causing school administrators to resort to reactive measures. Finding the means to create and preserve social tranquility in the classroom becomes their primary priority. While that reflex is understandable, because the protection and safety of students, staff and faculty is important, it doesn't address the core problem. Nor does stressing political correctness and multiculturalism, because they fail to address the core problem: the poison of prejudice in human hearts.

At best, multiculturalism can create a sense of toleration, but that's a fragile condition. At worst, political correctness can cause students and parents to rebel against institutions or individuals who try to impose what often amounts to superficial codes of conduct upon them. The end result is that any small incident or irrational act is able to dash the condition of "correctness", and humans end up reverting to deep-seated attitudes which can set off racist behavior in overt and subtle ways.

The challenge facing our educational institutions is how to inculcate in students healthy attitudes towards people of different cultures, and an understanding of the reality of the oneness of humankind, a principle to which many of the contributors of this book allude. An additional challenge is to provide teachers, administrators and parents with the mechanism to deal with their own biases and prejudices. None of us is completely free of prejudice.

This book provides educators and parents with penetrating insights into the nature of the problem, and practical approaches on how to solve it. Some may feel that the ideas are too difficult to apply to their own work, but a new approach is necessary; what we're doing now is not working. While teachers and scholars may have given up hope and remain steadfastly cynical about solving the problems of racism, we haven't.

A wide range of subjects is covered. For example: the sacredness of the child; the parent's role in producing a prejudice-free human being; ideas for pre-school; why students should learn how racism developed in America, and how to teach about it; an explanation of the pathology of the disease of racism; two chapters on how racism affects students of color; the role of the principal in creating a school-wide campaign to heal racism; cooperative learning as a means of creating racial harmony.

Since we view the internalization of the principle of the oneness of mankind as a vaccine for the disease of racism, we are devoting a chapter to the subject of how to integrate that principle into school curricula. To help teachers, administrators and parents work at overcoming their own prejudices, we offer a chapter on how to set up ongoing, non-threatening and healing mechanisms in their schools. There is also a chapter on the success of the University of Louisville in operating on-campus Institutes for the Healing of Racism. (Guidelines on how to set up an Institute for the Healing of Racism are given in the appendix of this book.)

An English professor at another university, the co-editor of this book, describes how he helps his students develop a commitment to overcome their personal prejudices and aid others in their struggle. The final chapter, by the other co-editor of this book, challenges schools of education to take a proactive role in healing racism. It provides practical steps as to how this can be done, including the kinds of undergraduate and graduate courses and programs that should be taught.

Most of the contributing writers, who come from a variety of racial, ethnic and professional backgrounds, have tried and tested what they offer as a solution. Some of the contributors are university professors and administrators, some are public school teachers and administrators, some are professionals in other areas, while some are simply enlightened individuals who have no formal degrees or titles, but know, and care deeply about healing racism.

Some writers are represented more than once in this book, and this is because their expertise extends to more than one aspect of the disease of racism. A few share family memberships, and their presence is more than coincidental. It is a measure of the concern often felt by persons who are in close touch with each other, and in a position to exchange views on vital subjects.

Because of the diversity of the backgrounds of these writers, this text is diverse in its manner of presentation. Some chapters are more traditionally "scholarly", while others are first-person narrative. When asking individuals to contribute to this book, we did not seek to obtain work high on theory and academic approaches, although some writers, indeed, come from that background. What we intended was to present a collection of work which inspires and informs, and which distinguishes itself by the depth of its healing capacity rather than by the depth of its sources or citations.

Nathan Rutstein
Michael Morgan

Chapter 1

Racism as a Disease

by John Woodall

The author, a psychiatrist and professor at Harvard University School of Medicine, asserts that racism is a disease. He believes that both the condition of racism, and its subsequent denial, are pathological in the personal, social and institutional character of this country. Furthermore, he believes that the country's failure to address the issue of race as a disease has made it much easier to neglect a host of other social ills which have contributed, in his opinion, to the "balkanization of America." He asserts that blacks have internalized a "pathological" suspicion of whites, and that, similarly, whites have pathologically internalized their view that people of color are inferior.

If we want to solve a problem we have to understand its nature. Educators have failed to understand that racism is a disease, not a fad, ideology or simple prejudice. It is, as the author points out, deeply rooted in the collective consciousness of the American population. Because it is important to understand the pathological aspect of racism, this chapter serves as a preface to the entire book. Ed.

The intent of this chapter is not to advocate for specific policy approaches to racism. Rather, the concern of this chapter is to look at over-arching principles that can guide the discussion. Considering racism as a disease is a powerful model. We will delve into principles inherent in all healthy living things, including the human body, as well as those found to be of benefit in psychotherapy to explore the perimeters of the notion of racism as disease. But first, I would be remiss as a physician if certain health care demographics that appear to be greatly influenced by race were ignored.

There are many ways to evaluate the general health of a group. Infant mortality is a particularly sensitive indicator of general health standards in a population. To quote Congressman John Dingle in the congressional hearings on "Infant Mortality Rates: Failure to Close the Black-White Gap," in March, 1984, "... black infant mortality remains twice the white race rate in the United States." Congressman Mikey Leland pointed out in those same congressional hearings that in some districts in Texas, black infant mortality was up to 95 percent higher than whites in the same district. Jeffrey Taylor, chief of the Division of Maternal and Child Health of the Michigan Department of Public Health, testified at the same hearings that in Michigan this statewide gap between black and white was 152 percent and in Detroit, 186 percent! These rates compare with the bleak health status in Haiti, and other of the world's most prostrate nations.

In that year, 1984, this country spent $26 billion on 226 MX missiles, $120 million each. One of those missiles would have fully funded a national pre-natal care program that could have dramatically alleviated this terrible human suffering and loss. Yet, even if these funds were available for pre-natal care, it is unlikely that they would have been distributed in ways that would equally benefit people of color in this country. The issue of race plays a role in the distribution of these resources, as Congressman Leland's point implies. In this way alone, one's color influences one's health.

For instance, a black child, Martin, born in 1995, has twice the chance of dying before his first birthday as Charles, born at the same time to white parents. Martin will be at greater risk for an early death from preventable and chronic illnesses including heart disease, stroke, cancer, diabetes and others. But first, little Martin will have to survive his teens and early twenties, when he will have a 1 in 21 chance of dying from homicide, compared to Charles, who will experience a chance of 1 in 131.

Martin's baby sister, Vanessa, will have a greater chance of dying of breast cancer than Charles's sister, Jenny. Vanessa, if she grows to be an old woman, is likely to die in a house fire. First, she will have to escape the poverty trap of teen pregnancy in which she might doom herself and another generation to a cycle of limited opportunity. Although Martin and Vanessa can expect to live longer lives than their parents will, Martin is likely to die six and one half years before Charles, and Vanessa five years before Jenny. While the life expectancy for blacks is increasing, the gap between black and whites is also increasing.

There are certain illnesses which blacks have at disproportionate rates over whites. Some of these have genetic predispositions. Yet, each of the chronic illnesses to which black Americans are most prone have risk factors affected by educational and social factors. The risk factors for blacks that contribute most to the disproportion in health statistics included cigarette consumption, alcohol consumption, socioeconomic differentials, differences in sexual and reproductive behavior, nutritional and dietary differences, hypertension, and obesity. These risk factors are all subject to considerations of access to educational and social resources. That access is influenced by race.

Cancer mortality rates are an example. If black and white persons are both presented to a doctor with their cancer at a similar stage in its progression, the black person still will have a shorter life expectancy. Socioeconomic factors can explain most of this difference. These factors have been identified as: (l) a greater occupational and social exposure to many cancer-causing agents*; (2) his image of cancer as a lethal disease, which causes him not to seek treatment as aggressively; (3) economic and medical access variables that cause him to be less effectively treated; (4) differences in disease type, with many histological types attacking blacks more aggressively; and (5) general differences in health status resulting in lower resistance to the tumor. Four of these five risk factors are directly related to the social position many blacks find themselves in due to their race. Disease itself is part of the disease of racism.

**Toxic waste dumping tends to occur near poor urban areas which are disproportionately populated by blacks.*

These statistics are a sign of a larger personal and social bleakness a black child growing up in America must endure. To many, these pressures crush the spirit. The subsequent loss of hope feeds a growing sense of desperation and then anger, which too often is turned against himself and society. Certainly, this is no small part of the disease of racism.

Although statistics cannot prove that racism is the cause of these health differentials, it is unquestionable that race is a critical risk factor in one's health. The science of statistics does not allow us to categorically state that these health discrepancies are caused by racism. But, these statistics clearly show that to be a person of color in America, particularly black, is a health hazard. One can dispute the ability of statistics to prove racism itself. But to ignore the issue of race as a critical risk factor in health is a classic example of the type of racism that continues to alienate black America from the national community. This form of racism uses the all too common psychological defense of denial to clip the discussion before it starts.

Racism is rarely expressed as virulent hatred. It is more destructive when it is unexamined, perpetrated by omission rather than commission. Similarly, most marriages die not from overt hostility, but from a long series of missed cues leading to indifference. When one spouse ignores the pain of the other, the basis of a trusting relationship can be severely damaged. This style of ignoring the pain and suffering of a segment of our nation has profound implications. This denial guarantees the continued presence of racism in our society. Both the condition of racism and its denial are pathological to the personal, social and institutional character of America.

UNITY

It is often helpful to ground a discussion as volatile as racism in easily understood and universal principles. Nature provides some examples that will be helpful for this discussion. Certain principles seem to always be present in healthy living systems whether these systems are in nature, the human body, or in society. Deviations from these principles tend to result in the disorder and disease of the system. One of the ways racism can be considered a disease is in the context of deviations from these universal principles.

First, is the principle that health represents a reciprocal interplay between parts of a system and the whole. In the body, for instance, when we are healthy, all the systems are harmonized and work in perfect unison. Our lungs provide sufficient oxygen to fuel each cell of the body. The heart circulates adequate blood for all the body's needs, our digestive tract absorbs nutrients and eliminates waste efficiently, and our liver disposes of toxins and performs its unnumbered metabolic functions with wonderful proficiency. Our endocrine system regulates the various body rhythms to deal with all manner of environmental stresses, metabolic and reproductive needs. The immune and repair systems fight anything that would disturb this marvelous balance. All of this regulated by a nervous system infinite in its complexity.

Anyone alive knows that this harmony of function does not describe the relations between races and peoples in the world, let alone America's ethnic subgroups. Not only is there no harmony among the component parts of our body politic, there is barely a concept of a body politic. This is especially true when it comes to racial identity. The division along racial lines is so ingrained, so much a part of our assumptions, that we cannot honestly visualize any other type of America. Consequently, a state of paralysis has marked the social dialogue about race. One wonders if the failure to address the issue of race has made it easier to neglect a host of other social ills that have contributed to the balkanization of America. We need some new infusion of ideas, some new paradigm within which we might move in ways that can give hope to the promise that America can be a land of opportunity for all its citizens.

In a healthy system, there is a reciprocal relationship between each part and the whole. The healthy function of one system has a strengthening effect on the whole. In turn, the harmonious functioning of the whole body has a directing and nurturing effect on each system. The oxygen exchange of the lungs, for example, becomes important only when we see the vital role it plays in the life of each cell of the body. This oxygen can't get to the cells without the pumping action of the heart, which is regulated by complex neural and hormonal feed-back loops, through the medium of healthy blood in healthy vessels, and in a narrow acid-base equilibrium supported by the kidneys and the entire metabolic rhythm of the body! We appreciate the role of one organ only when we see it in the context of the whole body as life shows itself to be an intricate web of balanced interconnectedness.

This balance between parts and the whole is referred to as the principle of unity in diversity. In this case, unity is not intended to mean uniformity or similarity in function or ability. In living systems, unity does not mean sameness or uniformity. Rather, unity describes a dynamic reciprocal process between all the parts in relation to the whole. Unity implies and requires both diversity of component parts, and a dynamic interplay between them and the whole. This diversity and dynamism are both required elements of the idea of unity. For our purposes, unity will be defined in this organic way as seen in nature.

The opposite holds true for the context of the racial dialogue in America. We use stilted notions of racial identity that betray the opposite of an appreciation of diversity. Also, the dynamism between society as a whole and its component racial elements is painfully lacking. Uniformity, not unity, marks the current state of the racial dialogue in America. Uniformity lacks these two principles of diversity and dynamism, and is therefore the opposite of unity.

This principle of unity in diversity has tremendous organizational power in the natural world. The nuances of this principle offer essential insights into the requirements for, and the nature of life itself. The degree of a living system's compliance with its requirements determines the degree of that system's health or disease. Racism represents the exact opposite of this principle of life, and is the archetype of social disease for this reason. For America to become socially healthy a dispassionate and careful study of the subtleties of the principle of unity in diversity must be made. Balancing these requirements in society is the task before us as we set the context for healing the disease of racism.

BALANCE

A corollary to the idea of the harmony of parts with the whole is the principle that, in health, the value of each part lies only in its balanced relationship to other parts. As in a Calder mobile sculpture, we see that even the most unlikely and preposterous shapes can achieve an elegant balance if the relationship between them is correct. To achieve balance, one must consider more than the needs of each piece. Balance is an over-arching perspective that sets the relationships between the parts. Everyone who has learned to ride a bike knows that it can't be done so long as the act is attempted in discrete parts. Once the student gets a "feel" for the whole process, balance and rhythm are achieved and bike riding happens. If the parts of the mobile are strung together without an over-arching understanding of the balance of the whole, chaos ensues as gravity pulls the heaviest pieces down, entangling the entire mobile on itself.

The dilemma in society is similar. Without a clear idea of what principle can act as the "scale" to achieve our social balance (or without the idea that balance itself is important!), we have become victims of the appeals of each segment of society demanding its own idea of what it needs to sustain itself with no regard for how this will affect the balance of the entire body politic. The absence of a clear unifying social principle has led to the collapse of social identity into smaller and smaller racial, ethnic, neighborhood, family, and personal identities. It is the absence of a central unifying idea for society that has sustained and worsened the progressive estrangement of social subgroups, ultimately leading to the personal alienation that feeds the violence and unhappiness in our world.

As a result of this absence of a cohesive social vision, a grim despair shows itself in the meager social goals we set for ourselves. Even the language we use betrays a falling back from the ideals of years ago. No one speaks of an integrated society any more. Rather, we hope that different racial groups can learn to tolerate each other. While African-American studies departments exist on campuses throughout the country, because of the lack of change in the fundamental relationship between black and white, the progress in status these departments represent also symbolize an institutionalization of the concept of separate-but-equal. Losing hope in the idea of real integration, we now assume that, first, blacks must be strong amongst themselves and develop their own sense of identity and pride before integration can occur. Isn't this in itself a statement of despair? Isn't this strategy a tacit acceptance that blacks must do all the work in developing improvements in race relations in this country. What does the current state of affairs call from white America?

An analogy is found in a marriage. It is often said that marriages work best when each member is strong and confident in himself. The reality of most marriages is different. One is strong where another needs help. The safety and support conferred by the marriage provides a context in which both can discover and work on developing their inherent strengths. Weaknesses of character can be addressed in the context of the reciprocity and mutuality of a supportive relationship. The two don't live in separate parts of the house waiting for one partner to "catch up" or gain an equal access to power. It is in the acceptance by both that they are involved in something bigger than themselves that weaknesses are corrected and inherent strengths are brought out.

Continuing the analogy, if each partner lived in a separate part of the house, had to develop his own economic stability without the other, did not consider the pains and needs of the other in building the relationship, and ignored the history of abuse that marked the early years of their relationship, we could not say there was much chance for a successful marriage here. Yet, we hold these assumptions in black-white relations and wonder why things have not improved enough. Is it reasonable to assume that black community efforts to build social and economic independence can be successful without integration into the greater social fabric of the larger American community? To what extent can economic expansion of inner-city black neighborhoods occur separate from the larger economy? This hope of achieving separate but equal status can only lead to further imbalance in race relations as the historic disparity between blacks and whites in virtually every socio-economic indicator will continue to put blacks at a disadvantage. Yet, the inability of white America to fully grasp the implications of racism in our society has left no other option than pursuing this course. This, then, has not been a strategy of preference, but one of despair at the ability of white America to understand the crisis racism presents to our entire body politic.

We have capitulated to the despair that there is no hope for fundamental change in the relations between racial groups. There is no longer an assumption that meaningful integration is possible or even desirable. As understandable as it is for blacks to consider pursuing a separate course, one must wonder if this trend shows that the road to a united society must pass through several more generations of Americans before the fundamental relationship between black and white is changed. But one can only further despair at the cost to those children who have not yet had their hopes dashed.

The principle of balance will require a fundamental change in the way component parts of America view themselves and society at large. This will be especially true of white America, which needs to take a fresh look at the historic principles of equality, freedom and justice for all that built this country. A nation which did not intend for blacks to be cosharers in this vision for freedom, justice and equality, that labeled a black in its constitution as three-fifths of a person, cannot ignore the fact that these roots have sent long and strong branches throughout our society. The fruit of that historic inequity is the racial divide we witness today. These principles must be examined anew and freed from the historic limitations given by the Founding Fathers. As we approach a new century, they must be allowed to grow into the full maturity of their millennial meaning.

These principles can call out the best of any person. But, unexamined, they can also be shields behind which we hide and ignore certain painful truths of our national or personal history. With a sense of inner conviction and poise which comes from honest reflection, we can approach the examination of the acts of inhumanity that marked the rise of slavery in this country and the central role it played in its economic and social past, without a sense of personal threat or guilt. This dispassionate examination will show that much of the meaning of black charges of racism have been misunderstood by white America. This misunderstanding has corrosive effects, not only on American culture, but ultimately on the character of those who refuse to examine this cry with open eyes and quiet calm. If we do not engage in this self-examination, the future of race relations in this country will continue on its desperate course.

The ability to weigh in a dispassionate way the truth of a situation, regardless of the personal cost, is a mark of maturity. This becomes possible when a larger context is available to the person. All will say they have a desire to be truthful. But when we feel frightened or threatened, our sense of what is true becomes limited. It is a conviction in the essential oneness of all humanity, and a desire to play a role in the betterment of this whole that provides one with the poise necessary for such a self-examination. It is this poise engendered by a conviction in the essential oneness of humanity that we must first seek to establish in the discussion of race.

A certain imbalance occurs in the moral thinking of many white Americans when it comes to race. On the one hand, they will see the gross inhumanity that is the legacy of slavery, and acknowledge the terrible moral cost it represented to this country. Yet, many will also feel that if they personally have done nothing to mistreat a black American, and, if they had nothing to do with slavery, then they can not be a part of a racial problem. While this thinking is logical, there is more to the story than this simple formula. The racism that plagues America is not the one that most whites typically imagine.

This formulation of racism has more to do with absolving oneself from a sense of personal culpability than examination at a deeper level. This self-absolution many whites engage in leads to a sense of non-attachment to the issue of race. By not examining the issue closer, most white people become vulnerable to subtler forms of racism. While most white people would not consciously harm or take advantage of a black person, their actions do just that. It is the unexamined assumption about the value of white Americans versus black Americans that is at the heart of the imbalance. The core of racism is a deep-seated presumption, with strong emotional overtones, that whites are inherently superior to blacks.

A husband may say and mean it that he is deeply committed to the equality of men and women. Yet, in his marital relationship, he may never question the way in which he assumes his point of view is more important, that he has the right to interrupt or correct his wife, that he is the one who defines the priorities of the relationship, that he is the one who needs to solve all of his wife's problems, usually without her input. The society in which we live has acculturated him to make certain assumptions about his inherent superiority in these areas. He, therefore, never questions their veracity, and is unaware of the corrosive effect they play in the relationship. If the man states he has never beaten a woman and was not involved in the sale of women in the past, this has little bearing on his need to examine the assumptions he acts on that are oppressing his wife and corroding his relationship.

There are basic privileges which whites assume are a given in the lives of each American. It is difficult for a white person to fathom the notion that basic acts in day-to-day life do not play out the same for a black man versus a white man. The average white persons, for instance, do not expect to be followed by security guards in a shopping mall. They do not expect everyone in a store to look at them when they enter. They do not expect extra checks on their identification when they are making a purchase. If they stop in a restroom, they do not expect others to presume they are the janitor. If they accidentally touch someone, they do not expect that other people will assume they are dirty. If they drive a nice car, they do not presume the police will stop them to ask how they acquired their car. When driving home, if they happen to drive through a black section of town, they do not expect to be stopped by the police. They do not presume that others will be afraid of them, that mothers will walk their children to the other side of the street. These presumptions on the part of every white person cannot be presumed by a black person. Although it should go without saying that every American should not have to worry about these things, black people do.

It is the unexamined assumptions that set the racial dialogue out of balance. It is the idea of the inherent superiority of whites that our society inculcates in our young that isolates our thinking from the larger picture of the effects of racism in our society. For many children of color, identifying with a community of people sharing the same pain and sense of inferiority becomes more compelling and real than with a community of opportunity defined by the "American Dream."

For example, attempts by blacks to find a sympathetic ear to their historic and personal suffering can be heard by whites as a repudiation of the community of opportunity most whites live in. Having firsthand experience in struggling to ascend in this identity group of opportunity, whites interpret black expressions of pain as an unwillingness to similarly struggle. This, of course, is experienced in the black community as either an overt attempt to subvert blacks or callous indifference to the history that has historically all but excluded blacks from these opportunities. Failure to recognize the different assumptions both communities bring to the table has led to an increasing sense of frustration and polarization in the racial dialogue. Without an understanding of the genesis of these two identity groups, one of oppression and inculcated inferiority, and one of opportunity and presumed superiority, it will be difficult to bridge the racial communication gap.

The body provides an example of the ultimate effect of this type of distortion. In the body, when one cell type disturbs the balanced relationship it has with the entire system and puts its needs above those of the body, disease ensues. The classic example is cancer. A cancer cell, if we were to anthropomorphize the process, sees itself as the reason the organism as a whole exists. A cancer is basically a cell type deciding to grow without regard for the balance of the whole body. There can be bone cancers, liver cancers, colon cancers, or brain cancers. Any cell type can develop cancerous tendencies. Each simply describes a cell type which decided to reproduce itself without regard for the natural balance of the whole body. If you will, it assumes its inherent superiority.

Unrestrained by the requirements inherent in a balanced system, cancer cells multiply without limit, robbing the rest of the body of its fair share of nutrients. Enormous amounts of energy resources must go to feed the hyperactive cancer cells. Even though they are no longer acting within the natural balance of the body, the cancer cells may still perform the function of their cell type, but in an imbalanced way. Thinking in terms of the simultaneous levels at which each cell exists at the same time, we may see that there is no problem or a lethal one.

For instance, on the cellular level, a thyroid cell in a thyroid tumor keeps producing thyroid hormone as it is supposed to. On its own scale it is "doing nothing wrong". Yet on the scale of the entire body, the growing thyroid tumor has become unresponsive to the actual needs of the body as a whole. It becomes unresponsive to the regulating signals of the rest of the body, producing far more hormone then the body actually needs. It may grow beyond its normal site or even invade other organs, upsetting the delicate balance of the entire body, ultimately leading to death. What is "healthy" behavior for the cancer cells becomes lethal to the whole system.

Much of the discussion of race is "cancerous" in this sense. The degree to which we begin the discussion from the exclusive vantage point of one racial group or another is the degree to which we are engaged in a debate with 'cancerous" consequences for the whole of society. Yet, a problem arises when we realize that there are historic pains and persistent injustices that compel us to plead the case from the vantage point of the dispossessed. This is the dilemma most blacks feel themselves to be in. An understandable but pathological response by many in the black community is to harbor deep-seated suspicion of white motives.

While there is a compelling moral reason to plead the case of our inherent oneness as a nation, the persistent and painful consequences of white society failing to examine itself has led many black Americans to abandon the high road of the principle of our common heritage as humans, and to plead instead for a separate economic and social justice. This pleading for a separate justice is complicated by the pemicious effects of suspicion. The natural appeal for justice becomes distorted and corrosive by this presumed suspicion. As in any human communication, the tone of the discussion often conveys more than the content. In fact, most arguments are about the tone rather then the content.

The tone of suspicion and its accompanying anger in pleas for social justice become blurred in the racial dialogue. As justifiable as the plea for justice may be, it may not be heard by the majority population, which hears only an angry tone. The tone is interpreted as the major message and not the plea for justice. Whites then see blacks as demanding and threatening. Blacks see whites as heartless and only interested in maintaining their status. Both miss the essential point of the other due to the presumptions brought to the discussion.

An over-arching principle is required so that the discussion of these inequalities and historic pains can be heard and dealt with in a way equitable for the parts and the whole. The question of justice is intrinsic to the discussion of race. Yet, how do we define what is just? More pragmatically, how do we ensure that our requests for justice are heard?

JUSTICE

The language of conflict is essentially that of justice. People argue over what they perceive to be their just rights. The problem is, of course, that people perceive differently. Our interest now turns to what influences that perception? I am not interested in defining what is or isn't just. Nor do I wish to entertain public policy options to issues of injustice, obviously important as that is. Another conversation should happen first. As a clinician, I am more interested in how it is that people come to see that one thing is fair and another isn't. And why it is people become hardened to the cry of others for justice. If we can gain insight into these problems, we will be able to break out of the cycle of polarized debate about race and see the issue with new eyes. Basically, the identity we assume for ourselves defines what we perceive to be just.

For instance, I made this statement about justice being defined by our identity to a colleague on a tour bus in Israel many years ago. She expressed her confusion with my point. Just then, a man who was sitting across the isle from us realized he couldn't see out his window when he hung his coat up on the hook in front of him. Without missing a beat, and without asking us, he quietly reached in front of us, said, "Excuse me," and hung his coat on our hook! Now we couldn't see out our window! "See, there it is!" I said, "He does not include us in his identity group, so he saw no injustice in hanging his coat in front of us so we can't see! He was even polite! But he was completely unfair to us."

If we had contested his action, he might have become defensive and thought we were argumentative. Seeing himself as benign, he might have responded to what he perceived as our belligerence. This might have enraged us, that he not only committed an insensitive act, but then had the gall to argue with us! And so, a conflict might have started. Each side feeling they were arguing for what was just: him, to not be attacked; us, for having our view obstructed. Of course, in a short time layers of hurts and perceived injustices would be accumulated on each side, raising the emotional stakes. Trying to identity the victims and perpetrators then becomes the name of the game. The feeling of injustice can then allow each to "justify" his acts, even if these acts are themselves inflammatory.*

These dynamics are the same in the discussion of race. Just as the man with the coat did not see that he was unfair to us by hanging his coat in front of us, whites tend to not see the unfairness of their actions on blacks. Just as this man had been polite to us, he had also been unfair. His failure to see the consequences of his actions became the first stumbling block in communication. So it is in the racial dynamics in America. Since whites tend to not consider blacks as equal members of American society, they do not see that their actions have any effect on blacks.

A perception of injustice has the effect of forcing the victim into a limited identity role he might not have otherwise chosen for himself. In this case, my friend and I saw ourselves as part of a tour of professionals. The coat incident might have constricted our identity to us against our colleague. In the discussion of racism, an individual might be perfectly comfortable with any number of social identities, but when the subject of race comes up, he is forced to become either "black" or "white." This constriction of our identity is one of the pathological effects of racism and one of its most tiring elements. Our sense of identity can shift, then, depending upon our experience of justice or in justice.

Couples will be tremendously hurt from the pain each feels by the injustice perpetrated by the other. Our experience of pain has a way of making us feel more isolated, "shrinking" our identity, if you will. With a constricted identity, each fails to hear the pain of the other, so each tries with mounting desperation to make his case. The growing desperation of one is perceived as self absorption by the other, who can't understand why his spouse can't see the pain he is causing. This, of course, leads to a greater sense of unfairness and

**This process was called "the narcissism of victimization" by John Mack, M.D., a psychiatrist at Harvard, who used it to describe the intransigence of both sides in the generational conflict in the Middle East.*

even louder protestations for justice. Inevitably, it becomes more and more difficult to see the identity of the marriage as a whole. Without this shared sense of identity in the marriage, both are caught in a struggle for dominance to be heard. This strategy invariably fails. Both parties wind up feeling misunderstood, isolated and suspicious of the motives of the other.

A vicious cycle ensues when both sides to a conflict, each starting with differences in identity, perceives the acts of the other as unjust. The resulting hurt leads to a moving away from any common identity and intensifies a sense of a separate identity. This increases the propensity to perceive injustice. The cycle goes round and round with hurt and estrangement increasing as the appeals for justice by one sounds more and more foreign, irrelevant and manipulative to the other. These dynamics are no less true in the discussion of race.

In the example on the bus, failing to prevail over the other, one side or the other might have felt compelled to seek out some authority – the bus driver, the tour director, the company of peers, the police – to ensure that his own version of justice prevailed. Injustice not only forces us into smaller identities, but as a result, human interactions cease to be regulated by dynamic reciprocal processes. Instead, relations are reduced to finding ways to prevail over an adversary. The use of power, instead of mutual respect, becomes the final arbiter in human relations. Relations become dehumanized in the process. This reversion to using power as the arbiter of human interactions betrays the fundamental principle of living systems, the unified dynamic interplay between component parts. It intensifies the identification of the parts as separate entities and diminishes the identification and response to the whole. And, like the thyroid tumor, the end result is the dissolution of both the whole and the part.

To begin the discussion of race from the perspective of injustice tends to lead to a discussion of acquiring power to prevail over others who will themselves feel this attempt as an injustice. As a result, separate identifications can only be intensified and further injustices perpetrated. Alternatively, by starting at the point of a shared identity, a common perception of justice is possible that takes into account the dynamic interaction and needs between the parts and the whole. The point of this section shows that the central issue in conflict resolution is not to begin with competing ideas of what is just, but to decide what the barriers are in perceiving a shared identity. In regard to the discussion of race, the history of white America's presumption of its inherent superiority and the suspicion and pain this has caused in black America are the primary barriers to this shared identity.

IDENTITY

The loss of a cohesive social identity can be seen everywhere. This fragmentation of society is all the more disturbing as it becomes plainly clear that the problems in effect in humanity at the close of the twentieth century are increasingly global in nature. And this defines the crisis of our times: that human social allegiance is shrinking and becoming more rigid just as humanity's problems require the largest and most flexible world views. This shrinking of our social allegiance is pitting one element of society against another, locking the social discourse into increasingly shrill fights for power over who will have and who will not. Trapped in our parochialism, our minds do not have sufficient breadth to wrap around the enormity of today's social ills. Therefore, with inadequate vision, the solutions we devise fall short. Because of our limited world-views, we are left with a never ending cycle of inadequate analysis leading to ineffectual solutions, which breed ever more complex problems. Racism is the quintessential example of this dilemma.

The first step out is to find the correct level of analysis, to view the problems we face from the correct vantage point. Once this is done, the solutions we construct will at least be at the correct scale of the problem. They may not always be the best solution, but we will at least have gotten the first step right.

We can view our sense of identity as a series of concentric circles moving outward. As we move outward from the core of these concentric circles, our identity includes larger and larger social groupings. Beginning from our sense of an inner self, we move out, say, to our identity as a spouse or family member, then to our vocation, then to some larger community. Any central idea around which the social identity is organized is known as a collective center for that identity. One can construct any number of such concentric rings.

Figure 1: Examples of concentric levels of identity:

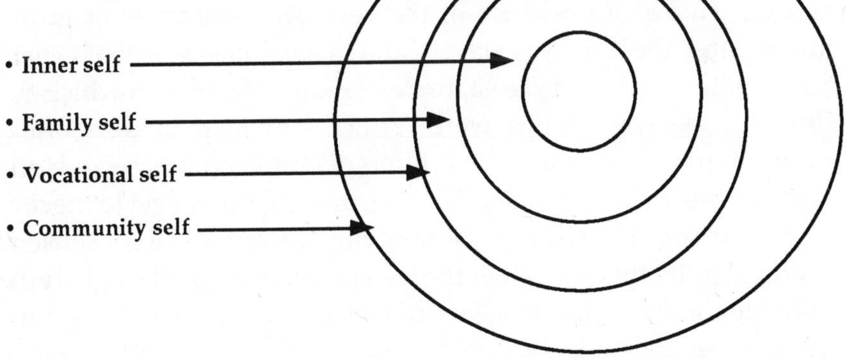

Our identity defines for us what it is we feel we need. It has been suggested that all humans have a fixed number of needs that they will always seek to fulfill. Among them are the need for security, self expression and recognition, and access to resources to determine one's destiny. But these needs are themselves sought out in the context of an identity. It is one's identity that one tries to secure. It is one's identity that seeks to be expressed and understood. And it is one's identity that seeks resources for self fulfillment.

As mentioned in the discussion on justice, our identity is not fixed. It can move. As our identity moves, so does our perception of what is good for us. Our sense of justice moves with our expanding or contracting identity. For instance, a woman walking down the street may jump out of the way of a car to preserve her security. But the same woman may jump in front of a train to save her child. In the first case, her identity includes only herself. In the later, her identity includes her child. Her identity has moved outward from one concentric center of identity to another, from self to mother. As she moves her identity outward, her idea of what needs security expands from herself to her child. So it is with all human needs. As our identity changes, so does our idea of what we need. We feel justice is served when our needs are being met. Those who share different identity groups will define their needs differently, therefore justice will be perceived differently.

Much of the miscommunication between the races in this country has to do with the misperception of the other's sense of what is just. This arises because of the very different sense of group identity that the history of slavery and the ongoing legacy of racism perpetuate. At the very least, understanding the way in which the different identity groups were formed can help in developing insight into the ways in which different ethnic groups see what is fair. But this historical understanding, in itself, cannot get to the root of the problem of racism. In the long run, fostering a larger sense of group identity that subsumes the lesser groups of racial origin is the antidote for the crippling legacy of racism.

Figure 2: Our allegiance to a particular identity can shift. The exercise of justice is a prime factor in this shifting.

If we experience fair play from a larger identity group, we tend to extend our identity to include it. Our identity moves outward in this case as we see ourselves as part of larger and larger communities. As our identity expands, our idea of justice becomes more inclusive.

If we experience unfairness from a larger identity group, we withdraw our allegiance from it. Our identity moves inward in this case, increasing isolation and alienation. As our identity shrinks, our sense of justice becomes less inclusive.

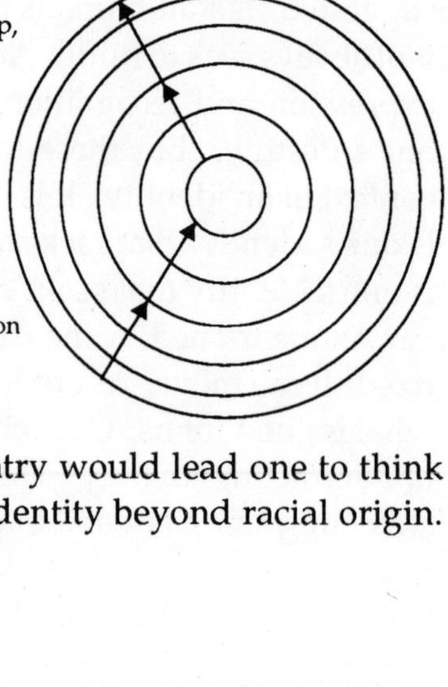

The discussion of race in this country would lead one to think that there is a barrier to seeing one's identity beyond racial origin.

The natural instincts of a mother show that there are inborn mechanisms that can expand the identity of an individual beyond himself. But how far? And what forces might push the identity back inward? What will anchor an identity at one level or another? What will anchor the identity at the widest and most inclusive collective center? If it is impossible for people to see beyond their racial identity group, then attempts to build beyond the limited goals set by social policies of mutual tolerance and separate-but-equal status would be vain.

We know from our own experience that it is possible for human beings to see themselves as part of the whole world, identifying with all people everywhere. The ability to have empathy for others, a quality that makes America the most generous country in the world in supporting charitable organizations, is a proof of this capacity. Yet, despite its presence in our lives, it has remained a largely undeveloped endowment in human nature in need of maturation.

Being able to reflect on the pain of another in an empathic way is liberating for the injured party. It allows for his identity to expand. Through recognition of the pain of another, a fundamental human need is met. Once this happens, the one in pain is given a new perspective that allows him more of a sense of empowerment over the situation. So, empathy and the experience of fairness can expand the identity. In fact, on a personal level, empathy is a type of justice in that it acknowledges the reality of another person's need.

In therapy, it is sometimes said that the nature of the relationship between the therapist and the patient is the "bowl" into which the work and interpretations of therapy are poured. The context set by the relationship, like a bowl, defines the shape of the work in therapy. Most discussions of race move to the liquid content without regard for the shape of the bowl into which it is poured. The characteristics of the "bowl" that make therapy most successful are also true for any relationship.

The therapist must demonstrate, (not merely through lip service), that patients are safe, that they will not be judged or demeaned, that they will be respected and that their experience (especially their pain), will not be minimized or inflated, but understood by the therapist for the full impact it has on the patient. Most importantly, the therapist must not let his own sense of fear or unease with what the patient is saying prevent him from hearing accurately what is being said.

It is a common failure of most therapy trainees that they feel personally powerless to help their patients. This sense of helplessness can make the young therapists feel incompetent. But, they also know that they have finished a lot of schooling and they very much want to be helpful professionals. This feeling of powerlessness contradicts the image the young trainee has of himself. If he is not careful, the therapist can resent his patient for inadvertently pointing out his weaknesses. The young trainee can then resent the patient and become punitive in his style with the patient. This style gets justified as "therapeutic" when in fact it is simply sadistic. Patients cease to look like people and more like needy and demanding beggars in proportion to the sense of loss of control and anxiety in the trainee.

A large part of supervision of such trainees is helping them overcome their own sense of helplessness and fear of their patients' pain so that they can become agents of growth. In the long run, it is the therapist who grows with the patient, as both must explore the painful realities of life. These characteristics of the alliance between therapist and patient allow the patient to trust the relationship and therefore, begin to reflect on his own life with a new perspective. In this way, a larger identity is conferred by the therapeutic relationship. The trust and safety of the larger identity of the relationship allows the individual to reflect on his own individual identity in a way that is not restricted by the perceived need to be defensive to protect that smaller personal identity.

Of course, by this analogy to therapy, I do not mean to put white America in the dominant position of "therapist" to blacks in the dependent role of "patients." Rather, I am trying to point out the natural human tendency to recoil from the pain of another as experienced in the therapeutic situation. These same dynamics hold true in intimate relationships. This comparison can serve as an example to white America, not of its dominant role as caregiver, but to the necessary inner strength and maturity required to examine one's own discomfort, and, sometimes, one's sense of helplessness when hearing the pain of others, and how failure to examine this discomfort can lead to denial that the pain of another is real.

It is a major step in the maturity of the trainee when he can begin to see his own anxiety as a measure of the level of pain of the patient. As the professional identity of the trainee as a healer unfolds, he becomes better able to hear the pain of his patients without feeling judged or threatened. In this way, his anxiety and discomfort with the pain of his patient begins to draw him closer to the patient, instead of pushing him away in denial and blame. The trainee begins to see his own anxiety and discomfort as a sign that he must pay extra close attention to the nuances of his patient's story. The pain and anxiety, which at first drove the trainee away from his patient, becomes his therapeutic ally. So, it is true in all mature relationships and so should it be in the discussion of racism.

CHARACTER

The identity conferred by the empathic therapeutic relationship allows for the calling forth, strengthening and stabilization of qualities latent within the patient that nurture self-esteem. The stability modeled by the relationship calls out the further latent capacities for healthy interactions with others, and builds confidence in doing so. So, the willingness to listen dispassionately allows for the creation of a mutual identity that allows for growth. The relationship creates an identity context in which the patient can explore new ways of being. Self-esteem, then, is conferred by, and within, the context of a trusting relationship, a larger identity.

It is a larger identity that calls up and organizes the inborn strengths and capacities of a developing personality. A teen-ager, for example, actively looks for a larger identity group to join. Adolescence is characterized by profound ambivalence. On one hand, the teen has many of the dependent needs of a child. On the other, he feels the need to strike out and begin to engage life independently. This is played out in every generation of teen-ager that stridently claims through fashion and music to be independent. But, any two given teen-agers will look and dress remarkably the same. It is the identity conferred by the group which allows the adolescent to begin to test his inherent strengths. The group identity helps organize and give direction to the latent abilities of the adolescent. In this way, the adolescent begins to gain a sense of competence in life.

It is an interesting paradox to note that an adolescent will seek out something beyond himself to gain confidence in himself. Here, we have an example of the dynamic nature of human character with different levels of our being operating at the same time and dependent on each other. Our inner life is dependent on a social identity, and vice versa. There appears to be an inborn urge for transcendence that serves not only a social function, but is an essential organizing factor in the development of a mature personality. The transcendent nature of the larger group identity helps the individual feel connected and confers meaning in the young life.

Without a sense of connection to an empathic group, the adolescent is caught in his ambivalence. The dependent part of the child personality gains the ascendant. If this condition persists, a problem develops. The personality does not have the experience of developing confidence in its own inherent strengths. A type of paralysis ensues in the young person's motivation. He feels incapable of moving effectively in the world. This provokes anxiety in the adolescent. This anxiety is what compels the child to join any group to avoid this sense of personal incompetence. If there are no constructive and empathic group models that can bring out the strengths of the personality, any group will do.

Unfortunately, for many youths the choices available are limited. In the extreme, the option is to join a gang of other similarly distressed and desperate individuals. If this occurs, a critical opportunity has been missed to call on the best of the young personality. The opportunity to encourage the individual to develop his most noble personality traits is sacrificed, and baser traits that are built upon dependence and the entitlement of his smallest immature identity come to the fore. The paralysis of motivation becomes ingrained as a tragic element of the character, justified and supported by the similarly demoralized group.

So it is for all people. A child in the most stable of homes will face the same challenges. But certain family and social conditions will tip the scale against the child in this natural struggle. If the child is from a home where abuse is present, where great deprivation exists, he has direct evidence that he is not competent to keep himself safe, for instance. The natural ambivalence of the adolescent is then knocked off kilter. He feels less ambivalents in a sense. He is more sure of his dependence and incompetence then his inherent strengths. Personal despair and paralysis of the will are the outcomes. The disabling of the natural cycle of personality development is the dynamic that racism plays upon. And this outcome is one of the chief legacies of the disease of racism.

A society that conveys to children of color in unnumbered ways that they are inherently inferior stacks the deck against the child, as it would any child. The years of overt and subtle messages conveying, the inferiority of blacks weighs heavily in the balance. By adolescence, it is not necessarily clear at all to a black child that he possesses inherent strengths that are of value to a larger society. As they would for anyone, these messages hinder the mature expansion of the child's identity. There are at least two consequences that act as intractable symptoms of racism. The first affects the individual identity in that the person becomes trapped in his sense of personal inadequacy by the paralysis of his motivation. The second is that it becomes infinitely harder for the individual to identify beyond the identity group of his race. The result of these two is an ingrained sense of despair, reflected in the fact that twice as many blacks as whites commit suicide, there are more blacks in prison than in college, and the epidemic of violence in the black community.

The effects on the character of white children are no less disastrous. The unwillingness to examine harsh realities stunts the natural development of depth in character and leads to moral weakness. The natural ambivalence of the adolescent is never truly resolved in white culture because of racism. Recall that each adolescent carries a natural ambivalence between his own sense of dependence from childhood and his desire to demonstrate a sense of personal mastery and social competence. Recall also, that, as the adolescent acquires more and more experiences of competence, he feels less and less inclined to invest his identity in the stereotypical adolescent peer group. These peer groups claim to be independent and self-sufficient, but demonstrate rigid conformity and neediness on the approval of the group.

These peer groups will label everyone outside their membership as bad. All the members are labeled good. This is a simplistic mind-set used to allay the anxiety of an inner sense of incompetence that has not been challenged. It is easier to "project" the negative part of one's own ambivalence onto an external group than it is to deal with the anxiety of examining this negativity. Couples do this, too. It is uncanny how, when you listen to an argument, the loudest protestations tend to be made by the person most in need of heeding his own advice. "Projection" is considered a primitive defense mechanism used to protect the inner sense from the anxiety of life. It is called primitive because it seems to be an inborn and immature defense that distorts the perception of reality and causes disruption in relationships.

If parts of our inner self remain unexamined, (i.e., those parts of us that comprise our motivation, thinking, feeling and behavior), they can direct our life in ways that make us a prisoner to them. Perhaps it is for this reason that Socrates said, "The unexamined life is not worth living." Freud stated that the purpose of psychoanalysis was to "make the unconscious, conscious," Or, to bring to conscious awareness all those patterns of motivation, thinking, feeling and behavior that go unexamined. Once this has been done the individual can exercise his free will to liberate himself from their control. In a sense, one is not free of one's own worst tendencies if the task of self examination does not occur.

If the group is excessively rigid, or if members don't begin to challenge the assumptions of the group over time, they will not explore their own capacity or challenge themselves to find the depth of their character in solving life's complex problems. A group that should act as a "cocoon" for the incubation for a mature personality, can then become a box imprisoning the adolescent personality in its own sense of incompetence. Over time, the personality begins to realize at a deep level its own weakness and failure to strive. An increasing sense of shame at one's inadequacy develops. This failure to examine this inner struggle allows this shame to corrode one's self esteem. Over time, without the capacity of character to deal with life's anxieties and challenges, the primitive personality projects these negative feelings onto scapegoats. Of course, freed of worry about its own weakness, this leaves the primitive personality assured of its own goodness. Projection is a primitive defense mechanism largely because it sanctions the freezing of personality development. The natural reciprocity of adult thinking is subverted.

Purged of the negativity that has been projected onto a scapegoat, the primitive personality now assumes it is inherently superior. All bad is projected onto a scapegoat. All good reverts to itself. This tendency to all-or-nothing thinking, black and white if you will, drastically oversimplifies the complexity of the world. These oversimplifications lead to ineffectual coping with the world's real challenges. To avoid the anxiety provoked by the sense of helplessness over the these challenges, the primitive personality then uses denial as a means of ignoring that a problem exists. Of course, the problem still exists. It simply is ignored. The denial of the existence of a problem of racism by individual white Americans, therefore, has drastic implications in their emotional maturity and development of character.

Unfortunately, these implications reach beyond the individual and extend to the quality of social relations and the goals of a society's institutions. As has been said, the use of race as a social identity from which personality is formed influences the way social justice is perceived. For the purposes of this discussion, we can say that there are three levels of activity that both influence and are influenced by our identity. These three areas are:

1. The inner life of an individual
2. The interpersonal interactions amongst individuals
3. Institutions and social structures that regulate human interactions

Each of these levels has an effect on the others. The way an individual thinks and perceives, for instance, affects the way he interacts with others. Group interactions affect both the individual's sense of self and influences the way these interactions are codified and regulated in the mores, traditions, laws and institutions of a society. Reciprocally, laws and institutions regulate the way people interact, which then reinforces how people think of themselves. Each of these levels, then, influences and is affected by the other in a dynamic interplay.

An example of how these three levels interact in the corruption of personal and social character is seen in the life of Adolf Hitler.* Horribly abused by an alcoholic father and neglected by a distant mother, this person developed a host of distorted views of the world. He fell prey, in an extreme form, to a number of unconscious processes to which, deprived of the appropriate nurturance and guidance, all humans are prone. Classical psychiatry describes a process by which rage and self-deprecation if experienced at a very early age are repressed if the child can find no safe outlet. This is particularly true when the child is made unsafe by negligence or abuse. In later life, the person no longer consciously identifies with this rage and self hate. Instead, he projects it outwardly onto someone or something else. In the case of Hitler, it was Jews in

* *For interesting psychoanalytic interpretations of the life of Adolph Hitler, see Alice Miller, "For Your Own Good", Farrar, Straus, Giroux, New York, 1984.*

particular, as well as other "auslanders."

This distorted inner life led to perversions in his interactions with others. But, he lived in a social milieu that had an ingrained historic presumption of superiority over the Jews.* The German nation had experienced profound and prolonged agony after the First World War. We recall that the pain of injustice is one of the factors that can rigidify the sense of self in the identity group that received the pain. So, by the 1930s Germany had experienced enough pain to make it vulnerable to extreme identifications of nationalism. Once this identity was empowered with the force of governrnent by the Nazi rise to power, the repressed rage and self-hate could be projected without inhibition onto a target long felt to be inferior by historic tradition.

The most virulent expressions of bigotry always seem to have in common a combination of distorted inner lives in key players, a history of limited healthy interaction between perpetrators and victims, and an historic assumption of superiority on the part of the perpetrators. Combined with the right social conditions, this volatile mixture has predictable results. The distorted inner identifications of Nazi officials led to a perverse justification for persecuting Jews. This inner turmoil led to interpersonal relations corrupted by the perverse fruits of these distortions. These perversions included the lack of rational communication, the convoluted fear of the threat the victims themselves represented to the persecutors, and the depersonalization of the victims. Once made into something less than human, Jews became the objects of the violence of the projection of the worst repressed elements of the Nazis, this being justified in order to preserve the identity of the Nazi perpetrators that was, paradoxically, perceived to be threatened by the Jewish victims.

Supported by deeply troubled inner lives, these malignant

**Anti-semitism was not a unique characteristic of Germany. It is a common feature of most traditionally Christian and Islamic nations.*

interactions were then codified into the Nuremberg Laws forbidding contact with Jews, and paving the way for the Holocaust. There is a maxim in psychiatry that people alwavs have at least two feelings for everything. Good people will have dark recesses of the soul that are evil. We call these people good because they choose the good more often than the evil. But given the circumstances of great deprivation and fear, the restraints on our lower nature weakens. Many previously decent people, with unresolved inner conflicts of their own, stirred by the fear of uncertainty of the times, became vulnerable to this reactionary psychology. The Nazis enacted the Nuremberg Laws and developed institutional supports for their extreme identification in German superiority. This over-identification with National Socialism offered an easy resolution of the inner turmoil of these people who followed suit and threw their identification in with this regressed ideology. The circle is complete in showing how the inner life effects social interactions and institutions, which in turn reciprocates these effects down to the group interactions and the individual.

While all people are prone to limitations in their identity, there is a limitation to using the Nazi analogy to racism in America. The tendencies that drove the Nazis are only partly at work in racism. Two important variables are not always present in American racism. The first is that few people prone to limitations in their identification have hatefully perverse inner lives, as did Hitler. Some few do, most do not. Second, the historic conditions present in Germany after World War I were so extreme as to be almost unrepeatable. Yet, we can expect that in times of social unrest, those leaders with perverse inner lives will be heard more by those who are simply afraid.

These distinctions are important in that most white people in America do not fit into the mold of a venomous hate monger. To put the issue of racism to the average white person as an issue of deliberate hatred or attempts to control is to miss the real and subtler point. It also elicits from whites a sense that the real problem must be with blacks, since most whites can't find in their personal experience any example of their deliberately trying to hurt or restrict a black. Most whites have little or no contact with blacks so, they reason, "How could I be responsible for their situation?" Racism plays in a subtler way.

The unique history of slavery in America has made the issue of racism more complicated. There are two historic distortions in this country that have influenced the way individuals, groups and institutions have responded to this issue of race. These are rooted in the historic fact of slavery. Slavery solidified two of the baser human traits that poison the social dialogue about race in this country some 400 years after its terrible introduction into the Western Hemisphere. The first is the human tendency to unconsciously presume one's own superiority over others. The second is the tendency to bear suspicion against historic oppressors. Because of the unique history of slavery, there is an unquestioned social presumption in the white community of its own inherent superiority. In the black community, there is a resultant unmalleable suspicion of whites. These two traits continue to anchor the social identities of blacks and whites in their ethnic roots to the virtual exclusion of the other.

Both of these traits are inherent in all humans. Since they have not been consciously examined by our society, they have become fixed elements in the personal, group and institutional levels of American identity since the time of slavery in this country. When these constant irritants that prevent the dynamic functioning of our culture are extricated forever from our lives by healthy, frequent and open communication, the healing of America can begin.

Instead, what we see now is that each side continues to reinforce the pathology of the other by failing to see the consequences of their own acts. The failure to recognize the hidden assumption of superiority in the white community continues to incense the black community and justify the stance of suspicion against whites. The insistence that every problem facing the black community has roots in white malevolence contributes to the white communities sense of black intransigence. A bitter dance ensues in which both sides self-justify their acts and compound the problem.

One wonders if this bald-faced primitive projection of the superiority of whites and inferiority of blacks, conveyed throughout American society for centuries, has stunted the character development of the nation! The signs seem to be present when we note the hyper-simplistic analysis of public events. The tendency to frame all social discourse in absolute good and bad terms, the absence of more than two viable political parties, each considering the other its mortal enemy and inferior. Could these social trends have, at least in part, their roots in the inability of American society to grow past the primitive projections made against black Americans by white America? Just as an individual's character is stunted by clinging to projections from adolescence, should we not assume the same holds true for the society as a whole? Are there further signs of this tendency to project in our foreign policy which dehumanizes "enemies" of America? How many times in U.S. history have we presumed our inherent superiority over developing nations and peoples? Of course, this same tendency occurs in all nations. But, until recently, America was the only nation dedicated to principles of universal freedom. It should not be surprising that we are subject to the same paradoxes and contradictions as a people, but to deny our darker side is to condemn ourselves to repeating the mistakes of the past. It is to ensure that we, as a nation, never mature in character. Defined in this way, racism is the most challenging social issue in America.

In this sense, our addressing the issue of racism in America can have an effect on the global stage. Not only does the world cry out for a model by which diverse peoples can live in harmony, but it desperately needs an evolution of human character and the putting away of childish ways. Ways which now are causing the death and wastage of entire peoples and nations. Could the goal of eradicating racism from American society have a maturational effect on global culture?

THE ONENESS OF HUMANITY

Since Darwin*, the law of the struggle for survival has been assumed to be the guiding principle in social as well as natural systems. It has long been considered naive to think that social justice for minorities will be realized as a result of a willful act by those in the majority. Social justice is assumed to be impossible without a struggle for power to force change to have one's needs met. It doesn't sound pretty, but this is essentially the assumed tone of discussions about justice. This point is particularly true for the discussion of racism in America. Racism has come to mean institutional manifestations of discrimination. Consequently, the solutions to the problem of racism have been largely formulated around the institutional administration of justice. For years, the social dialogue about race has been economic and legalistic.

As important as these issues are, however, we have seen that approaching the issue of racism only from this perspective has not appreciably changed the position of blacks in America. Nor has it addressed the fundamental relationship between black and white. The unquestioned assumptions whites harbor about their inherent superiority, and the unmalleable suspicion this has engendered in the black community have not been addressed. The failure to provide an antidote to these assumptions has led to distortions in the inner lives of all Americans, in our interpersonal relations and, finally, our institutions. Attempting to address the problem of racism only at the institutional level is doomed to failure because it ignores the roots of racism in these other more basic psychological and interpersonal levels.

In an effort to provide a solution to this problem, social and educational programs designed on the principle of tolerance have spread over the past several years. This is certainly a step in the right

* *Thomas Huxley, Darwin's apologist, actually championed the notion of the survival of the fittest, Darwin's main contribution being the notion of natural selection.*

direction in that it attempts to personalize the issue of race and has opened the doors to the possibility of true appreciation of diversity. Yet, there is a nuance here that requires clarification. The principle of tolerance itself carries some assumptions.

We must see by now that tolerance of diversity is a far cry from appreciation of its necessity. There is an ambiguity in the principle of tolerance that saps its strength as an organizing pnnciple in social programming. Implicit in the notion of tolerance is the idea that diverse peoples are irreconcilably different. You may tolerate my presence, but feel no affinity for me. I may tolerate your culture, but feel indifferent to its value to me. Does tolerance as a principle hold within it a subtle capitulation to the idea that we can never be truly united? Must we only tolerate each other? We owe other human beings much more. While tolerance as a motif for social programming to deal with racism is certainly better than no discussion at all of the value of ethnic diversity, we need a more assertive and explicitly encompassing principle.

The ultimate proof of the limitation of the idea of tolerance is held within this question. If you are white, would you be happy to see your daughter marry a black? If you are black, would you be happy to see your daughter marry a white? Aside from statements that we would not want such a marriage because of the difficulties it would present to any children of such a union, the fact remains that, at a deeply emotional level, people are appalled by the prospect of such unions. The inherent problems of racism come out in this emotional response. If we are truly one people, then such unions should have no emotional loading other than excitement over the potential qualities that may be expressed with the joining of diverse cultures. The pathologies of the white assumption of inherent superiority and the black assumption of deep suspicion of whites are played out here.

The ambiguity of the principle of tolerance is codified in the trend towards separate but equal status of blacks and whites in universities, for example. We may tolerate Afro-American studies departments, but these programs have made no impact on the fundamental relationship between blacks and whites. In fact, we may have done more to solidify our social distance. The vagaries of the principle of tolerance naturally lead us to such social isolation between ethnic groups, and justify within us the impossibility of true integration. This is the capitulation to despair that saps our social vitality. In contrast, the principle of the oneness of humanity provides a first principle that gives context for an appreciation of diversity as an essential and valued part of the whole.

We have seen that people will perceive justice differently so long as they see themselves in different social identity groups. Unless we find ways to instill an abiding sense of our common humanity, we will never be able to have a context in which a discussion of social justice will be all-inclusive. This inability to see our common human identity will inevitably lead to a struggle between groups for power. In a pinch, the notion of tolerance cannot prevent a person from acting to support only his own racial group. What is needed is a social principle that can mobilize all of a society's diverse components to act in concert for the common good. The passivity inherent in the principle of tolerance is not enough, despite how much better it may be in comparison to the evil of outright hate.

The principle that gives the most meaning to appreciating diversity is the idea of the oneness of humanity. The principle of the oneness of humanity is the "bowl" into which we can pour our appreciation of the various ethnic components of society. True appreciation of our diversity is impossible without it. This principle gives the largest possible social identity, and therefore, allows for a discussion of social justice that appreciates the needs of all.

If the principle of the oneness of humanity in all of its implications were taught to children from the earliest age, a foundation would be laid for the social cohesion we desire. By teaching this principle as the essential first lesson, we would be able to demonstrate the context within which an ethical life based on the need for justice for all makes sense. The principle of the oneness of humanity gives a context for ethical decision making. It provides a context for examining communication styles that foster cooperation. It serves as the only sure basis upon which diversity can be truly appreciated for its necessity to the whole of society, and not simply tolerated. The principle of the oneness of humanity denotes a cohesion and transcendence of the human spirit. From this confidence in human nature, hope is engendered for solving complex social ills.

Because it eliminates the perception of others as fundamentally different in nature, the principle of the oneness of humanity abrogates the law of the struggle for survival. When this principle is internalized in one's emotional and intellectual life, one's highest values become the preservation of the best interests of all people. It feeds a natural desire to abandon the use of force as the inevitable means of achieving social justice. It allows the natural social graces to develop and become valued. It becomes possible to see the loss of others as a loss to oneself. Similarly, the gain of others becomes one's own gain.

This principle grounds one's ethical life in the widest possible embrace. In its sphere, the value of each part of society becomes evident. The power of the Golden Rule as a foundation for personal and social action becomes justified without dogmatic overtones. Since other ethnic groups are not seen as intrinsically inferior or superior they are not perceived as threats. By putting the value of the entirety of humanity first, the sense of fear and need is diminished. Free from these emotional pulls, one's thinking is free to explore the world without resort to defensiveness. One can see the pain and paradox of human struggle. Empathy for the human condition overtakes resentment of others' advantage. Psychologically, the mind is free to abandon the primitive defenses of projection and denial and move into the mature character skills of reciprocity and empathy.

By giving priority to study of the nuances of the oneness of humanity, a safe context is provided which makes an exploration of human diversity meaningful. It provides an antidote to our diseased racist thinking by providing the context in which primitive psychological defense mechanisms can give way to mature personality development. Taught in ways that show its applications on the personal, interpersonal and institutional levels of human activity, the principle of the oneness of humanity provides the vaccine to prevent future generations from acquiring the infection of racism.

Americans have always arisen in times of need when a crisis has been clearly laid out before them. We can see now that the disease of racism has far too long plagued our nation's soul. We also now see that a conviction to root out this patent evil from ourselves, our relationships and our institutions itself will have ramifications far beyond the quality of black/white relations. We know that it is our destiny to bravely live up to the noble principles espoused in our nation's founding. As we approach the change of a decade in the year 2000, we face also, on a far grander scale, the revolution of a century of untold bloodshed and division. Might we not rise up now, as one people, to root out this disease of racism from our national character, and by the power of a conviction in the essential oneness of all humanity and in all the inherent beauty of its diversity, fulfill the promise of the millennial vision for which our nation stands?

Chapter 2

Children as Sacred Beings

by Robert Atkinson and Patricia Locke

In this chapter, the writers, professors who specialize in American and Native American cultures, present an idea crucial to the elimination of prejudice in our society: that all living things are sacred, and that children must be trained to understand this fundamental concept. In reading this chapter, parents and teachers can acquire valuable insights from traditional Lakota moral principles, such as the concept of mitakuye oyasin, *which means, simply, that we are all related. Imagine if all young children were taught this principle at home and in their pre-schools. These and other Lakota teachings provide a valuable foundation from which teachers and parents might present the issue of racism within a moral context. Ed.*

When children are given support and encouragement in their interests, endeavors, and dreams, they will flourish. They will retain their natural optimism and hope. What could best facilitate this is a collective call to spirit, built upon a code of ethics we can respect and live by, and fostered by a moral education that will guide and inspire its members toward a vision of greatness and a life that matters. To this end, we offer a look at three powerful underlying principles in the Lakota world view that might serve as a basic frame of reference for parents, educators, and helping professionals everywhere. These principles provide a way of seeing life and seeing children that could dramatically influence the way we relate to children and to each other.

The word for child in the Lakota language is *wakan yeja*. In English this translates into "sacred being." This is not just a different way of perceiving children than most of us are used to. This is a belief central to the ancient Lakota worldview in which **all** things in the created world are sacred, the two-leggeds, the four-leggeds, the winged creatures, the crawling ones, the finned ones, and the rooted ones. Recognizing children as sacred beings, and treating them as such, is one of three underlying principles in the Lakota belief system that we will explore here as a basis for understanding and internalizing racial harmony.

In the Lakota tradition, as with other American Indian traditions, there is no clear division between the sacred and the secular. All life is sacred. Human beings are essentially sacred beings. As a sacred being in a sacred creation in which every other created thing is sacred, it becomes our primary responsibility to honor and respect everything around us as sacred. We are both spirit and flesh, sacred and material, but when we put the sacred aspect of our being first, that could change the way we see everything else. This may be a way of seeing life that is fundamentally different from, even antithetical to, the way schools and the rest of society view life. We want to examine this contrasting American Indian picture of life, and to propose how this view of seeing all life as sacred could help eliminate many of the social ills that stem from ways of viewing life that permit inequality and prejudice.

Life, for the Lakota, was from the beginning like a huge, interwoven design in which each element, or strand, played an important and equal part in contributing to the whole. Each part of the design is what it is due to the interaction of all other parts. Each part is connected to and influences the other parts. This inherent order and connectedness in the creation gives the Lakota people a glimpse of the Great Mystery that is life, and a sense of their basic purpose in life, which is to care for the land and live in harmony with all of creation.

It is true that many of the Lakota and people of other Indian nations in the past 150 years have been schooled away from their ancient values of fortitude, respect, wisdom, and generosity toward the white society's primary values of individualism, acquisitiveness, and materialism. Hundreds of native languages and ceremonial songs have been forgotten. Yet, such life-giving and life-affirming values can never really lose their power. They are what ultimately connect the human spirit to its Creator. Kinship with all creatures is a real, active, and living principle. Native peoples are renewing the innate capacity to dream, and are rediscovering the essential spirituality that all humans share. The ancient Lakota values that support all of humanity's essential sacredness can be understood as auxiliary to the three primary principles that follow.

1. Mitakuye Oyasin

The first underlying principle of the Lakota world view that establishes a strong foundation for seeing children as sacred beings, and which every child learns and relearns throughout his life, is the healing concept of *mitakuye oyasin.* This Lakota word means, "We are all related." Kinship with all creatures above, below, and in the water is a living principle that gives the Lakota a feeling of safety in the world, as well as a feeling of reverence for all life, a sense of purpose for all things in the scheme of existence with equal importance to all, and an abiding love. This concept of life and its relations fills the Lakota with the joy and mystery of life. As Standing Bear (1933) puts it, the Lakota could not despise any creature, because all creatures are of one blood, made by the same hand, and filled with the essence of the Great Mystery.

This principle implies that there is really only one human family, though there are people of many colors. A Lakota holy man, Black Elk (Neidardt, 1972), understood this fundamental concept through his vision:

> I saw more than I can tell, and I understood more than I saw; for I was seeing in a sacred manner the shapes of all things in the spirit, and the shape of all shapes as they must live together like one being. And I saw that the sacred hoop of my people was one of many hoops that made one circle, wide as daylight and as starlight, and in the center grew one

mighty flowering tree to shelter all the children of one mother and one father. And I saw that it was holy. (p. 36)

The four sacred colors used in Lakota ceremonies - red, yellow, black, and white - represent the colors of humankind. Traditional Lakota believe that one day all will hold hands on this earth in peace. The idea of prejudice against any particular people is a foreign one to Lakota who have been raised to understand the sacredness of all beings. Of course, Indian children living in isolated South Dakota reservations have little opportunity to meet their African-American or Asian-American relatives, so the idea of respect for the four sacred colors is not often tested.

When a troupe of Australian Aboriginal dancers of the Yolgna tribe in Arnham Land were taken on a Trail of Light to schools on six Lakota reservations in December of 1992, such an opportunity arose. Before each performance, the Dreamtime Dancers were introduced in these ways to maximize the Lakota perspective: "You know how we use the four sacred colors in our ceremonies to honor Wakan Tanka's creation? Now we have a chance to show a real Lakota welcome to black fathers, brothers, and sons who have traveled thousands of miles from their homes to meet you, to dance for you, and to tell you about their people. Watch how their dances are different from ours. Show them our famous Lakota bravery when they ask you to dance with them. Listen to why they paint their bodies in such beautiful designs." Without exception, the hundreds of Lakota school children showed rapt attention during the performances. They danced with the Aboriginals, and afterwards shook their hands, smiled at them and lined up to thank them for their sharing of culture. At community meetings, adults showed this same warmth. When the four Aboriginals were adopted by one Hunkpapa Lakota family and given names, three hundred Lakota stood in respect when the honoring song using their new names was sung.

Mitakuye oyasin – we are all related – is said upon entering the sweat lodge, when smoking the sacred pipe, before eating, and after drinking water in a ceremony. It is an affirmation of an all-inclusive unity, a connectedness that includes all created things. Upon saying this, children and all others are reminded often that all of creation is related and deserves respect and protection, that the animals, the birds, the crawling beings, the plants and trees and even the mountains, rivers, and stones on our mother, the earth, are all related to one another. This is a principle, a view of life, that supports family, community, complete interdependence, and unity on all levels, and disallows prejudice of any kind.

2. *Wolakota*

A second principle upon which the Lakota world view is founded is that of *wolakota*, or harmony and balance. The core of Lakota wisdom is to achieve harmony and balance with the creation so that life will be good for each of the seven generations to come. When individuals take things into their own hands, or forget their sacred obligations, such as prayer and participating in the ceremonies, they can find themselves out of balance, or in a state of inner confusion and chaos. It is then that one of the seven sacred ceremonies is undergone to help restore and achieve harmony and balance. Traditional Lakota seek to achieve this state of balance, and then to live it.

In the case when someone is the target of another's unbalanced behavior, an unusual approach is used to help that person regain his balance. A woman was once given a rough time by a couple of men, to the point where they were being overly critical. "You're never going to be the people's advocate the way Delores is," one of them said. This made the woman feel awful. Someone close to her said, "It's them. They're way off the path. If you were at home you could sponsor a ceremony for them. Then everyone could help guide them back to the state of wolakota. But since you're in the city, the most you can do is pray for them."

Lakota are also taught to strive for harmony on two levels, with nature and with other human beings. The good life consists of living in harmony with the creation since nature is a manifestation of the power of the Creator. The cornerstone of Lakota ethics is a deep concern for the "innerness" of another human being. People are expected to always act in a kind and thoughtful manner toward others, due to a basic regard for another's feelings, and a basic need for balance in life. Striving to be in balance on this sacred path, and in harmony with all creatures, is the sign of truly understanding the principle of "we are all related."

3. *Wakan Yeja*

A third principle, which is essential to planning for the education of children, is the principle that explains who children are. The Lakota view of the child as a sacred being is central to a way of life that fills each person with a sense of an abiding love and joy for the mystery of life. It gives each person a reverence for all life, and makes it possible to see all things in the scheme of existence as equal. *Wakan yeja*, in its fullest sense, means sacred one, consecrated one, the being endowed with a spiritual quality.

When children are not only intentionally included in this sacred world view, but given the guidance to understand their own nature and what this all-pervasive sacredness of life really means, the ramifications are very significant. The sacred being is, first of all, perceived as a gift from the Creator. A Lakota belief is that the *wakan yeja*, before it is born, looks down from the spirit world to search for the parents and family who need a sacred being. In anticipation of the arrival of a Beloved Child, some Lakota mothers even today bead the soles of the *wakan yeja's* first moccasins.

From conception on, the transmission of unconditional love to the sacred being is the primary role of the parents. This is the foundation of life for the Lakota. Unconditional love means that the child is loved no matter what. Regardless of whatever weight, size, or appearance the child may have, regardless of whatever mistakes, performance, or limitations are manifested, at whatever age, the child is loved unconditionally. This is an intrinsic part of the Lakota value system and world view. Unconditional love is transmitted by focused attention, physical contact, playfulness, and gentle discipline.

Focused attention is when parents give the child their complete watchfulness, appreciation, and regard through direct eye contact. It is from this undivided attention that the child feels valued and develops a healthy self-esteem.

Nurturing through physical and spiritual contact is also considered essential to the child's growth. Even before they can see it, Lakota parents sing, talk to, and massage their gift from God. In utero, the sacred being begins to receive this genuine love from the parents as well as other family members and friends. The mother's spiritual influence counts for most, as it is her private meditations that instill into the receptive soul of the unborn child the love of the "Great Mystery" and a sense of relationship to all of creation. The mother even wanders prayerfully in the beauty and stillness of nature, or the silent prairie, in anticipation of the day of days in her life.

When the sacred being is born into a traditional home, it is a time of joyousness and thankfulness. Rather than coming into this world with original sin, the sacred being arrives carrying within it divine qualities. These spiritual qualities are meant to be nurtured so that they can flourish.

Birthing is a calm and gentle time, with family arriving immediately after the joyous birth. The first sounds the newborn Lakota baby hears are soft, loving voices. The infant is touched and caressed by the parents and family members. The Lakota mother nurses her baby for at least the first two years of its life. The Lakota baby is not permitted to cry and is carried about by family members. The Lakota cradle-board is making a comeback so the baby can be securely carried on walks and propped up against a tree in the summertime to watch family activities. When the baby is bathed, dried or changed, the arms, hands, back, chest, legs, and feet are massaged with oil or powder, with the parent all the while talking, singing, or smiling, and looking into the sacred being's eyes.

This affectionate touching, holding, cuddling, and hugging from both parents and family continues until puberty. At that time, a change in the age-appropriate affectionate behavior on the part of the parents toward their children of the opposite sex is evident. Both adolescent boys and girls still need physical affection, but this affection is modified to show respect. Teenagers will accept kisses on the cheek and forehead, quick bear-hugs and touching of the arms, hands and shoulders from parents and grandparents. Eye contact will be modified slightly; men and women lower their eyes and make only sporadic eye contact - conveying respect when talking to one another. It remains appropriate for mothers and daughters to show affection toward one another all of their lives.

Playfulness and joyfulness are expressed by Lakota parents toward their sacred being. It is not true that Indian parents are solemn, stern and stoic with their children. Instead, laughing, smiling and playfulness are the norm for Lakota parents and the extended family.

Another way to show unconditional love of the sacred being is through gentle discipline. In families where predominate society schooling has been avoided or unlearned, the sacred being is never slapped, spanked, beaten or physically abused as a means of discipline, but is touched only with loving hands. The traditional Lakota parent disciplines the child indirectly and never in public. A mother would say such things as, "Lakota boys and girls are always kind to one another, especially brothers and sisters and boy cousins and girl cousins. It is always this way." Or perhaps, "Lakota girls and boys are kind to animals; they think of others." Or maybe, "Did I hear someone being noisy? It must have been the older ones; they forgot." The older ones know they weren't guilty, but would understand that the little ones would learn eventually.

All of this creates a strong basis of guided and deliberate nurturing that helps build a sense of wonder in the child. Again, as Luther Standing Bear (1933) has written:

> Reflection upon life and its meaning, consideration of its wonders, and observation of the world of creatures, began with childhood. Knowledge was inherent in all things. The world was a library and its books were the stones, leaves, grass, brooks, and the birds and animals that shared, alike

> with us, the storms and blessings of earth... In talking to children, the old Lakota would place a hand on the ground and explain: "We sit in the lap of our Mother. From her we, and all other living things, come. We shall soon pass, but the place where we now rest will last forever." So we, too, learned to sit or lie on the ground and become conscious of life about us in its multitude of forms. (p. 193)

The sense of wonder, which is this conscious awareness of the world all around us, is nurtured further by the utilization of the second of two types of education known by the Lakota. The first kind, *kaonspe*, is education by force. This is the approach used in breaking a horse. The second kind is *woksapa*, a gradual adjustment to nature and all its aspects. An uncle or grandfather will begin to guide the child along the *woksapa* path as soon as he begins to crawl. The grandfather will tell the child, "Ablejayo!" (beware, take notice). Then for a few minutes, and periodically throughout the day, the grandfather will help the child to hear, smell, feel and see everything in his environment. This training will continue as the child begins to walk and play outdoors. Soon, when the child hears "Ablejeyo!" he is able to concentrate and then describe textures, bird songs, breezes, moss on a tree, and even distant animal hooves that his prone body has felt through earth vibrations.

This is the way sacred beings are helped to achieve responsibility, wisdom, and happiness. It is through observing and participating in nature that we come to understand and appreciate the beauty and patterns of nature, and in the process gain a greater sense of meaning for the way nature works and its role in our lives. This practical, gradual, way of learning through adjusting to what we find around us can be applied to other areas of education, especially when it comes to acquiring virtues, or developing spiritual qualities.

The Four Lakota Values

Children raised as sacred beings in a Lakota home come to know, understand, and enact in their everyday behavior the four primary Lakota values of courage, respect, generosity, and wisdom. The quality of courage or fortitude is an important one that relates directly to the survival of the Lakota people 500 years ago when the estimated native population north of the Rio Grande was a conservative 12 to 30 million. Today the U.S. Department of the Interior recognizes about one million Indians. Courage can be defined as the strength of character which equips us to meet and survive danger and troubles. In today's world, this means developing a strong moral capacity to be able to know right from wrong and true from false, **and** being able to act upon that knowledge.

Traditionally, there is a category of behavior among the Lakota known as "the brave-hearted woman." In earlier times certain women were trained to be physically strong and to exhibit fearlessness. A brave-hearted woman was in every way feminine, but when the occasion demanded, she would perform tasks beyond her normal responsibilities. This meant becoming a hunter if the men were not around and there was hunger in camp, or even assisting in battle.

In one battle, while the brave-hearted women were on their ponies at the edge of the battlefield, one young woman saw her brother fall, his horse shot out from beneath him, and without hesitation, she rode toward her brother, leaning low over the belly of her horse and zig-zagging to dodge the cavalry's bullets. She swooped him up and carried him beyond the battlefield's edge. To white historians this battle is known as the Battle of the Rosebud. To the Lakota and Cheyenne, it is known as the Battle When the Girl Saved Her Brother. Today there are many brave-hearted women in every reservation community raising children on very little income, going back to school while supporting their families, and advocating for better housing and health programs. Contemporary brave-hearted women are attorneys, medical doctors, judges, and politicians.

Lakota men and women both exhibit extraordinary bravery when they participate in the sacred ceremonies, especially the sun dance where they go without food and water during four days of prayer, sacrificing for the benefit of all human beings. Children grow up observing from the example of their elders that the journey of life is "to lead an upright life, to go through life bravely without a whimper, bearing slander and misrepresentation without stooping to correct them, and enduring loss upon loss without discouragement."

The second Lakota value, *wacekiya*, or respect, means both "to address a relative" and "to pray or smoke ceremoniously." There is a respectful obligation inherent in the relationship and the natural reciprocal trust that is implied in addressing a relative. The same is true of the respectful trust and attitude that is assumed when praying with the Pipe to the Creator. This is also the same kinship structure upon which the principle of *mitakuye oyasin* is based. We are related to all, and therefore respectful of all.

Respect is actually built into the Lakota language. This determines the way in which relatives are naturally addressed and helps bring about the proper respectful behavior that characterizes the Lakota kinship system. In a traditional society, the Lakota child not only has a natural mother and father, and brothers and sisters, but also secondary parents. The child's "fathers" are all the men the natural father calls brother or cousin. The mother's brothers and cousins are the child's uncles. The child's "mothers" are all the women the natural mother calls sister or cousin. The father's sisters and cousins are the child's aunts. When blood relatives marry, all the new relatives by marriage are added to the kinship system, too. Because of the wide range of ages possible among secondary fathers and mothers, and among their married sons and daughters, it is possible for a child, at birth, to already have parents-in-law, daughters, sons, nieces, nephews, grandchildren, daughters-in-law, and sons-in-law because all the spouses of the child's siblings and cousins become its sisters- and brothers-in-law. With all these relations, the child grows up learning the correct usage of terms and practicing the respectful behaviors suitable to each relationship while also experiencing the honoring that goes along with the reciprocity in this vast network of interpersonal responsibility.

This extended kinship system, however, has been nearly destroyed by government policies that removed children to boarding schools, relocated males to the cities, and forbade the practicing of native religion and the speaking of native languages.

Beginning in 1963, a renewal of Indian culture has occurred. Many who are fighting for this revival of culture and who see the integrity of traditional social structures and systems of justice are inspired by Lakota histories.

There is a story of a murderer who was not punished, but made a loyal relative instead, showing how the power of this traditional kinship system can rise "to its sublime height," even when there are violations of these relationships. The angry younger relatives debated the kind of punishment fitting the crime while their wise elder listened. Later he spoke, first seeming to go along with them, but then describing a better way. He challenged them to choose "the hard way, but the only certain way to put out the fire in all their hearts and in the murderer's." He said to them, "Was the dead your brother? Then this man shall be your brother. Or your uncle? Or your cousin? As for me, he was my nephew; and so this man shall be my nephew. And from now on, he shall be one of us, and our endless concern shall be to regard him as though he were truly our loved one come back to us." And they did just that. When the slayer was brought to the council, they offered him the peace pipe saying, "Smoke now with these your new relatives, for they have chosen to take you to themselves in place of one who is not here," and his heart began to melt. Then the council's speaker said, "It is their heart's wish that henceforth you shall be one of them, that you shall go out and come in without fear. Be confident that their love and compassion which were his are now yours forever!" And tears trickled down the murderer's face. He had been trapped by loving kinship. Children can be the greatest beneficiaries of such an all-encompassing social fabric of respect.

The third value is generosity, and this is in terms of not only material possessions, but with food, time, and experiences, too. Generosity is closely tied to compassion for other beings. Children are taught from the earliest years to be generous to all, and they see this in the home when visitors come. Guests are always served drink and food. Without asking, the best that one has is simply placed before the visitor. Parents can get the idea across to young children by saying, "We Lakota always share our food with guests. We share our toys (our books, our pencils, our crayons, etc.) too." Traditional stories are also told to underscore the foolishness of greed and selfishness. When young children exhibit sharing and other forms of generosity and compassion, the parent should give them much praise.

The value of generosity is also woven into the sacred rites of the Lakota. In the ceremony "Preparing a Girl for Womanhood," the young girl who has just begun menstruating not only learns the meaning of this change to womanhood, but also is instructed in the duties which she will now fulfill. She is told, "As Wakan Tanka has been merciful to you, so must you be merciful to others, especially those children who are without parents. If such a child should ever come to your lodge, and if you should have but one piece of meat which you have already placed in your mouth, you should take it out and give it to her. You should be as generous as this!"

In "the keeping of the soul" ceremony, food is brought by relatives, purified, given to four virgins who have participated in the Sun Dance, then shared with the poor and the elders first, and then with all others who participate in the feast. In the "give-away" that is a part of other ceremonies, certain people are honored first. Those who are bereaved, those who have been ill or suffered other hardships, those who have made special sacrifices for others, or those who have traveled a long way may receive gifts before others. Give-aways are usually a part of memorials, namings, and some of the seven sacred ceremonies. Many Lakota spend hours making jewelry, beaded goods, quilts and other objects for a future give-away that a family will have. By preparing for and participating in give-aways and by being generous in other ways, the traditional Lakota is saying that human relationships are more important than mere material things.

Generosity of spirit in today's world means trying to understand and love others beyond the immediate family, because true generosity is another value that supports the principle of *mitakuye oyasin*. It means trying to be compassionate to people of other communities and nations, and the people of all the colors of humanity.

The fourth value is wisdom. This is understood as being something sought and gained over the course of one's entire life, but not just by adding years to one's life. Wisdom has to do with understanding the meaning within natural processes and patterns. It means knowing the design and purpose of life. It also has to do with understanding and living the spiritual values and beliefs upon which one's culture is founded, and being able to share these with others. It means being able to incorporate the sacred way of life into one's own life, and to respect and honor all life. It means being open to the dreams of the day and the night when spiritual direction may come to a receptive child or adult seeking wisdom.

Again, there are ceremonies designed to help bring this wisdom about, such as the vision quest for men. This is a ceremony when young men pray for a vision for guidance in life. It is a private time in a remote place where the supplicant fasts and prays for four days. Wisdom is continually sought, though it may never be achieved. But when the gift of wisdom is received, understanding, compassion for all, and a depth of gratitude come with it. And of course, with the passing on of this wisdom, children are again the beneficiaries.

Gateways for Wakan Yejas of all the Sacred Colors

Perhaps we need to ask ourselves, who are we, really? Are we a body with a soul? Or, are we sacred beings? Are we a soul with a body? The way we answer these questions will determine the way we relate to others. The Lakota view would be: we are a soul with a body. That's why children are seen as sacred beings first. Everything else follows from that. When children observe the four primary values, and see each of them put into practice all around them, and when they see that adults are responsible for their safety, welfare, and happiness, children come to really understand that they **are** sacred beings. The effect of this love on the children is a strong feeling of security and self-assurance.

However, children that have flourished in traditional Lakota homes as *wakan yeja* are often brutally shocked when they are then subjected to *kaonspe*, education by force, in the public school system. The Lakota child begins to doubt all that he has been so lovingly taught: he is not precious; he and his parents and family speak an inferior language; his ceremonies and religious practices are evil and pagan; he is punished for daydreaming in class; his "savagery " can be punished by beatings with impunity (corporal punishment is legal in several states); his values are wrong and out of date. Worst of all, he begins to feel alienated from his family, who have been the source of *woksapa*, traditional education, in his life. Then, horror of horrors, he reads on the printed page that U.S. presidents who murdered his people, stole their lands, and broke treaties are actually honored.

While many children have been irreversibly damaged by *kaonspe*, many have survived. Significant numbers of Indian educators declared their intention to revitalize *woksapa* at the 1992 White House Conference on Indian Education. Families as well as educators from many Indian nations are committed to making life joyful for the sacred beings.

The principles and values in the Lakota world view have important implications for all of us. If the rest of society really **did** see children first and foremost as sacred beings, that would have a significant effect on how we would relate to them. If teachers really saw their students not as human beings first, but as sacred beings first, and acted upon that vision, that would significantly change their approach in the classroom in many important ways. In fact, we can propose nine ways in which society as a whole might be transformed if the Lakota view of the child as a sacred being, the related principles, and the four primary values were understood and practiced generally.

First, teachers, and others, would be operating on a different assumption of **who** children are. They would not see them initially and only as miniature adults, they would see them first as integral to an essentially sacred creation, in which all things are sacred and equal.

Second, this would considerably alter everyone's perception of who we as adults are, as well. We would see that we are all sacred beings, too. The Lakota view also includes the idea that all stages of life are within us all the time. No matter what age we are, whether it is a teenager, an adult, or an elder, the sacred child is still within us, and we always have access to its perspective on the world.

Third, if teachers, and others, saw children as sacred beings first, and second as human beings, the whole focus of education might shift from needing to forcefully fill that human being up with facts from "out there" to wanting to assist that sacred being in bringing about their full potential from within. It would then be as important to nurture each sacred being's inner development to bring forth latent spiritual qualities.

Fourth, the issue of racism as an endemic disease in this country, forced upon unwilling, peaceful peoples, would be directly addressed and alleviated. Racism has made life miserable for native and non-native children in school, has turned many off on education, **and** made it next to impossible for many to realize their potential. Teachers and administrators might be able to face this deep problem if they saw children differently. Textbook writers, if they understood the sacred nature of all life, might be able to provide curriculum materials that, rather than reinforcing, would help eradicate racism.

The Lakota world view (with these three of its primary principles: "we are all related," "harmony with all of creation," and "children as sacred beings"), is really a very clear and strong statement recognizing the oneness of humankind. This is something the Lakota people have understood for untold generations. Science is now recognizing this as a reality, too. The writers of this chapter encourage educators to consider these truths and teach them to their students, as this will contribute to the personal transformation that has to take place in order for us to move beyond racism and realize harmony in the family, the classroom, and society.

What is really needed is a proactive approach, especially on the part of teachers and administrators, to help create an understanding of racial harmony in order for this to be enacted and carried out in the classrooms. It is primarily up to the **teachers** to make sure this happens. It means teachers will have to explore and examine their own beliefs, values, **and** biases, and even work together with one another to overcome individual prejudices. Teachers could establish in their own schools a time and a place for a gathering of their peers to share their inner thoughts and experiences around the issues of racial harmony and relatedness. This sharing could become a version of the traditional American Indian "talking circle" where persons, one by one, speak truthfully on matters that touch the heart. Groups of teachers could meet regularly to speak openly on the topic of racial harmony. Groups of students could also carry out a similar process amongst themselves. The effects of these in-school "talking circles" could be far reaching.

Fifth, with an understanding of all life as sacred, children would be prepared to live in harmony with their environment. This would bring about a major shift in the values that have permitted the practice of unmitigated dominion over the soil, air, and water. Children would become planners and caretakers who would see the earth as mother, provider, and as a sacred creation to be treated with respect and love.

Sixth, this view of all life as sacred and related would prepare students to live in a global society. With age and grade appropriate education, children would learn to understand and appreciate the people of all ages and cultures in their own communities, their regions, their country or nation, their continent, their hemisphere, and finally the planet.

Seventh, when teachers, administrators, curriculum developers, other helping professionals, and parents act upon their understanding of this world view, children would be taught the truth of past and present history. We would be ready and willing to look bravely at how justice and ethics would be taught and learned in our schools. History would be rewritten to present the story of what really happened, and current events would be looked at more closely to understand what is really still happening in our world now. Information from Amnesty International's 1992 Annual Report, such as that 143 countries are in violation of human rights, would be considered in schools so that children would be able to voice their concern over such actions and advocate for improved records supporting human rights in this country and around the world. Children will want to know and defend the idea that we are all one people of one planet.

Eighth, understanding and accepting this world view would enable us to become more comfortable with sharing the many gifts of life. Children would learn at an early age to share what they have with others at home, in school, and in other settings. It would be understood that time is a gift to be shared with others, that visiting relatives and people in retirement homes is an important way of sharing. Growing up with the value of generosity and the idea that human beings are more important than material things would enable adults to view their world as one, and all the resources of the earth as valuable and to be shared by all.

Ninth, When we understand that we are all sacred beings, and that we are all related, we, as well as our children, will understand the empowering value of seeking our own personal truth. We will understand the importance of a personal quest for meaning and purpose, to find our place and role in the world, and to live in accordance with our sacred nature. When we have found this, and respect ourselves as sacred, we will respect all creatures as sacred, too.

In order to find our personal truth, and align our purpose with the larger whole, we first need to clear out our mind of negative emotions, attitudes, habits, doubts, questions, or anything else that would limit our growth and our acceptance of others. This is a process that Frank Fools Crow (1979) describes as becoming "hollow bones for the spirit to work through". (p.30) Then, cleansed and purified and filled with hope, a new power comes to one, and finally this new understanding and power can then be given away to benefit others. This is the essence of the traditional vision quest, and requires solitude and sacrifice. It is as Black Elk (Epes, 1971) has said, "Peace comes within the souls of men when they realize their relationship, their oneness, with the universe and all its powers, and realize that the center is really everywhere. It is within each of us." (p.115)

The Lakota principles, spiritual values, and world view of children and of all other created things as sacred leaves no room for prejudice or inequality. This world view teaches that the creation is sacred, and that every particle of our beings is nourished by this sacredness. All things on earth are related through the Creator. Frank Fools Crow (Mails, 1991) makes very clear the implications of this world view: "The survival of the world depends upon our sharing what we have and working together". (p.18) "We need peace and understanding and unity of young and old, Indian and non-Indians alike. We must all stand together for the reason of peace and tranquility of life for all". (p. 199)

References

Amnesty International Staff (1992). *Amnesty International Report on Human Rights Around the World*. Alameda, Calif: Hunter House.

Epes Brown, Joseph (1971). *The Sacred Pipe: Black Elk's Account of the Seven Rights of the Oglala Sioux*. New York: Penguin Books.

Mails, Thomas (1991). *Fools Crow: Wisdom and Power.* Tulsa: Connaol Oaks Books.

Neidardt, John G. (1972). *Black Elk Speaks.* New York: Simon and Schuster Pocket Books.

Standing Bear, Luther (1933). *Land of the Spotted Eagle.* Lincoln, Neb: University of Nebraska Press.

Chapter 3

Racism and Anxiety: Talk to Kids about Unity

by Anita Remignanti

The author, a child psychologist, compares racism to a mental illness which begins developing in children when they are very young. She believes that racism stems from confusion and fear, and that parents and teachers need to talk to children in ways which inhibit them from developing negative and damaging stereotypes regarding race and ethnicity. Ed.

Racism can be likened to anxiety. Anxiety is excessive and unrealistic worry about a perceived problem. When we are anxious, we push an internal panic button even though there is no emergency. When we are racist, we push an external panic button when there is no need for alarm. It is usually easier to understand and accept ideas about anxiety than it is to understand and accept ideas about racism.

For example, a young man arranges a luscious picnic with a young woman who he has admired for quite a while. After the carefully prepared food is all set up under a beautiful maple tree, the man notices a large branch wobbling and creaking up above. He begins to worry about the branch and climbs up the tree to inspect it. The branch looks stable and secure from above, but when the man is down on the ground he begins to worry about the branch again. He thinks, "That branch is going to fall. It will hurt us if it falls on us." These thoughts lead to feelings of anxiety.

When our thinking goes awry and causes feelings out of

proportion to reality, we experience anxiety. In this case the man had a recurrent thought (the branch is going to fall), and even though he checked the branch, he could not figure out how to stop his thought. The recurrent thought of the branch falling ultimately made him feel anxious. Thinking about the branch is excessive and worrying about it is unrealistic, yet when a person becomes anxious a vicious cycle takes place where increasing anxiety leads to decreasing objectivity. As we are less able to think clearly, our thoughts become excessive and unrealistic, which makes us feel out of control.

When a person develops an anxiety disorder, he continually misinterprets the likelihood of worrisome events, such as the branch breaking. In reality, let's say there is a one in one-thousand chance that the branch will break; but the anxious person does not perceive this probability, and remains convinced the chances are one in ten. The probability or likelihood of situations occurring is misperceived in anxiety, and dire conclusions are drawn from the misperception. The inaccurate thoughts generate feelings of fear and anxiety and the individual is plagued by tension, worry, stress and confusion. David Burns (1989) writes about anxiety.

> ...Your thoughts, not external events, make you upset. This is as true for anxiety and panic as for any other negative emotion. You have to interpret a situation and give it a meaning before you can feel worried or nervous about it. This idea has tremendous practical importance, because when you change the way you think, you can change the way you feel. You can overcome fear, worry, anxiety, nervousness and panic. (p. 210)

To give an example of how anxiety comes about, consider Tina as a child of four or five years old. Tina was told she was a bad girl if she spilled her milk, and when she accidentally did so, her parents slapped her and told her she was careless, clumsy and spiteful. In Tina's mind, the idea of spilling her milk became a frightening and horrifying thought. She tried hard to avoid spilling anything, but, alas, she was a child, and children have accidents (as do adults). Then the boom fell. Tina's thought developed in the following way:

Distorted Thoughts in Anxiety
1. I am scared that I will spill my milk.
2. I better hold my cup very carefully.
3. My hand will probably slip.
4. If my hand slips that means I am bad and spiteful.
5. I feel continuous anxiety.

Tina's overriding motivation was to please people and when she saw that she could not avoid accidents, she began to punish herself by scolding herself and calling herself names inside her head, just as her parents did on the outside. Now, Tina was set up to become anxious because her thoughts were centered in the thinking error, "If my hand slips that means I am bad and spiteful." Of course, this process of thinking (it is bad and spiteful to make a mistake) and feeling (worry about making a mistake) came together to make her anxious. The following dialogue illustrates Tina's thinking as she matures:

Adult: Tina, what do you think it means when someone makes a mistake?

Tina: When I was young I thought it meant they were a bad person and they were really spiteful. My parents interpreted all accidents to mean that you were really trying to get back at them. With my parents, a mistake meant you were really getting revenge on them

Adult: So what did you come to believe about accidents?

Tina: I believed I should go to extreme measures to try to avoid them. If I made a mistake then I would get into big trouble with my parents.

Adult: But aren't accidents and mistakes inevitable?

Tina: Yes. So I could not win. This made me anxious all the time.

Adult: Did you eventually learn to separate your parents'

reaction from a more balanced point of view? Did you see that most people could easily accept and understand accidents?

Tina: Yes, when I was a teenager I worked as a waitress. One day I broke a number of glasses accidently. I was mortified and I went to the owner of the restaurant to apologize, I expected to be fired. Instead she told me that I was a good worker and that she appreciated how careful and fast I was with the bills. The broken glasses were not a big problem for her.

Adult: It sounds like you began to re-evaluate what is meant to make a mistake. You saw that people in general are tolerant and focus on the positive aspects of behavior.

Tina: Yes, it was a gradual process of learning and eventually I felt less anxious.

It is hard to get rid of anxiety once you have gotten into a pattern of thinking that way. The anxiety which was created inside Tina had to be considered and thought out more fully to help her form more balanced ideas about herself. As Tina got older and moved away from her parents she was able to rework her thoughts to reflect more accurate and careful observations, and, thus, her feelings became more comfortable and relaxed. Anxiety is considered a serious mental disorder and requires treatment by a trained psychotherapist.

You may be wondering, at this point, if this chapter is going to deal with anxiety or racism. I began by making an analogy between racism and anxiety, then went on to describe what anxiety is from a clinical point of view. It is usually easy for people to understand that anxiety is a departure from accurate and honest appraisal of the facts of our environment and experience. I have attempted to show that anxiety is a distortion of what is really happening in our present life and has more to do with the hurts and problems from our childhood. As I have pointed out, anxiety results from inaccurate interpretation and thinking. When we interpret and analyze the events and behavior in our life and figure out what they really mean, then we can begin to rid ourselves of anxiety and confusion.

The same is true for racism. Let's stop here for one moment and use David Burns' (1989) description of anxiety as it applies to racism:

> ...Your thoughts, not external events, make you upset. This is just as true for "racism" as for any other negative emotion. You have to interpret a situation and give it meaning before you can feel "racist" about it. The idea has tremendous practical importance, because when you change the way you think, you can change the way you feel. You can overcome "racism". (p.210)

Racism is the systematic denigration of a group of people, based on confusion and distortions. Racism is based on the thinking error that whites are superior and people of color are inferior. This inaccurate view put forth in racist thinking implies there are clear divisions between "races" of people. In reality, there are no separate races; human beings have never been bred like dogs to get pure breeds or races. A more accurate observation of humankind portrays people as individuals with characteristics more or less similar to others. All human beings are inherently and undeniably more similar than they are different. Racist thinking comes from confusion and fear just as anxiety does. Take a look at the steps in thinking that go wrong in racism just as they do in anxiety:

Distorted Thinking in Racism

1. I am scared that people of color are similar to me.
2. I am going to make any differences between us look much bigger than they are. This will help to convince me that I am different and better.
3. I want to band together with others who are worried about similarities between whites and people of color, and we can all encourage each other to exaggerate the difference.
4. If I am viewed as similar to people of color, then I will have their bad traits, too, and that is why I have to accentuate differences.

5. I feel I belong to a separate and superior race.

Racism has been around for a long time, probably as long as people have been around. Psychologists have studied racism and found that there is some inherently human predisposition to cast people as same or different from the self. When people take this discrimination too far they begin to view "sameness" as good and "differentness" as bad. Racism rears its ugly head as "sameness" becomes an excuse to form an in-group and "differentness" means an out-group." These distinctions are dangerous because they involve distortions and misperceptions. For millennia, groups of people have segregated other people into in-groups or out-groups.

Why is racism like anxiety? The main reason is that both are based on distortions of reality which result in mental illness. The troubles in Tina's family involved distortions in the way her parents perceived her behavior, talk and motivation. It is not surprising that Tina's parents misperceived other people as well. When there is distorted perception and interpretation of behavior within the family, it is likely that this will occur on the outside also. Given that Tina's parents misconstrued her behavior and motives, it is likely that they will misconstrue others' behavior and motives. What do you think of this conversation between Tina and her father?

Father: Black people are inferior to white people

Tina: I don't think that is true. I think we are all people, black or white.

Father: There are studies that prove black people score lower on intelligence tests than white people.

Tina: That does not prove that blacks are less intelligent. It only points out that white people have used black people as slaves, then continued to treat them as inferior and deny them privilege and opportunity, including education.

Father: Why are you such a bleeding heart? Where are your brains?

Tina: I know that all people are equal and I feel bad that there are large groups of people of color that have been discriminated against and treated unfairly for centuries.

Father: You are a stupid female. You have not even read these important studies that prove black people are stupid and will always be stupid.

Racism is a misperception and a misinterpretation of the characteristics and traits of a group of people, based on confused thinking and emotional reasoning. Racism, based upon confusion and misinterpretation of reality is, like anxiety, a serious mental illness. It is a more virulent illness than anxiety because it destroys the lives, hopes, and potentialities of millions of people in one fell swoop.

The facts about the human race are compelling and lead to the understanding that there is a "oneness" that bonds all people together. In reality, there are no separate races; all people possess more or less of various characteristics based on their particular genetic makeup. As a matter of fact, we, as a people, are profoundly similar in our biological, psychological and spiritual realities. Consider our biological similarity: All human beings are related to one another and we all are at least fiftieth cousins to every other person, and often more closely related than fiftieth cousins. When people of all races recognize the "oneness" of humanity we will be able to achieve unity and begin to work together.

> This "coming together," the achievement of unity, is a social process that stems from the recognition, understanding, and internalization of the reality of oneness. The resulting unity does not mean uniformity, but implies a celebration of diversity, because once the reality of oneness is understood, diversity becomes an asset rather than an obstacle. (Aull et al, 1989, p. 5)

When we concentrate on what is true about all people based on scientific facts and reason, then we have a chance to dispel the myths and distortions of racism. It is only when we refuse to acknowledge the truth about our common genetic structure, our relatedness and our heritage, that the mental illness of racism will spread. By sticking to the facts we can view reality as it is and get on with the task of unity.

In the next pages I hope to shed some light on the problems that racism causes for children and families. I am going to examine the way families discuss racism and racist language, keeping it in mind that racism is a serious mental illness. It is inevitable that children will be exposed to racist acts or language at some point in their home, school or community. If a parent is there to observe the racist event, then he or she can open up the topic for discussion and work on the problems. At times, a child will open up the topic with a parent by reporting a racial incident. This is a prime time to begin a talk on racism and what it means, how it affects the child, the family, other people and how to respond in these situations.

As parents, we need to understand the devastation that racism brings to children's lives. We need to understand that racism is a virulent mental illness that comes from mental processes gone awry in the same way that anxiety disorders result from thinking what has gone wrong. It is important for parents to examine their own issues on the topic of racism. We can use the motivation-thinking-feeling-talking process to assist us here. First, we must ask what is our motivation in working on the issue of racism? Are we motivated to view humanity as one? Can we regard people as people regardless of their skin color? Do we understand the idea of unity? Can we grasp the idea that humankind is one? The answers to these important questions must be absolutely "yes" before we can proceed with the task of educating and nurturing our children.

After we square away our motivation on the issue of racism and become clear about the oneness of humankind, we can move on to our thoughts. Examining our thoughts is a continuous, ongoing, inexorable process that must never end. You see, we are all susceptible to the widespread mental illness that has swept through our society, our culture and even our homes. No one has been unaffected by the pernicious and destructive distortions that cause racism. We are influenced by racist messages sent to us directly and impacting on us subliminally. You can not have lived at any time during the twentieth century and not have been overtly or covertly swayed by the blatant racism of our times. Therefore, scrupulous efforts to examine motivations and thoughts for traces of racism is vital for each parent.

How do you go about examining your thoughts? Capture every phrase and statement that passes through your mind on any and all racial topics. Be honest with yourself. If you capture a negative racial thought, pull it out, inspect it, understand it and above all, rethink and rework it to match your most pure and heart-felt motivation. Let me give an example. I was driving through town and was cut off in traffic by a young, black man. I felt angry and realized that my automatic thought was, "He cut me off to show that he does not have to wait his turn with me because I am white and he is black." After I allowed this thought to pass through my mind, I began to feel resentful. If I could have spoken to the man at this point, the conversation would have gone badly. My thinking was negative and distorted, my feelings were resentful and, because of this, my talk would have taken a wrong turn.

After the thought ("He cut me off to get back at me and to show that he does not have to wait his turn with me because I am white and he is black.") went through my mind, it was crucial for me to capture the thought and rework it. First, I had to ask myself, in what way is this thought guesswork? In what way does this thought lack objectivity and moderation? To answer these questions, I had to consider that the man probably did not do this to me personally; any person in my lane at that time would have gotten the same treatment. My thinking error was that I personalized his behavior when, in fact, it was probably just a mistake. Most likely, he made an error or predicted the timing of his turn wrong.

The next thinking error involves racism. I noticed the color of the man's skin. I jumped to the conclusion that his behavior was related to his race and his behavior was a statement about his feelings toward me. This is a leap; it is not reasonable, moderate or helpful.

To view the man's behavior in traffic as a racial put-down is going to make me feel resentful and it is going to create harmful relations between groups of people. After I realized that I personalized the incident inappropriately I became motivated to rethink my response.

I changed my thought to, "He cut me off in traffic and although it was momentarily annoying I am going to think of it as an accident. Also, I am going to keep in mind the time when I recently cut off another person in traffic. Most important of all, I am going to keep racial issues out of this. I have to face the truth in myself that I noticed the man was black and I let that idea lull me into misperceiving his motives. I have to accept that I lapsed into some prejudiced thinking and that this thinking is not in line with how I feel about racial equality. I have to take note that I fall prey to racist thoughts at times, and I want to work on those thoughts and change them to get in line with my more overriding value of racial equality and the oneness of all people."

If we keep in mind that racism is a mental illness where negative thoughts of people of color are distortions and based on faulty thinking, then we can begin to see how to solve the problem on a personal basis. We live in a racist society and so it is understandable that each one of us is going to allow racist thoughts to pass through our mind. We cannot help the fact that we are immersed in a prejudiced and confused society, but we can check out thoughts and rework them in order to keep our mind and heart pure and our talk balanced and healthy. Parents not only have to work on their own thoughts and feelings regarding racism, but they have the job of communicating about it with their children. All parents are going to observe their children experiencing racism. The best time to talk about racism with children is before they notice it and before it has a negative impact on them. It has been shown that preschool children, black or white, are clearly aware of racism, and that at about three years old, white children are apt to form negative stereotypes of people of color. This suggests that parents need to talk to their young children of three and four years old to prepare them to deal with racist stereotypes. One of the most potent ways to prevent racism in children is for parents to speak openly about the equality and oneness of all human beings. Preschool children do not have lengthy and deep conversations about racism, or anything else, but they respond with their minds and hearts to these kinds of brief comments and questions from their parents:

STATEMENTS TO PROMOTE RACIAL UNITY

1. All people of all colors have the same kinds of feelings inside.
2. All children of all colors have the same kinds of feelings inside.
3. People are the same inside even when they look different on the outside.
4. I like brown (black, yellow, red, dark or any other descriptive word) skin.
5. Different kinds of people are beautiful to me.
6. I like to look at different colored flowers and I like to see different skin colors on people.
7. Different people, put all together, are like a garden of colorful flowers.
8. I love people and I love all different kinds of people.
9. I care about people and I care about all different kinds of people.
10. I love you and I feel some of the same love for all people of all colors.

QUESTIONS TO PROMOTE RACIAL UNITY

1. Do you notice different skin color?
2. What does it mean to have different color skin?
3. How does a person feel when his skin is different from yours?
4. Is any person better than anyone else because of his skin color?
5. Did you ever hear the word "racism"?
6. Do you know what the word "racism" means?
7. Are there words that you have heard that might be racist and that bother you?
8. How do you feel when you hear words that would hurt people?
9. Do you think there are any differences between people of

different colors?
10. Who would you like to be friends with, a person the same color as you or different?

When parents of minority group children talk to their children about racial issues and present a clear and positive view of their racial group, children from an early age develop healthy self-concepts and self-esteem. Children of color can be aware of prejudice and understand racial stereotypes, but at the same time develop a confident and well-integrated view of themselves. This process is vastly improved when parents discuss race issues in an open and balanced way. A parent might say to a child, "Yes, I know the man in that restaurant said something mean to us, but I want you to know that I do not believe what he said and I do not like it. I do not want you to think he is right, I know he is not."

When children are given support by talking in a direct and honest way about racial problems they can grow up feeling good about themselves. When children hear their parents speaking and listening with concern and empathy they come to realize their worth and value, even if society does not.

Here is an example of the kind of situation that occurs in life to unsuspecting children. This example of racism in action is both puzzling and upsetting to the nine-year-old boy, Dave, who experienced racist language directed at him. You will see that Dave's mother is trying to support him and empathize with his hurt and confusion while, at the same time, she is trying to be balanced and realistic about the racial prejudice that exists and that Dave will have to learn how to cope with it.

Dave: Mommy, Pat called me a nigger when we were out on the playground.

Mom: Son, let's talk about that. How did you feel about that?

Dave: I felt bad and ashamed because he said it in front of all the other kids. I didn't do anything bad to him; he just started picking on me. Then I got really mad.

Mom: I can understand your hurt and anger. I have felt that way myself when someone called me a bad name. I feel hurt and angry now for you. It sounds like Pat was trying to be mean.

Dave: Why did he call me that? I have never been mean to him.

Mom: Pat is suffering from the mental illness called racism. Do you remember when we talked about racism before?

Dave: Yeah, I remember. You said that racism is all around us and that it was very harmful.

Mom: Yes, what happened to you is an example of racism, and it is cutting and destructive. I feel so bad that you were a victim of racism today, but let's talk more about why it happens. Would you like to know more?

Dave: Yeah.

Mom: Some white people do not feel good about themselves, so they look around to try to figure out how they could make themselves feel better. They notice that they are part of an in-group, a bunch of white people who band together for the sole purpose of excluding people of color. These white people feel better about themselves if there is an out-group that they can look down on.

Dave: So we are the out-group because we have darker skin color?

Mom: Yes, but this does not make much sense since there are no differences on the inside between whites and people of color.

Dave: You have told me that we share most of the same genes with all people?

Mom: Yes, that is right. The in-group searches for any reason to exclude the out-group, even when substantial differences do not exist. When an in-group and an out-group form, this happens for an important reason. The people in the in-group do not feel good about themselves, so, in order to feel better, they put down another group of people. They try to put themselves up by putting others down. Does it sound like this is going to really make the in-group feel better?

Dave: No, it will not make them feel better. So, when Pat called me a bad name, he was trying to make himself look better than me.

Mom: Yes, and it is not going to work. He is not going to feel better about himself. And he is going to inflict pain upon you and me. I am wondering what you said to him after he called you a bad name?

Dave: I told him that was bad, and that I could think of something much worse to call him. Then I just kept on playing ball with the other kids. Pat finally just walked away.

Mom: You handled that really well. What you did is a good strategy, because you let him know what you think of his behavior without sinking to his level. Then you went on playing ball and enjoying the game.

The mother in this example is trying to teach her child that he will have to face racism in his life, and she is encouraging him to face it, understand it and plan effective strategies to maintain his self-esteem. Dave learned more about racism and why it exists from a good talk with his mother. Her patience and willingness to discuss the problem with her son showed him that it is important to understand this pernicious illness, and that it requires great patience and forbearance to recognize it, process it and form a solid plan of action to combat it. This mother was able to describe racism accurately without overreacting to the pain of it, and encourage her son to work to overcome it.

The next conversation takes place between a daughter and her father. The daughter is also nine years old, and she comes home from school with a problem involving racism on her mind. She begins by telling her father about it with the hope that her father will talk about it with her and help her to straighten out her feelings on the issue.

Cindy: Dad, today at school some kids were teasing Tricia and calling her a spic. I don't know why they were being so mean.

Dad: Well, what happened? How did it start?

Cindy: Well, some kids said that Tricia and some of the other children of color had to swing on the old swings and only the white kids could use the new swings.

Dad: This sounds like the problem that we talked about before: racism.

Cindy: Yeah, it is racism because the kids wouldn't let Tricia on the new swings because she has dark skin.

Dad: Cindy, I do not like that. We have talked about the fact that there are no real differences between people based on skin color. How do you feel about that?

Cindy: I know there are no real differences, and I know you told me that all people are really from the same family. We are all at least 50th cousins or closer. But if we know this, why do the kids still use bad names and keep the children of color out?

Dad: Because there is a serious mental illness in our society and it is getting worse. It is racism and each one of us has a duty to do something to stop this illness.

Cindy: I don't know what to do. I feel so bad for Tricia.

Dad: Cindy, what did you do today while the name calling was going on?

Cindy: Nothing.

Dad: What did you think? What was going on in your mind?

Cindy: I just felt confused and awful.

Dad: OK, let's start there. I understand your feelings because we all have a hard time knowing what to do. I will tell you what I would do. First, I would look into my own heart and I'd say to myself that I have to be clear about racism inside of me. I have to straighten out my motivation and thinking to go this way: People of color are equal to all other people, and this is true for me always, even if other people around me are acting racist.

Cindy: So you have to rehearse inside your mind what you believe?

Dad: Yes I do, because I know that I could be influenced by the racism all around me. It is a daily process of getting my motivations and thoughts straightened out and clear. I am sharing this with you because it would probably help for you to think this out every day when you are at school observing the racial problems. We all must continually work on our own thoughts.

Cindy: I can do that. It helps me to know that you really do that too.

Dad: It is very important to me, Cindy, because I care about all people. I care about you, and I am interested in knowing what you would like to have done differently when Tricia was being called racist names.

Cindy: I wanted to stand up for Tricia.

Dad: Why didn't you do that? What happened inside of you?

Cindy: I got scared and I wasn't sure of what I could say.

Dad: So maybe if we worked every day together on our thoughts and our motivations, then it would all be fresh in your mind when racial problems come up at school. You know a friend of mine at work told a racist joke once, and, although I liked him, I told him that I did not think it was funny because it was hurtful to a whole group of people. If I was not working on the racial problem in my mind, then I would not have been able to come back so quickly with my answer to him. Think of something you could say to the kids who say racist things.

Cindy: When they call Tricia a bad name, I want to say that is mean and I do not like it. I think that Tricia is a good person and she is my friend. I am going to have her swing on the new swings with me.

Dad: That sounds like a good start!

Dad is trying to encourage Cindy to keep working on her own issues with racism. He is trying to model a person who continually processes their own motivations, thoughts and feelings, language and behavior on racism. Dad is insisting that even people committed to the value of equality get lax in their thinking unless they are actively working on themselves. He is saying that it is not enough to adopt the position of racial equality, that it is only the first step. After the first step, motivation and thinking must be examined and re-examined as a life process to avoid the disease of racism that has, unfortunately, spread.

Compare the messages from Dave's mom and Cindy's dad. Dave's family is black and Cindy's family is white. Their parents are talking to each child about racism but there is, necessarily, a different message coming through for each child because of their different racial position. Cindy's father is encouraging her to stand up for the equality of the races. He is telling her plainly about his own conviction of the equality of the races, but he is doing more than that. He is coaching Cindy to be extremely cautious and introspective about her own inner motivations and thoughts. He is telling her that daily housecleaning needs to be done in her heart and mind on the topic of racism; the issue is that vital and insidious. Dad is urging his child to be capable of speaking and acting on the spot. Dad has learned that it is not enough to confront the racial problem intermittently, it is essential to keep it alive inside himself; it is work in progress.

Dave's mother takes a different approach. Dave's mother has lived her life constantly aware of her out-group status; she cannot forget this. Now, Dave's mother must watch her son experience the devastation of racial prejudice, and help him to separate it from his own self-esteem and self-concept. Mother knows this is not an easy developmental task, and, for her, continual reassurance and self-acceptance is the way to counteract the destruction that hatred can wreak on the heart and mind. Dave's Mom must help him to develop a strong sense of self, and assert himself when he is put down. She knows that everyday work in this will put Dave in a position of strength and confidence. The next issue that Mom tries to include in her talk with Dave is patience and forbearance. The racist talk and behavior that will be inflicted upon Dave will come from mean-spirited individuals, but there will be hurts from well-intentioned individuals who are not processing their own racist thought on an ongoing basis. It is too easy to slip up, living in a racist environment, even if your basic beliefs are of equality. So, for Dave to survive he will need to be assertive, but he will need patience to cope with the roadblocks that will be thrust in his path.

References

Aull, Brian, Hacker, Barbara, Postlewaite, Robert & Rutstein, Nathan (1988). "Healing Racism: Education's Role". A chapter in this book.

Burns, David (1989). *The Feeling Good Handbook.* New York: Penguin Books.

Chapter 4

Creating Racial Harmony in the Learning Center

by Bernie Streets

Development of children who are prejudice-free can begin at preschool. The author, a retired industrial scientist who now directs a child-care center, has had a profoundly significant experience organizing learning at the preschool level. As part of the process, he has been attempting to make his students aware of the prejudices potentially taking root in their minds. The writer shares his thoughts on the mind-set necessary for the preschool teacher seeking to help students overcome attitudes of racism which may prevent them from becoming aware of the essential oneness of humankind. He also provides numerous ideas on methods for showing young children how to love and appreciate all human beings, no matter who they are, what they look like, how they worship, or where they live. Ed.

Knowing is not enough; we must apply.
Willing is not enough; we must do.
— Goethe

I have happily come to realize that one of the greatest bounties received is my recent opportunity at age sixty to be a teacher of young children at a learning day-care center.

First of all, I would like to make a disclaimer about being an expert on childhood education and training. The truth is, I have never taken a course in education. Actually, my only experience with children up to this point was in raising my two wonderful daughters, Karen and Kimberly. And, even with them, I did not have any special training. In my family, my brother, Dr. Donald Streets, is the expert on education, and, even though he does not know it, what I have learned from him – especially the loving way he interacts with the children he teaches – represents much of the model for my own actions. So, really, what I brought into this teaching position were his example and my strong personal belief in the principle of the oneness of humankind.

I am a scientist by experience and background, with undergraduate and graduate training in the areas of microbiology and chemistry. Prior to this, I spent some thirty-odd years in the corporate world as a researcher and later as a technical director of scientific personnel and laboratories. I have traveled all around the world and served on several international technical commissions. Plus, I have interacted extensively with people of many ethnic, racial, cultural, and religious backgrounds. I must admit that all of this has been truly rewarding, and, for the most part, enjoyable. Still, none of the things I was privileged to do in my corporate life – the research, methods and process development, publications and patents, and travelling – ever brought me the feelings of pure joy and satisfaction that I have experienced in working with "my kids." In fact, I have found greater fulfillment and rewards here than I ever did in the corporate world.

Then, why? I have always had in the back of my mind a desire to work with children – a longing that just lay dormant for many years, until now. All of the time I worked for "big business" in a number of assignments and positions of relative prestige, periodically I would ask myself if what I was doing actually made a contribution to humankind, really was worthwhile, honestly made a difference in the lives of people. At the time, I liked to believe that the work I was doing was important and of value. Some of the research I did on ingredients and enzymes for food and medicinal applications, I suppose, made some marginal, positive impact upon the welfare of people. But, for the most part, working simply meant making money to take care of my family comfortably, and to live the so-called good life.

There is a time for all things, and I know this time is mine to do what I am doing now. How I came upon this job is interesting, if not providential.

One day, while reading the Sunday newspaper, I happened to pick up the employment section. Usually, I just skip over that portion of the paper and read the world and local news, the sports section, and the travel and entertainment stuff. Yet, this time I had the inclination to peruse the want ads. I did not look for long until my eye caught a small, almost inconspicuous ad for a teacher at this particular learning center, which, even though not affiliated with it, was located on the campus of one of the area colleges. Immediately, I sensed that this was for me, and, so, I jumped at the opportunity. I called, asked for, and was granted an interview. I was hired. The executive director seemed very pleased that I was a man. I would be the only male among the six-member teaching staff. I thought to myself how different this experience was going to be in a situation where I as the only male would be in the minority, because the corporate world that I knew was totally dominated by men, and, in my opinion, it is still given to tokenism for females, as well as for other minorities. In addition, I hold another distinction. I am the only African-American staff member. I have plenty of experience in being in the minority in this regard.

What motivates me is a desire to be of service, and I find it very satisfying to share my experiences and any knowledge I have with the children. I have been so blessed in my life that I want to give something back. When I am with the children in class, on field trips, on the playground, or wherever, I feel so good– sort of on a "natural high." And, I am very grateful for having been given the bounty and opportunity to bring some happiness and value into the children's lives, and the chance to help them build self-esteem, respect and caring, and loving qualities.

What now is to follow is a description of what a learning center is, and how I attempt to create racial understanding and harmony in my children and others at the learning center through focusing everything I do around the principle of the oneness of humankind. I will share also my thoughts on what I see as the most vital requirements and mind-set a child-care center teacher should possess in order to "teach" the oneness of humankind and equality. In addition, I will offer my own opinions and beliefs as to what the teacher's role should be in helping his children avoid, deal with, or overcome attitudes and feelings of racism or racist behavior. And, where appropriate, I will share examples of real life situations and scenarios I have encountered at the learning center.

THE LEARNING CENTER

Definition and Goal

Our learning center is a non-profit, non-sectarian social agency pledged to provide quality child-care to people of all income levels. It is licensed for fifty-five children from ages two to nine, and is open fifty-one weeks a year, Monday through Friday, 7 a.m.-5:30 p.m. Payment is based on a sliding scale fee system and is determined by income and ability to pay. Over half of our children come from one-parent homes.

The center is more than a day-care facility to baby-sit children while their parents work or attend school. Our purpose is to not only offer optimal substitute parental care in a group environment, but also to promote, emphasize and enhance certain developmental social, behavioral, language, and academic skills.

Demographics: The Students

We presently have fifty-five children in attendance, and of this number twenty-four children are in the preschool group, ages two to four. It comprises two African-Americans, one Saudi Arabian, and twenty-one white youngsters.

The kindergarten group has fourteen children, and is made up of one African-American and thirteen white youngsters. I might add that our kindergarten program is fully approved by the New Hampshire Department of Education, and the children can go from here into the first grade or readiness program at public school after completion of one year and receipt of their teacher's evaluation and recommendation.

The after-school contingent has twelve children who range from six to nine years of age. Unlike the children in the other two groups who attend full time, the after-school children, during the autumn, winter, and spring, attend from 2:30-5:30 p.m., Monday through Friday, and often during public school vacation periods all day. In the summer, they attend full time. In this group are two African-Americans, one Pakistani, and nine white youngsters.

The Environment

Three of the teaching personnel are involved almost exclusively with the preschool children. There are three of us who primarily are involved with the kindergarten and after-school children. We come together in the afternoon on the playground, which offers a nice opportunity for all the children and teachers to interact. This composite of humanity of different age levels is a "laboratory of opportunity" which encourages work on human understanding and cooperation.

As to the education process, it varies. Depending on the age of the group, attention for the most part has been given to "traditional" education and the utilization of current generally accepted methods of teaching and imparting information based on the writings on multi-cultural and anti-bias curricula by various present-day pundits and pedagogues. My fellow teachers are very caring, dedicated, and loving people, and they do a wonderful job utilizing these methodologies. I, on the other hand, tend to depart from the traditional mode of imparting facts and figures, in that my curriculum is based entirely on the principle of the oneness of humankind, the objective of which is to facilitate a process which will stimulate and enhance my kids' acquisition and internalization of human virtues and values. My lesson plans revolve around this – and it does not matter whether we are discussing science, nature, history, geography, sports, or how to make Indian pudding. More about this later.

The Potential

I believe sincerely that child-care centers have tremendous potential – not to mention unlimited opportunity – to start very young students on the pathway to human understanding and racial harmony. Ideally, parents should assume more of an active role in educating their children before they start school, but, many do not. So, more and more the responsibility for preschool education, by default, is falling upon child-care centers, and this trend most likely will continue to grow. For example, consider the following figures for the United States: (1) More than 50 percent of all mothers of preschoolers work outside the house, and by the year 2000 this figure is expected to be 70 percent; (2) there are only 5 million licensed or registered day-care slots available, yet, it is estimated that there are 35 million children under fourteen years of age whose mothers work; (3) one out of four working parents with young children uses child care centers, which is nearly twice the number that did so ten years ago, and the percentage is increasing. (Shell, 1992)

What we have here is a tremendous opportunity to educate these kids early on, in a positive way, about the principle of the oneness of the human family. If we just do this, we can begin to help them avoid the soul and spirit damaging pitfalls and consequences of racism and intolerance. I consider this my most important duty – nay, obligation – as a teacher.

WHAT THE TEACHER NEEDS TO KNOW

Need Number One

The teacher has to know what the problem of racism is, its true nature, and its real cause. It is vitally important to realize that racism is not merely prejudice expressed in action by one group with economic, societal, and political power over another group which lacks power, but, in reality, is a disease – a highly infectious social and spiritual disease. The reason this disease has persisted in these United States for almost 400 years is that we have not dealt with and treated the disease directly. Instead, we have concerned ourselves only with its symptoms of discrimination and segregation via a multitude of civil rights legislation, executive orders, and pronouncements. Laws do not in themselves change hearts. This is made obvious by the fact that whites have discovered and are using many devious ways to circumvent the laws.

The teacher first must recognize, confront and address the disease in herself or himself before approaching the children. After all, for nearly four centuries this disease of racism has been passed along from generation to generation; so nobody has been spared its contamination or left unblemished or unaffected in some way. Racism is a condition that blights human progress, seriously wrongs and impairs its victims, and corrupts, perverts and debases its perpetrators.

The fact that this disease is so widespread throughout every component of society is alarming. Still more alarming is that too many people do not, or cannot, even recognize it in its most subtle forms, and continue day after day to unconsciously perpetuate it. The teacher must learn what these subtle forms are, then look for them in himself. Only then can the teacher be tuned in on this thing and be able to handle it on a personal basis. None of the teachers at my learning center are racists, in my opinion. However, from time to time, I have observed subtle, unconscious racist attitudes or behavior. Let me cite a couple of examples.

When I first began teaching at the learning center, I observed that often, whenever the teachers wanted the children to sit quietly on the floor and listen, they would say, "Please, everyone sit like Indians." Dutifully, the kids would do what was asked, like robots. The first time I heard it, I immediately felt uncomfortable and uneasy. The words by themselves seem harmless, do they not? The intent is for the children to gather, sit on the floor with legs crossed, and be quiet. This suggests or implies that Native Americans naturally do this and are good at listening and controlling or restraining themselves. Now, let's look beyond the words and see how the message is received and perceived. This is how children perceive it: that all Native Americans sit on the floor or ground in the same way, are by nature quiet when doing so, and submit without complaint to unavoidable necessity. A typical Hollywood image of the stoic "red man." Though intended to be complimentary, the statement actually is a backhanded compliment.

I decided to say something to the teachers, particularly to those who used the expression often. However, before doing this, I thought I would first find out from the kids how they interpreted the message. So, a number of them were asked individually, "Tell me about sitting like Indians. What does this mean?" Without exception, they perceived it as something characteristic of all Native Americans, past and present, something different from how "we" usually sit, and something one is forced to do. One youngster said he thought "Indians just sit this way all the time." Another thought that Native Americans probably sat on the floor this way "because they don't like chairs." And, still another believed that if he did not sit like an Indian he would be in trouble and be punished.

The other example of subtle racism is one that occurred one November. As Thanksgiving, 1992, approached during that year of the celebration of the 500th Anniversary of Columbus's "discovery" of the New World, the teachers were engaged in various projects with the children which revolved around the European discovery of America and the traditional celebration of Thanksgiving. Emphasis was placed on the Pilgrims and the first Thanksgiving. Stories were told about the food and how the Indians were invited guests. The children sang songs, under the direction of their teachers, like "Ten Little Indians." It goes, "One little, two little, three little Indians, four little, five little, six little Indians" and so on. It is not hard to imagine what perceptions the children hold of all this. I facetiously suggested to one of the teachers that she change the song to "Ten Little Pilgrims." She looked at me rather strangely, then with a smile said, "I think I get your meaning."

The cute, humorous little ditty about the ten little Indians, in my mind is just one of a number of things that subconsciously implants in the childrens' minds an "us and them" attitude. I found the song rather degrading and offensive and shared this with my fellow teachers, who incidentally received my comments very well. They did not realize that someone could find the song objectionable.

As for Thanksgiving, I decided that fairness and truth should prevail. So, I discussed with the children some "facts." They were told how Benjamin Franklin and President George Washington patterned our government after the government of the great Iroquois Nation. We then talked about the reasons why Native American people are not happy with the way Thanksgiving is celebrated because it does not tell the whole story or truth about the part the Native Americans played in teaching the white settlers how to survive in the new land, as well as how to prepare delicious meals from the numerous plants and animals found here in the new world, most of which were not native to England and therefore unknown to the settlers before arriving upon these shores.

We discussed why Columbus is not considered a hero by Native American people. We talked about "subtle" prejudice and racism. Without exception, when told the reasons, the kids understood. Their comments verified this. One of the children said: "Mr. Streets, the Native Americans were really smart, weren't they?" I thought to myself, nobody would have gotten that impression from "Ten Little Indians."

I say again, the teacher has to know and understand that a condition of racism does not exist only when overt elements of prejudice are imposed upon a group by another group which holds societal, economic, and political dominance. It exists in abundance by "good," well-meaning people who subconsciously and passively manifest it condescendingly in a multitude of subtle ways. The active and passive white racist both benefit immensely from "white privilege." And, the fact of the matter is that the actual cause of the disease of racism is the inherent and often subconscious attitudes and feelings of superiority by whites toward people of color.

Need Number Two

The teacher has to know and understand what a true human being is. In his book, *Education on Trial*, Nathan Rutstein (1992) states that a new standard of education is needed "....that's dedicated to discovering, releasing, and developing a student's potential and helping him understand what a human being is, who he really is, and what the purpose of life is". (p. 141)

Human nature has two distinct features – the material and the spiritual. Our material nature, if allowed to dominate our consciousness, can lead to such consequences as egotism, injustice, cruelty, and selfishness. On the other hand, it is our spiritual nature which nurtures such qualities as love, justice, courtesy, generosity, kindness, and compassion. The teacher has to recognize this and be committed to a belief that education is more than a process of teaching children academic skills. Children need a strong sense of purpose as human beings that will, from a personal aspect, point them towards the development of their immense potentialities, which include those qualities and virtues that every human being should possess and those specific characteristics and talents that are unique to them as individuals; and, from a social aspect, engender within them the desire to promote the welfare of the entire human family. Material learning lacks purpose and is of questionable value unless the children have a sense of what a human being is and an understanding of what constitutes a good person.

Need Number Three

There is an old saying that goes, "If you don't believe it, you can't promote it." The teacher has to really believe in the principle of the oneness of humankind and practice it before she or he can promote racial harmony. In connection with this, the ideal teacher must appreciate diversity in people, and possess a worldwide consciousness in order to successfully incorporate this principle into his course of study.

I personally have discovered that young children truly tend to look up to their teachers and, more often than not, they will place more credence in what the teacher says than even their parents. Given this, what a wonderful opportunity the teacher has to be a "healer" of the disease of racism. By acquainting young children at a child care school with the reality of the oneness of humankind, the teacher can significantly make an early start in exposing the myths of white superiority and of people-of-color inferiority. If these kids can begin to feel they are part of the human family, and realize that harm to any portion of it results in harm to all, and that their happiness and well-being lies in the happiness and well-being of their fellow human family members, then this awareness will be one step forward in easing the conflicts that have historically characterized relations between peoples in every part of the world.

Need Number Four

Love. Love for humankind. Manifesting through action and deeds the feelings of warm personal affection, regard, respect, and understanding towards each student no matter what their background, condition, or behavior may be. This quality of love is perhaps the most important requirement, because if it is truly genuine, impartial, and unconditional, it serves as the cornerstone for all the other needs and mind-sets the teacher must have in order to effectively teach human understanding and equality and promote racial harmony.

It is my sincere belief that teaching is one of the highest callings to which a person can be summoned. For, not only can a dedicated, knowledgeable teacher stimulate a child's intellect, he can, when sincere feelings of love and service are internalized, reach, enkindle, and nurture the spiritual nature of the child and be a source of emotional nourishment. In other words, a contributor to the child's becoming a true and "complete" human being.

HELPING CHILDREN AVOID THE DISEASE OF RACISM

I now would like to draw from my experiences and share my beliefs, thoughts, and opinions about the role of the teacher as an instrument to help children develop feelings and attitudes of oneness, become "immunized" against the disease of racism, and begin to recognize and appreciate themselves and others as members of one large human family. Throughout this effort I have reminded myself of the works of Erik Erikson (1989) on childhood development and the stages in a child's life when he develops a sense of trust, autonomy, initiative, and industry.

Setting The Proper Example, Tone, and Educational Climate

When I arrived at the learning center, I found my students to be an interesting mixture of personalities and contradictions. This seemed normal. I had seen similar things in my own children. I was new; so, the children started to test me. Alas, I was not quite ready for such behavioral outbursts, havoc, and confusion. You name it, they did it. I reacted. My impatience blossomed like the proverbial rose, and my predilection to criticize was given maximum opportunity to be challenged. Yelling did not work, and it became readily apparent that an army drill sergeant approach definitely was not the answer to achieving unity and harmony. Well, it became obvious that I had to work on a way to establish an understanding between us, and develop a sense of mutual trust and respect.

The first item of business was me. I had to seriously look at myself and determine if my mind-set was right, and, if it was not, I had to make it right. That meant examining my motives and looking to see whether I actually had a proper sense of direction, conduct, and conscientiousness. I knew that I really wanted the challenge of teaching these children how to become true human beings. So, that was not a problem. It was my approach on how to properly accomplish this that had to be defined and become an integral part of me. I had to mirror forth the virtues I was attempting to teach. This was part of the "way", and the other part was the application of all aspects of the principle of the oneness of humankind to every activity undertaken at the school. The second item of business was the children. I wanted them to be partners with me in this learning adventure. So, we talked about our not just becoming friends but looking at ourselves as members of a family. "Family" is not some abstract term to them. They know and understand what the word means. I merely enlarged and expanded upon its meaning by talking about us all being members of the same "human family." In fact, we now talk all the time about being members of a worldwide family, and that we at our little school are simply a small part of that larger family, which, like a beautiful flower garden, has members of many different and radiant colors – all of which are important and of value.

Children often tend to be extremely inwardly directed, preoccupied with themselves as "centers of the universe", and selfish. This is not surprising. We adults wrote the book on this. On the other hand, young children possess a tremendous capacity for such virtues as caring, compassion, sharing, and loving. Every human soul is imbued with this capacity. My job was to help them bring these traits into the open. Radke-Yarrow and Zahn-Waxler reported in one of their studies of preschoolers during a forty-minute observation period that sixty-seven of the seventy-seven children observed helped, shared with, or comforted another child at least once. In another study to find out why children behaved positively toward each other, Eisenberg-Berg and Neal discovered that the children helped because another child needed help, not because of fear of punishment or that an adult expected it. If preschool children naturally possess some altruistic impulses, it seems logical that these impulses can still be nurtured in kindergarten and elementary school kids. This has become my goal.

I have mentioned that the children carefully watch my reactions to things they do and say. Sometimes I believe they are testing me to see if I put my money where my mouth is. I have learned that our actions, more often than not, do speak louder than words. "Let deeds, not words, be your adorning" does make sense, because it is correct. Here is an example.

One day we were having a scavenger hunt. There were three groups of children, each with a teacher assigned. My group was the Blue Team. We, as well as the Red and Green Teams, had twenty of the same items on our lists, but they were not listed in the exact order. We were supposed to collect these items within 45 minutes. They included such things as a vial of pond water, three white rocks, five live ants, twenty pine needles, and a piece of skunk cabbage, to name a few. We were instructed to gather the items in the exact order as they appeared on our lists. Now, here is where the temptation to be devious entered. Several of the items noted on the middle and bottom of our list were readily available near our starting point. Yet, item number one was to get the signature of the maintenance supervisor whose office was across campus, and item number two was that vial of water from the pond which was even farther. Temptation set in, and the kids many times asked if they could collect the items as they found them. I must admit I was tempted, too. Then, I thought, "No, there are some very basic moral principles involved here, like honesty, obedience, and trustworthiness." Our purpose was not to compete against the other teams; it was to have fun and accomplish our assignment. We teachers had figured that everything could be gathered easily within the allotted time. I told the children that I did not feel comfortable about breaking the rules and certainly would not feel good afterwards if we cheated, that it was more important to do it the right way than to collect all the items unfairly. One by one the kids agreed, some rather reluctantly. Then, six-year old Penny said, "We wouldn't be acting like human beings if we cheated, would we, Mr. Streets?"

We did as we were instructed and found everything well within the time period. Later, in consultation, we talked about how good we felt because we had done the right thing. We consult with each other after every activity and, when the circumstances warrant it, discuss the moral principles that apply. Our consultation sessions are based on universal participation, equal voicing and sharing of opinions and suggestions, respectfully listening to each other, and no criticism.

Setting high standards and expectations for basic human values is critical. We teachers of preschool, kindergarten, and other early-age children must be extremely vigilant in our actions because they help to mold the values that these children will hang onto as they continue to learn about the people in their world. One thing seems evident. If we do not do it, the kids will most likely by default learn the various and sundry messages which are currently prevalent out there. If we are remiss, then both we and they will be contributing to the perpetuation of past notions and ideas that we do not want repeated in our children's future. And, most definitely, we do not want them to harbor and pass on negative racial attitudes, opinions, and behavior.

I try to be very conscious of everything I do with and say to the children. This also includes my "body language" – the things not spoken but said nonverbally. Consistency, fairness, honesty, truthfulness, sincerity, and the ability to use consummate tact have to be my "adorning." It is critical that I be a true human being with them, because I do not want, ever, to unintentionally "teach" racial, gender, or even handicap biases. One check and balance I use is this: I have asked the other staff members to observe and quickly let me know if they ever detect anything in my behavior that is even remotely related to the aforementioned biases. They agreed, and I did not realize it at the time, but this has helped them to become more conscious of their interactions with the children.

The Teacher as a Facilitator and Discoverer

Many of our children have a low self-image, and they express it in various ways. Some have even come right out and said to me, "I'm just no good," or, "I don't do anything right." And, get this: a five-year-old white boy told me one day, "Mr. Streets, I'll never be a good basketball or baseball player because I'm not black." Some of them come from very unstable homes, dysfunctional families, and at times express extreme fear, anger, and antisocial behavior.

In order to be fully open and receptive to dialogue on the oneness of humankind, the children first have to appreciate and like themselves. One of my important jobs, then, is that of cheerleader. The kids constantly are reminded how special and unique they are. Praise is showered upon them continually, and most vociferously whenever they demonstrate a human virtue or kind act. In fact, one of the things we do on a regular basis is to sit in a circle and tell what we like about each other. They are encouraged to look only for and talk about the good they see in each other. The purpose here is to encourage them to be positive people.

At first, it was difficult for them to "accentuate the positive." It was so much easier for them to speak negatively about each other, and this was manifested in the form of tattletales, backbiting, and name-calling. Telling them not to do this did not work. That was when I decided to be dramatic. Using my whole body as a prop, I started running away from them when they began to speak unkindly or negatively about another child. As I would run away, I would cover my ears and yell, "I don't want that negative stuff in my head. I don't want to hear unkind words. I just won't listen!" They appear to remember my physical action more than my words. The visual effect of my six foot, four inch form bounding away with my hands over my ears is no doubt more easily remembered and associated with the offense than the wisdom of my words. Now, whenever one of the kids comes to me and begins to speak negatively about another, I just smile lovingly at her or him and put my hands over my ears. The child usually will stop, look at me sheepishly, and start to move away. At this point, I thank them for not continuing, and give a big hug.

The children come from varying backgrounds – social, economic, ethnic and otherwise. Their life experiences so far have been somewhat limited and the major influences on them, for the most part, have been various family members and TV. These, their own biological makeup, and whatever upheavals persist in their lives at home impact on their learning ability and receptivity. Some tend to be very verbal, precise, and reasonably organized; others are day-dreaming types, more intuitive, and artistically creative. I am not at all qualified to talk about left brain or right brain influences, effects, or stimulation on humans. I know very little about this. However, I do know that I must be flexible and innovative in my approach with each child in order to promote and develop understanding in them. I figure it is not really important that I am not able to give a succinct and erudite discourse on the neurological basis of childhood learning, or even pedagogical theories of education for that matter. To me, my job is that of a discoverer, facilitator, servant, and pathfinder – to find and use the best way to open the door to a child's powers of attention, recognition, and understanding. With my children, it cannot be done alone through words spoken by me appealing to their logic. I realize that what is logical to me may not be logical to the child. Yet, to the child's way of thinking, he's being logical – because it makes sense to him. Are we now at an impasse? Sort of. But, there are ways out of it – and not by the clash of wills, with my teacher's position power being pushed to the limit to overwhelm the poor kid to my way of thinking. No, they have to come to it on their own. They have to be an active participant in the solution process. Thus, here is where we go back to our mutual point of reference, the "human being." The child is asked, "How would a human being handle this situation? What would a human being do?" This procedure, I have found, removes the situation from "me against you" or one child against another and gives the child or children involved the responsibility for solution. We have gone to a non-threatening area of "neutral ground" and now have a common point of focus. Yes, how would a human being do this? They always answer the question correctly. After answering, I will say, "Do you want to be a true human being? The child says, "Yes." No need to lecture now. The answer or solution readily becomes apparent when everyone returns to the reference of the "human being."

I have discovered that the best learning by kids often comes about informally and spontaneously when I respond immediately to their behavior or comments. Every opportunity is used to emphasize or bring out a point about fairness, love, honesty, caring, truthfulness – any of the virtues of a human being, or anything that will help to engender an appreciation of human diversity and differences. I listen and watch like a hawk for spontaneous moments. Here are a couple of examples.

One morning, we went on an adventure trip to the State Historical Society Museum. I wanted the children to see a special geology and geography exhibit. This was going to be used as an example of how beautiful and exciting landscape diversity can be. This was done, and the children loved it. The "moment", however, came while we were gathered in a room which depicted the history of the logging industry in the state. As we were viewing a video presentation, a group of adults entered the room. They gathered near us, then became restless and started talking, not too coherently, about what was appearing on the screen; others just smiled or giggled at us. I sensed that this was a group of mentally-impaired individuals. My children also sensed that something was a little different about these folks, and as they became more and more apprehensive they began to move away. Several children asked if we could leave. One child blurted out, "Mr. Streets, I'm scared." Many "me too's" followed. As they were in near flight out of the room, I stopped them, and said we needed to talk about this and their feelings.

They were all eager to talk, and all at once. They were just plain frightened of these people they perceived as strange and very different. Everyone was allowed to express himself. Every other comment it seemed was, "Let's go!" I said no. We talked some more. It was important to acknowledge that their fears were real and that I understood. When asked if I was scared, I said no, then proceeded to explain why – that I recognized these were people who, for whatever reason, were born with a condition that made them not able to learn things as fast or as well as they could. The children were then asked to recall just how friendly and kind the people had been to them, and how happy they were to see and be with us. Some of the kids nodded, "Yes." I pointed out that by expressing such cheerfulness and friendliness these people were in fact acting like true human beings. There was relative calm now with my troops, and it was then that I decided to march them back into the room from which we had so hurriedly exited a few moments before.

I motioned to the supervisor of the adult group. He came over, and, as the children hovered behind me, I explained who we were and described what the kids were feeling. He was very understanding and told me that his group was from a sheltered workshop for mentally retarded adults. I mentioned that we were working on being able to accept and value differences in people, and asked his permission for the children to introduce themselves and meet his group. He was delighted. So, we brought the two groups together. It was a bit awkward and shaky at first. However, as they all began to interact and talk, laugh, and look at the exhibits in the room together, apprehension and nervousness subsided dramatically. We discovered that one of the adults had worked as a logger's helper and knew how to use many of the tools we saw. This really surprised the kids, and from him we learned something more practical about logging than was printed on the cards of the exhibits. Young Mickey, who had been one of the most frightened of the youngsters, walked over to me and said, "Mr. Streets, isn't this great?" I smiled as I watched him scurry off to rejoin the combined group.

Several days later, the children were still talking about what had happened at the museum and how happy they were. I told them again how very proud of them I was. They learned something about people and human understanding that day which touched their hearts, and the joy of that experience still persisted. As we sat in our circle of consultation, the moment seemed appropriate to continue talking about some things that are part of human understanding – knowledge, acceptance, appreciation, and love. We now know that our new friends were born with a handicap; we discovered how friendly they were; and, upon meeting them, we found out that they were kind and gentle people and meant no harm to us. We discovered how much we liked and enjoyed them, and they us. We really came to love and appreciate them. As we talked, it seemed fitting to also talk about something our Native American sisters and brothers have known and believed for centuries about those who are mentally handicapped: That these souls are specially blessed and touched by The Great Spirit and must be accorded the utmost courtesy, respect, and kindness.

Another moment occurred one day on the playground as a group of the children were playing basketball. As they were forming two teams, everyone started yelling out which National Basketball Association super star they wanted to be. Mickey yelled, "I'm Michael Jordan." A disappointed Johnny said, "Mickey, that's not fair. You were Michael Jordan yesterday. It's my turn." Mickey replied, "I said it first." The two boys, now quite irritable, approached me for resolution. "Mickey," I said, "how would a real human being handle this situation?" He thought for a moment, then said, "OK, Johnny, you can be Michael Jordan. I'll be Magic Johnson." Billy, looking rather puzzled, walked over to Mickey and said, "Why did you do that, Mickey. You said you were Michael Jordan first." Mickey then replied, "I know, but a human being takes turns." All Billy could say was, "Oh!" The dynamic here was that three children interacted, experienced, and learned directly one of the features of a human being.

While this was going on, something else happened. Another child who had been observing and standing quietly a short distance away came over to me. He had tears in his eyes. "What's the matter, Buddy?" I asked. He replied, "I want to bounce this ball and pretend

I'm Michael Jordan, but I'm scared." Tears were really flowing now. I put my arm around him and encouraged him to let it all out before we would talk about what was bothering him. After a few moments, he began to talk. One day, while visiting his father, he had been playing basketball with some of his friends, and he yelled out that he was "Michael Jordan." His father overheard this, called him over, and told him that he did not want him to be Jordan. Buddy was crushed and asked why. His father did not give him a reason. He told Buddy he wanted him to be "Larry Bird." Jordan is black and Bird is white. Get the picture? A prejudiced, insecure adult attempted to foist his own bias onto his child. So, now five year-old Buddy is puzzled why it is wrong to pretend he is Michael Jordan, but perfectly all right to be Larry Bird. Confused, Buddy asked, "Why can't I be Michael Jordan, Mr. Streets? I don't want to be Larry Bird." I replied, "You are not at your father's house now, Buddy. You are at the learning center, and here you can be Michael Jordan or anyone else for that matter. We can understand why you would want to be like Michael Jordan because he is perhaps the best player in basketball. I think it's a good choice." A big smile appeared, and a much-relieved child went merrily on his way, dribbling his basketball into his world of wonderment and make-believe.

It was on purpose that I did not tell Buddy the reason why his father was so upset with him. If I had, I would only have drawn attention to something negative about skin color differences. On the other hand, if Buddy would have recognized and mentioned that it was because Michael's skin is dark, then I would have been more direct. I wanted to counter his father by first having him hear from me, his teacher, that neither I nor any of the other teachers found anything wrong with this, and that his father's wishes did not apply at the learning center – and, in fact, were not endorsed here.

As a followup to this incident, I related to Buddy's mother what had happened. She is divorced from his father, and has remarried. She and Buddy's stepfather then told Buddy he could pretend to be Michael Jordan as often as he liked at home. Such reinforcement is always a morale builder. A point is made to talk regularly to the children's parents so they will know what I am trying to do. Everybody wants their children to develop good qualities and possess virtues. I have not found one parent who has been in disagreement with this, even though some, I know, have prejudices. Many have reported that they have seen some remarkable changes in their children regarding helpfulness, sharing, and the like.

Making the Classroom Rich in Possibilities

It never fails to amaze me how readily children can discern and assimilate things around them unconsciously. The classroom environment, then, can be used to enhance the teaching of human oneness and understanding. I have mentioned previously how the children watch my every move, and almost instinctively listen for contradictions in my spoken words. How I set up the visual displays, I have discovered, alerts them to those things I consider important or not important. Children are as vulnerable to racist thinking by omissions as they are to commissions of stereotypic comments and inaccuracies about a specific group. In other words, things not observed often can be as potent and effective contributors to racist attitudes as what is observed.

Therefore, a classroom environment that strongly depicts human diversity is what I endorse and have established. The whole world is brought into my classroom. Pictures of peoples from around the world of all ages and descriptions line our walls. Magazines, books, various forms of ethnic music and movement, items from different cultures and countries, and drama are used to demonstrate that the beauty and richness of the world can take many forms. The unfamiliar suddenly becomes familiar. What formerly was beyond the children's experience now takes on some meaning and relevance. Our world globe and map have been extensively used to point out where various peoples live. Whenever we study a group of people, such as we recently did with the Somalis, we look for, discover, and discuss them in the context of the family. Then we can relate these things to our own families, and we usually discover that we have so much in common.

I mentioned before how caring children can be. As often as possible, an attempt is made, especially with literature, to act on the "caring side" of the children's natures. Books which promote caring behavior or express caring themes are excellent in touching that side of children. Whenever possible, materials that deal with interracial themes are used. It is remarkable how my kids vicariously experience the joy of caring from books read to them which concern loving and empathetic characters. After a book or story has been read, we always discuss what we heard and felt. When books on caring or differences or any of the human virtues are shared the children vicariously internalize those attributes. And, whenever we consult about a particular story, I find that the expression of their opinions and concerns tends to help them value the moral lesson in the story more. It is not uncommon to hear a child say after a discussion, "Mr. Streets, this is how a human being should be."

One day I read out loud to the children *Colors Around Me,* a book by Vivian Church (1971) which creatively describes the varieties of skin tone and colors among African-Americans. The children loved it and were greatly interested in the illustrations which showed that African-American people range from white in complexion to very dark. One white child remarked, "That's neat. I could even be an African-American." Some of the other white children talked about complexion differences they have observed in their own relatives. One story stimulated a conversation on skin color in a positive way.

There is one book in particular that I have shown and read to the children many times. It is called *The Color of Man* (Cohen, 1968). It was first published by Random House in 1968 and is now out of publication, and very scarce. Hundreds of photographs of all types of people are wonderfully presented. This marvelous treasure contains seven chapters entitled, "What is Color?", "Where Does Color Come From?", "All Men Are Brothers", "Millions of Dark Skins", "Millions of Light Skins", "The World of Color", and, "The Idea of Color". Though not a children's book, per se, this beautifully written and illustrated text touches their hearts and excites my kids.

I think they have learned much about humanity from it; they identify with the people. Excerpts from it are read to them all the time.

Relative to the selection of materials, I avoid "token diversity" like the plague – that is, having only one object, book, picture, or item about a particular group. Since the population of my classes is predominantly white children, at least one-half of the images used depict diversity to counter the white-oriented images of the dominant culture.

Another practice is to not substitute information and images about people in other lands for life in the United States. As an example: African-American children do not live in the same culture as children in the various countries in Africa. Nor do Chinese-American children live like children in China or Taiwan. By the same token, try to avoid the dangers of stereotyping a group by implying that all African-Americans, for example, live the same way. We find out from various families how they practice their ethnic heritage.

Selecting good books often is difficult, because all of them in some way reflect social values and attitudes. Some are more obvious than others. I prefer those that reflect diversity – racial, cultural, age – and present accurate images and information. Minority faces should be depicted as representing real individuals with distinctive features. People from all groups should be shown living their daily lives in all aspects, and various family lifestyles and income levels, as well as different languages, should be described. To this end I have found *Guidelines For Selecting Bias-Free Textbooks and Storybooks* (1980), by the Council on Interracial Books For Children, to be very helpful in analyzing children's books for racism and sexism.

Find and Use Creative Approaches

I do not teach specific courses at the learning center. This is not our mission. I do, however, cover various topics such as nature and science, art, literature, conservation, geography, music, and history.

Woven into each topic is the theme of "unity in diversity." The kids are told that these two things – unity and diversity – go together like ice cream and cake. Both are unique and different in various ways. Yet, they go together well. The children are asked to name items that are different but fit well together. They have come up with the following, to name a few: cookies and milk, bread and peanut butter, French fries and ketchup, bacon and eggs, hands and gloves. So, with these analogies in mind, it is relatively easy to demonstrate unity in diversity in a geography / geology exercise as we walk up a mountain by calling the children's attention to differing strata of rock. They readily observe differences in color, texture, and feel. They see diversity among rock formations and within a rock formation, and they see how these formations unite to form a large part of the mountain. Then, on the surface they observe numerous types of vegetation growing. Next, they find insects, see birds, and other animals. Now they perceive that living things are also a part of this mountain, and are in harmony with the rocky non-living part. Pointed out to them is the interrelatedness of all things, including themselves who have become part of this mountain. They have started to learn firsthand and experience unity in diversity, as well as begin to recognize that there is order in the universe. This, then, provides a natural lead-in to talk about our common destiny with each other and all human beings. By using the analogy of the mountain, we can turn to the family of humankind and talk about the beauty and unity in human diversity.

Certain days are devoted to a particular activity that might concern a specific subject such as "Earth Day" or "Music Day." Or, it might deal with something to boost self-esteem and dramatize the attractiveness of human diversity, such as, "We and Everyone Look Special."

Just a few comments about each of these. First, "Earth Day." We talk in basic terms about the importance of clean air and water, the destruction of the forests here and abroad, and other natural resources. We discuss the earth as "home." The children are then asked to draw, paint, or write about their concerns and how we might solve our worldwide environmental problems. Once that is done, we consult and discuss as very concerned citizens of Planet Earth. Next is an act of service. We will form into groups and pick up trash and other debris on the playground and part of the campus. After this, we take time to put our voices away and quietly walk in the nearby woods and just listen, look, and send out thoughts of appreciation.

A "Music Day" may include listening to various types of ethnic music, videos of orchestras playing symphonic, jazz, or popular music, and to vocal groups. The children's attention is drawn to the various instruments, people, and harmony that is formed by playing all together. Sometimes we will spread out on the floor from a large roll of paper a long section, give the kids crayons or markers, and play a tape of various music styles and rhythm patterns. The children are instructed to listen, feel, and put on the paper markings that reflect what they are feeling as they hear the music. This really encourages freedom of expression and emotion. Some of the children make up songs about human beings. When we hang our long music mural on the wall, discuss our individual contributions, and share the joy of our collaborative efforts, we recognize again an example of "unity in diversity."

On looking special, the children compose a book about their physical characteristics. Photographs of each child are pasted in the book, and the kids are asked to describe themselves in detail. This will include hair color and texture, skin color, color and shape of eyes, birthmarks, freckles, body size and shape. Also included are descriptions of people and things they care about and like. Finally, we sit in a circle and I read to the children. Then follows a discussion of what we have heard and written. It is remarkable how even in a class that is predominantly white the children recognize and point out so many differences among themselves. When asked, "Are the differences among people such as yourselves likeable or unlikable?", the children loudly respond, "Likeable!" That leads us into further commentary on just exactly how likeable it is that there are so many different types of people in our human family throughout the world. And, as we look around the room at each other and the numerous pictures on the wall of various peoples of the world, we can once more experience a feeling of appreciation for human diversity.

WHAT DOES IT ALL MEAN?

The full integration of this vital principle of oneness and human diversity in teaching activities, in my opinion, provides a better means of combating racism and promoting human understanding than present-day multicultural education programs can. Most of these programs stress racial tolerance. We really need to go beyond that, because our educational focus should be on implanting in these youngsters a sense of belonging to one worldwide human family. My hope for them is that this sense of belonging will grow into an enduring respect, appreciation, and love for all human beings, no matter who they are, what they look like, how they worship, or where they live.

References

Church, Vivian (1971). *Colors Around Me.* Chicago, Ill.: Afro-American Publishing Co.

Cohen, Robert Carl (1968). *The Color of Man.* New York: Random House.

Eisenberg-Berg, N., and Neal, C. (1979). "Children's Moral Reasoning About Their Own Spontaneous Prosocial Behavior," *Developmental Psychology,* 15.

Erikson, Erik (1989). "Identity And The Life Cycle," *Psychological Issues,* Vol. I. New York: International University Press.

Guidelines For Selecting Bias-Free Textbooks And Storybooks. New York: Council On Interracial Books For Children, 1980.

Radke-Yarrow, M., and Zahn-Waxler, C. (1976). "Dimensions And Correlates Of Prosocial Behavior In Young Children." *Child Development*, 47.

Rutstein, Nathan (1992) *Education On Trial.* Oxford, One World.

Shell, Ellen Ruppel (1992). *A Year In The Life Of A Daycare Center.* Boston: Little, Brown, and Co.

Chapter 5

Why and How the History of Racism Should be Taught in Schools

by Tod Rutstein

In this chapter, the author, a middle-school social studies teacher, asks his readers to consider the wisdom and effectiveness of devoting time in a United States history course to teaching about the historical origins and development of racism in America, starting with slavery. Students, he finds, are eager to be helpful in finding solutions to moral problems, and once they understand that racism is dangerously epidemic in our historically-prejudiced society, they become potential agents for change. Ed.

A number of years ago, I had the opportunity to watch a documentary about a prestigious mid-western independent school. It was the experience of a female African-American student from Chicago that revealed the importance of understanding how our history shapes poor race relations today. Throughout the documentary, she spoke in great detail of the difficulties of gaining acceptance in a new community. Coupled with this anxiety was her concern about being rejected by her friends and some family members who began to see her as having assimilated too much, telling her, "You've become white."

In a few scenes she talks about a senior project which involved preparing an exhibit of her artwork for display in the school. All of the pieces addressed the theme of her racial alienation. It seemed to have been a therapeutic endeavor for her, since it was a means to express feelings that are not easily communicated. For some whites who saw the show, however, it only evoked defensiveness. They felt threatened by the notion that racial prejudice was operating in their environment. Because they believed any association with it to be taboo, they sought to challenge such a claim.

In one particular scene, a fellow senior began to question the validity of her perceptions. He rejected the idea that racial prejudice played any role in the cause of her feelings, preferring instead to see her anxieties as part of the universal experience of American adolescents. He remarked that all teenagers have to deal with the stress of *fitting in,* and to blame that struggle on race is ridiculous.

Their discussion continued for a few minutes and the young man's points were well articulated. In the end, he appeared to have gotten the best of her, for his final statement elicited only a non-verbal response from her that clearly indicated an inability to express such complicated and subtle feelings. Despite no comment, her body language seemed to reveal much pain and frustration. She knew how she felt. Even the arrogant posture of her opponent in debate reinforced those feelings. Though he did not outwardly flaunt what appeared to be verbal superiority, it was still a moment of triumph. It is likely that he thought, "My argument has to be truthful; she had no come-back."

This common kind of clash is a tragedy for a number of reasons, but the most important one is that such an intelligent boy seemed unwilling to consider the unique nature of his peer's life experiences. It is natural to perceive the world from your own frame of reference, but it is unhealthy to be blind to the reality of others. This point is not meant to belittle all he had to say, for there is truth to his comments about the difficulty of adolescence, and some of her feelings may have been based on suspicion. But on what grounds can he deny her *whole* reaction to that environment? Could he continue to deny it if he truly knew the dynamics of the history of racism in our society, and how it taints our hearts and minds today? When one immerses oneself in this study, it becomes clear that racial prejudice is woven thickly into the fiber of our culture, and the treatment of people of color by whites over the course of several centuries has created a legacy of oppression that requires the constant effort of everyone in this society to overcome. In light of this belief, I have sought to teach United States history with the goal of providing students with a firm understanding of the historical origins of racism.

I. Introduction to the Roots of Twentieth Century Slavery

At the Friends School of Baltimore, I like to begin the year with my eighth grade history students by establishing some important facts about the human family. I tell them that these facts should help form a framework of thinking deeply about race and racial prejudice in our society, and since these subjects are so central to what defines our culture, in turn, they will be essential to our study of history in general.

When they hear me begin to talk about the oneness of humanity, I'm sure they think "this isn't new stuff," especially since, at a Quaker school, they are regularly exposed to sentiments that reinforce a sense of world community. But they quickly find that there is much more to this concept than just celebrating the lofty principal of universal brotherhood. I tell them that the most distantly related any two human beings can be is roughly fiftieth cousins, and the closeness of relationship transcends our notion of race, making a Nigerian and a Norwegian potentially closer relatives than two individuals of either of those nationalities. Usually, at least a few students are openly skeptical, but I assure them that geneticists support this point. Since it remains an abstract claim, however, they don't become convinced that easily. So I provide them with an example using the student, usually white, who shows the greatest resistance to embracing this reality.

"Let me show you how even after just two generations James here could have relatives of a few different races. According to what we call races today, at least. We already know there's really just one race.

"Anyway, let's imagine James several years from now. Imagine that he develops an interest in African studies while in college, so much so that he decides to major in that subject. He ends up doing quite well in all of his courses and graduates with honor and decides to continue his studies in a doctoral program at a top university in Nairobi, Kenya. While pursuing this work, he meets and falls in love with a Kenyan woman and marries her. They settle down and raise a family, having three children, all of whom grow up to be adults who in turn marry other Kenyans and have children of their own. Of course, these children would be James' grandchildren. James, with his blond hair and blue eyes, grandfather of, most likely, fairly dark skinned African youngsters.

"Now just to make it a bit more interesting, let's imagine James' sister does something similar to what he did, but she goes to China. She marries a Chinese man and their children grow up to have families with other Chinese spouses. Now James is the great-uncle of several kids who are mostly Chinese. And what is the relationship of those children to his own grandchildren? Second cousins. Kenyan and Chinese: truly close relatives.

"This means that one family spanning three generations has members with ethnic origins in three continents, and this is only with respect to a couple of branches of the family tree."

This example usually inspires the students playfully to call me and other members of the class "cousin" for several days. More importantly, however, they are now ready to consider the human experience with a more refined understanding of what the interrelationship of the human family means. In turn, they gain sharper insight into the absurdity of prejudice.

Having set this foundation in the first or second day of classes, we then move through an overview of European exploration and colonial history in only a few days, the goal being to get to the framing and function of the Constitution as soon as possible. One of our focuses during this sprint through several hundred years of history is on the clash between the cultures of the European settlers and the American Indians living in the "New World." We discuss the importance of understanding that the European ways of life were materialistic and competitive, while those of the American Indians were essentially cooperative. In a sense, it was the graciousness of the indigenous peoples that contributed to their own exploitation, for without that quality, the newcomers might not have gained a foothold in the "New World".

Once they reach the Constitution, they receive about a two-week unit on the subject, with some focus on how issues of race figured into the debates and compromises that shaped this document. The importance of this is to give them background throughout the rest of the year for understanding the federal government's role in perpetuating racism. At this point, we cover in general terms such topics as the three-fifths clause and the notion of blacks being property, with essentially no civil rights.

The unit on the Constitution is followed by brief ones on the Civil War and Reconstruction. But in order to prepare them for that, they first receive a fairly detailed overview of the origins and early development of racism in the U. S.

We discuss the arrival of African people in North America in 1619, and the belief of historians that they were indentured servants rather than slaves. I point out that there were some Europeans who were kidnapped and forced into indentured servitude, but most resorted to this station by choice as a way to get to America. This raises the question of whether Africans, as indentured servants, were likely to come by choice. Clearly, as slaves they came unwillingly. But, even if these first Africans in America were indentured servants, it still seems certain that they could not have come by choice.

This subtle indication of a different attitude towards black people leads as well to addressing the beginning of legalized slavery in the American colonies. As one graphic example, I site the punishment of three runaway servants from Virginia, two white and one black, by the General Court of that colony in 1640. The whites were sentenced to an extra year of service to their masters and three to the colony itself, while the black man was condemned to service for the rest of his natural life.

Another important issue dealt with in this overview is the Middle Passage. They learn in graphic and horrifying details of how Africans were stuffed into slave ships, their physical welfare assured only to the degree that they could bring good prices on the auction block. In some cases, the only concern among the crew of the ship was to make sure they had a large number of slaves to sell once they arrived in the colonies. In other words, one theory of how to fill a slave ship revolved around the notion that if you pack six hundred slaves into a ship with a capacity for four hundred, a high number of one-hundred-fifty may die on the trip, but having the extra slaves for sale would be worth the loss.

The next period during slavery that merits some discussion as a part of this overview is the early 1800s. We talk about the significance of the government's putting an end to the international trade of slaves in 1808. The kids' first consideration is for the obvious good that came out of this legislation, for it clearly sought to stop one of the most heinous practices in history. (It continued to happen, illegally, until just a few years before the Civil War.) But, with deeper reflection, they see how in some ways the changes in the institution of slavery that resulted from this only helped to intensify blacks' degradation. This realization comes from a full discussion about which slave experience was worse: that of the kidnapped African or the African-American.

"There's no question that getting kidnapped from your home and treated with such brutality on those ships was worse," is their general, and almost unanimous comment. I allow a number of students to elaborate on that view.

"I mean, what could be worse than being chained in coffin-like compartments, with no fresh air, disease all around you. I would have tried to kill myself! Maybe starve myself, but even then you didn't have any freedom to do that. They'd strap some metal contraption on your head to force your mouth open and get you to eat. This whole thing makes me sick just thinking about it."

"Being repulsed by this is normal," I reply. "The Middle Passage was horrible. But can anyone argue the other view, that being born and raised as a slave in this country was worse?"

"What's the point of trying to say one was worse than the other?" someone adds. "I think they were equally horrible. Women getting raped by their owners to breed more slaves when you couldn't go to Africa anymore and kidnap them. Sun up to sun down, back breaking work, every day. Getting whipped. Having laws that say you can't learn to read and write. That's pretty awful stuff too."

"But all of that was happening to Africans right after they were sold to some plantation owner anyway," someone else interjects. "It seems the kidnapped African had the worst of both worlds."

After a few minutes of exchange, I try to focus the question a bit more narrowly.

"Well, all of these comments are well stated, but they show concern mostly for just physical suffering. Consider the psychological suffering that went on as well."

"The emotional damage of being forced to leave your homeland would be pretty rough."

"No doubt," I agree. "But how does it compare with never knowing freedom at all?"

This creates a pause in the discussion, followed by a clear shift in thinking. Some of the kids who argued strongly in favor of the other view make good points about the effects of a person's frame of reference on his attitudes and self-worth.

I try to summarize with the following thoughts. "We're dealing with the difference between the experience of an African who was kidnapped from his homeland and forced into slavery after living as a free person, and that of an African-American who was born and raised in slavery, knowing no other system, becoming fully enculturated to accept his imposed, lowly status. This distinction really occurred as early as the first African was born in this country under slavery. In that condition, when you are constantly bombarded by notions that you are destined to be dominated by others, and the laws protect those who treat you this way, it is natural to develop a sense of inferiority. Especially since the knowledge of the glorious past of your ancestors has been almost completely stripped from you. At least the man, woman or child who lived in Africa before becoming a slave knew a different experience. But with this new legislation, this would be true of fewer and fewer slaves."

Some students question how universal this experience could be, wondering if it is fair to characterize all African-Americans in this way. I assure them that, of course, it would be narrow-minded to assume that this psychological wound of inferiority manifests itself equally among members of a huge, diverse group. But, I assert that its existence is real and encourage them to investigate the issue for themselves over the course of the year. I add that there have been many individuals who have overcome most of this conditioning, facing great obstacles in the process, and a number of these men and women will be studied in great detail in just a few weeks.

After we finish the discussion of that important transition in slavery, we then address the origin of the Sambo stereotype. I tell the students that we will focus much attention on this subject all year, because it remains at the heart of racism as it exists today.

I begin by asking if any of them had ever heard of Sambo. A few students sometimes make vague references to the children's book, *Little Black Sambo,* but they know nothing of the nature of the stereotype. I proceed to explain that it first showed up around the 1830s, when southern white plantation owners began to feel the threat of the anti-slavery movement. With the growing polarization of the North and South over slavery during the last few decades before the Civil War, those who supported the "Peculiar Institution" sought to defend its existence on moral grounds. Their argument promoted the idea that blacks should be grateful for the effects of slavery, for they were taken out of savagery, Christianized and given civilization. If the system were to be abolished, these inferior beings would only revert to their previous condition, and the American society would be burdened with their presence. In addition, the male slave, in particular, commonly referred to as Sambo, would become a dangerous beast, intent on raping and killing white women. The only way to prevent this would be to keep him under the restraints of slavery. There he can thrive as a potentially lovable, simple-minded and child-like servant.

Having given this background information, I then solicit their thoughts about why this stereotype worked so well.

"Work so well? It was wrong!"

"Of course, it was wrong," I agree. "But this argument worked well in the sense that southern whites bought it. How?"

"I guess people see and believe what they want to see and believe."

"That's true. But there's more to it. They could point to what they considered evidence to support their claims. How?"

It usually does not take long for someone in the class to determine how African-Americans in this situation were condemned no matter what they did. "Wait, this is kind of ridiculous. There was no way to win. The only way to overcome slavery was to run away or rebel, probably violently. The slave owners could just say 'see, that's the beast in them'. But if a slave obeyed the master and even kissed up to him, then he was the good little Negro servant."

"That's right," I say. "And many blacks under slavery chose to play the role of the happy, simple slave, but this was done for the sake of survival. It was a con, and I imagine quite humiliating, but at least they could avoid some of the physical abuse."

Once we complete a thorough discussion of this stereotype, I teach them about a few last specific pre-Civil War issues, such as the Dred Scott decision. In this case the Supreme Court declared that blacks could not be citizens, and slaves, in particular, were property with no rights that any white man was bound to respect.

With a brief study of the Civil War now upon them, I feel the most important groundwork has been laid for understanding the nature of the race problem in this society. The students have been given a description of the forces that promote superiority and inferiority, thus developing a heightened awareness of how difficult it can be to overcome those feelings. But really, this point only marks the beginning, because despite getting all this good background, some kids still question the legitimacy of any claims that these attitudes still exist today. Actually, I welcome those queries and I consider them to reflect a healthy approach to the subject matter, for I expect them to spend the rest of the year investigating the connection between twentieth century issues of racism and those rooted in our early history.

II. A Unit on Reconstruction and Jim Crow Era

After the quick overview of the Civil War, I do a more detailed look at the Reconstruction period. The aim here is to learn that despite the passage of good laws, social equality among the races was not achieved. During the course of this unit, however, a more important project is undertaken. Since they have just finished a thorough overview of fairly depressing material, it is important to give them an opportunity to learn about some of the great historical figures of color of those time periods. I believe that if you only focus on the history of a people as victims, you subtly reinforce the notion that that is all they can be.

I start by creating a list of famous individuals, most of whom are African-Americans and American Indians. I include both women and men, but I consciously choose only one or two whites, because I want to provide the reverse of the white-dominated lists that are so often offered as the norm. In researching the lives of "famous people" it is easy to take for granted that the list will encompass a broad range of fields for whites. But when people of color are added to the list as isolated tokens, a student can get the idea that their achievements are limited. I want my students to consider what the effects would be if whites never appeared on these lists as anything but tokens. But since they also get some choice of whom they will research, I want the focus to be on those historical figures who are often left off the list.

Once the list is complete, including for example, Benjamin

Banneker, Sarah Winnemucca, Phillis Wheatley, Quannah Parker, Frederick Douglass, Susan B. Anthony, Chief Sitting Bull and George Washington Carver, to name a few, I then ask the students to pair up with another member of the class in order to do an interview project. Each student is responsible for studying the life of his chosen famous individual over the course of two weeks. At the end of this time, he must have two to three pages of notes on the individual's life which he will exchange with his partner. The next week or so is spent doing two things: (1) writing questions based on the gathered notes to use for a ten-minute interview of the partner, who assumes the identity of the person he researched; (2) mastering his own notes in order to successfully portray the famous person. The interviewee is allowed no notes during the interview. In the end, the students are evaluated for the quality of both the portrayal and the conducting of an interview.

After each interview, the students in the class are allowed to ask a few questions, and responses are given by the interviewee in character. In some cases, rich discussion ensues and this is where one of the most important values of the assignment lies. By assuming the identity of someone like Benjamin Banneker, a scientific genius of the late 1700s, whose achievements should have been significant in the process of healing racism in that time period, these kids gain greater insights into the more personal aspects of racial prejudice. Many wonder, as they learn of the reputation he earned even during his lifetime, why more people did not take note of the excellent role he played in dispelling the myths of blacks' intellectual inferiority.

"So at least the people running the government at the time must have overcome some of their prejudices. I mean, they hired him to plan the layout of the nation's capital. With that much faith in him, they'd have to also start thinking their attitudes about black people are wrong," one student remarks.

"You're right that it must have had some effect on some individuals' thinking," I comment. "And there were certainly a number of intellectuals at the time who challenged his view. But the dominant views of white superiority were formed and promoted despite Banneker's accomplishments. In fact, even a direct appeal on his part in the form of a letter to Thomas Jefferson in which he condemned the practice of slavery and offered his almanac as proof of blacks' intellectual capacity didn't change many attitudes. Yes, it did some good. But Jefferson, one of the most influential thinkers of his time, remained unconvinced. He was confused by Banneker, but continued to suspect that blacks were somewhere between apes and human beings."

"But that's a weird way to think. How come such an intelligent guy didn't get it? Banneker seems to have been the perfect proof of equality," someone else adds.

"Yes, but I think the point here is that intelligence doesn't necessarily solve the problem. I had a professor in graduate school a few years ago whose whole career was based on doing sociological studies to prove that black people are intellectually inferior to whites.

"Also, Jefferson did something else that is typical of prejudice, and it still happens all the time today. He saw Banneker as an exception to the rule, and he pushed him aside and built a fence around his own views to protect them as his reality."

Once the class is through with the unit on Reconstruction and well into the stage of presenting these interviews, they begin to do some reading on the beginning of the Jim Crow Era, and on immigration during the nineteenth and early part of the twentieth centuries. They learn about the development of radically racist groups who sought to "redeem the South" for whites, promoting ideas that revolved around the belief that blacks would ultimately self-destruct. While in the process, the argument went, they should be made to understand that their place in society was to remain the moral and intellectual inferiors of whites. In their study of immigration, students focus on the prejudices faced by European and Asian newcomers to the United States. As they investigate these issues, our class discussions are geared towards gaining an understanding of how the experiences of various groups differed, especially when compared to those of American Indians and African Americans, whom we also have defined as immigrants, based on a broad definition established at the outset of our work.

What they come to understand about this subject is that all immigrant groups have dealt with tremendous hardships in the process of becoming a part of this American society. But, a clear pattern emerges indicating that the degrees of their suffering have not been equally harsh. Since we cannot study every specific European nationality's experience, we consider the distinctions between northern and western Europeans versus southern and eastern Europeans. With regard to Asian immigrants, we deal with Chinese and Japanese. The goal of this unit is to develop a theme for understanding the reasons for differing treatments which will serve as a frame of reference for our study of racial prejudice throughout the rest of the year.

Once they have done enough background reading on this material, I like to open the discussion by first asking them to address how these two general European groups differed.

A common response: "Seems like there's more they have in common, really. They're all white folks to start with."

"So all whites are the same? Is that what you're saying?" I ask.

"No, but let's face it, skin color is the biggest difference people deal with when facing prejudice."

"I agree, and we'll talk about that soon, but be careful; that's not the only issue. Think about culture too. People with the same skin color don't necessarily behave the same way. That attitude helps fuel racial prejudice. Weren't there cultural and ethnic differences between these European groups?"

They get the point quickly and usually elaborate on it well. "The main cultural differences were found in language and religion, I guess. Weren't there more Jews in southern and eastern Europe? And the languages they spoke were more different from those spoken by other immigrants already in America."

"Yes. See, immigrants from places like Russia and Greece came in their largest numbers later than the northern and western

Europeans. The Dutch, British, French and German peoples, just to name a few, had been living here for generations already. When new immigrants came from those lands, they certainly were discriminated against because they were 'foreigners', probably with thick accents, if they spoke English. But, their cultures were already represented in this society. They were not as different from whites already here as Russians and Greeks, etc. were."

"In so far as religion is concerned, you're right, too, about Judaism. That was a big difference, also, because religion is one of the more obvious aspects of culture."

"What about ethnic differences, though? These differences help a lot in developing our theme."

This point is also reached without too much effort.

"I guess this is where we come back to physical stuff. People from Italy and countries in the Balkans and so forth were a bit darker. They had greater visible differences."

"Yes, and this is the most important point to understand. People from southern and eastern Europe had more difficulty being accepted because, over generations, while their cultural practices might change to become more 'American', whatever that means, they couldn't change their physical appearance. Well, they could, but they didn't, because they tended to stick together, marrying and raising families within their own ethnic groups. So despite changed names, genuine American accents and American upbringing, they still looked different from the standard white Anglo-Saxon Protestant, and therefore continued to face many of the same prejudices their parents and grandparents faced."

By establishing a relationship between the degree an immigrant group differed from the white American standard and the extent of the prejudice they faced, the rest of this pattern unfolds rather naturally. Students can easily see in the treatment of Chinese and Japanese immigrants of the nineteenth century how even greater differences brought on more intense hardships. Here were people who could be classified as belonging to an entirely different race, with even more unusual religious practices and customs. European immigrants never dealt with discrimination like that of the Chinese Exclusion Act, which forbade the immigration of Chinese workers in the 1880s, or laws that denied the right to own land or become citizens. Even in the early decades of the twentieth century, when European immigration was heavily restricted, more so for those coming from southern and eastern Europe, immigration for Asians was strictly forbidden.

When the students take this principle a couple of steps further, looking at its implications for American Indians and African-Americans, they gain confirmation of its validity.

The peoples who were here before the Europeans arrived were not even meant to be included in the white society. Of course, there were some notable examples of efforts of the U.S. government to force assimilation of Indians, such as the Dawes Act, but these usually required complete renunciation of their own ways of life. For the most part, the prevailing attitudes were that America's earliest settlers would have to make way for whites' progress, and their certain demise was just part of that process. Perhaps the clearest indication of the low regard for the American Indians held by the government is seen in the fact that it was fully acceptable to break every treaty made with them. In many respects, there wasn't even a pretense of a social relationship here.

With a fairly thorough background on the treatment of the unwilling immigrants, the students already have enough information to see how and why blacks have been kept on the bottom rung of the social ladder in the United States. The most extreme manifestations of racial prejudice have been reserved for their experience, because they represent the group most different from whites, and the most pronounced differences do not disappear through assimilation the way a language barrier or unusual customs can. Though few students at this point are able to question this viewpoint the way they might have at the beginning of the year, any who do need only to further consider the horrors of the Jim Crow Era which occurred before, during and after the height of immigration. Of course, this was supposed to mark a better time for blacks because slavery was abolished and they were now U. S. citizens, but in reality little changed for the better. In many parts of the country, the most basic political right, voting, was essentially denied through literacy tests, poll taxes and grandfather clauses, and if any of those methods failed, the ever-present lynch mob worked quite well. Economic conditions remained poor, too, for the sharecropping system was in many ways disguised slavery. Strict segregation, where institutions and facilities reserved for blacks were always separate and never equal, became social custom. But perhaps the most pernicious aspect of this way of life was found in the unwritten rules that required blacks to behave always as subservient to whites. Breaking those rules could bring on brutal punishments which were sanction by those in control of the power structure.

III. Twentieth Century Racism: Influences of History

With this newly established premise that contends that some groups of Americans have been wronged more than others, the kids are set to further explore these issues as they relate specifically to the rest of the twentieth century. Indeed, many are anxious to get to the question of how this history influences the present. I assure them we will get there in due time, but the first step in that direction is to do one last small project to personalize our studies of immigration.

I ask them to do some research into their own family histories, the goal being to see if they can uncover information about when and from where their ancestors first came to this country. Obviously, they are not expected to cover every branch of their family trees; that would be impossible. Instead, they are required to pick one side of the family, their mother's or their father's, and focus on that. It is also clear that many students of African descent will not be able to get even close to the goal, because their family histories have been mainly robbed from them. In these cases, it is important to set up the assignment carefully, for it could otherwise become a cause for shame or embarrassment. By allowing as an alternative to simply research to the earliest time in history where information is available about the family, tracing from that point up to the present, every kid has a story to tell, and the fact that some span many generations and others just a few, only adds to the diversity of experience.

One exciting benefit of this assignment is that once everyone has done a presentation on his findings, I share the list of countries of origin that represents the entire class. The students are surprised to see a long list that is far more varied than they would have guessed it would be. In this process, they discover a rich mix of ethnic diversity that is almost never apparent on the surface. Furthermore, when we review the point that this information reflects only a small portion of the family members that contributed to their existence, since the number of one's ancestors in each generation increases dramatically as one goes back in time, they come to realize that the labels placed on nationality and ethnicity are a bit artificial. The unknown ancestry must include a whole new range of diversity that makes each one of them a complex mix of the fruit of humanity.

For the next couple of months, until we reach the post-World War II period, our study of the history of racial prejudice in this country is dealt with in bits and pieces rather than by addressing intense, large issues. Because an overriding theme and core startup have already been established, the main objective is to let kids see for themselves how much racial prejudices are ingrained in the development of our society in the twentieth century.

They get to consider, for example, Booker T. Washington's approach to reform and how it may well have been influenced by the prevailing Sambo image, for he clearly sought to avoid alarming whites with radical ideas. He knew such challenging demands for change would be dangerous. Instead, it could be argued, he needed to be a shrewd con man to get economic support from wealthy, southern whites. Once that economic base was obtained, he could more effectively work towards achieving social equality, and this would be done slowly and under the guise of accommodation.

Another two examples of points addressed briefly during this time involve the two world wars. A resolution suggested by the Japanese to be included in the Treaty of Versailles, calling for universal recognition of racial equality, was rejected by President Wilson on the grounds that the United States Congress would never accept such a principle. The well-known treatment of Japanese-Americans, after the attack on Pearl Harbor propelled the U. S. into World War II, stands out as one of the purest forms of race prejudice because German- and Italian-Americans didn't suffer the same treatment.

Once the unit on World War II is completed, emphasis having been on the Holocaust and what it reveals about human nature, we begin a thorough preparation for the study of the Civil Rights movement. One or two class periods are used to review quickly the early history discussed at the beginning of the year and to finish the overview of the Jim Crow Era. Particular attention is placed on the Supreme Court's decisions on Plessey vs. Ferguson and Brown vs. Board of Education of Topeka, Kansas, in order to understand what inspired such an important struggle. During these discussions, the kids are presented with the details of the famous doll studies conducted by Drs. Mamie and Kenneth Clarke in the 1940s. When they learn that over two-thirds of young black children who were questioned about white and black dolls routinely preferred the white ones as those considered more attractive, intelligent, clean and good, they gain a sense of the degree to which racism can devastate its victims. But the most profound lesson of this work comes only when they realize that the same tests done in the late 1980s yielded identical statistical results. This marks such an important transition for the kids who doubted whether this problem really still exists today.

"I thought the Civil Rights movement was supposed to change all that. What went wrong?" someone typically asks.

"Well you can see for yourself as we get into "Eyes On The Prize". Some of you may have seen bits and pieces of this six-part TV documentary series on the Civil Rights years. We'll spend the next few weeks watching and discussing each episode. You'll see that one of the aims of the movement was to get rid of segregation, which is what the Supreme Court said was so unfair. A major point of the ruling written by Chief Justice Earl Warren was that even if schools had been truly equal, to separate on the basis that one group is inferior to another causes psychological damage.

"Now just think about it. Did segregation go away? How many of you live in really integrated neighborhoods?"

Few hands, if any, go up.

"So what's the answer then. Why didn't everything change?" I ask the class.

"Well, laws changed. You can't make people live certain places anymore. And you can't keep them out of restaurants and all that stuff. But laws don't change attitudes."

After elaborating on that observation for just a few minutes by pointing out that there are many creative ways to get around the good laws passed in the sixties, I usually stop the discussion so we don't get too far ahead of ourselves. To finish their preparation, however, I leave them with some overriding questions to consider. For example: What is true integration? How was integration implemented? If lessening racial hatred was achieved, what attitudes remained that are central to the problem?

The whole time this Civil Rights unit is being covered, each student is responsible for reading *The Autobiography of Malcolm X*. Since it is quite long, I simply assign ten pages a night for each weekday, therefore spreading it out over a long period. Fast or motivated readers can and do usually surge ahead, finishing well before the due date.

The purpose for reading this book is not just to investigate its value in analyzing racism in the United States, but to learn something profound about human nature. Of course, these two functions end up merging, because I am convinced that a major reason racial prejudice persists is that most Americans believe people are fundamentally evil. And despite much philosophical talk about our potential to overcome sociological disadvantages, and to improve character, we really assume that the capacity for good in an individual is fixed. Therefore, when we witness horrible behavior in someone, we sense that a person's worth can only be defined by those actions. In examining the life of Malcolm X, however, these notions are dispelled. Here was a man who had lived no better than an animal, but, when he discovered his true, essential nobility, he set in motion a process of change that involved dramatic, personal, spiritual and intellectual growth. It didn't matter that at first his high self-image was based on faulty premises. Obviously, those views were open to revision, for he later publicly renounced them. The key to the lesson of his being is in the evidence it offers of the lofty potential inherent in human nature and the empowerment one receives when it is discovered in one's self.

By the late spring, when each episode of "Eyes On The Prize" has been viewed and everyone has finished *Malcolm X*, a few more days are used to relate what they have learned to current conditions. To spark lively and thoughtful discussion I sometimes turn those overriding questions posed earlier into challenging statements. For example: Integration has never happened in the United States.

"I knew you were probably leading up to some point like that about integration," says one student, kicking off our exchange. "But I'm still not sure why you think that. Look at colleges across the country and even schools. I know they're not balanced, but kids from different races are attending them together. And what about service at restaurants? Sure, I agree with that idea that laws don't change attitudes, but the service is being given even if those attitudes aren't changed. Without the James Merediths and Little Rock Nines and lunch counter sit-ins, we wouldn't have gotten rid of discrimination."

"I have never doubted that those events were important. But, I don't agree that a little bit of interaction between different groups means integration has happened. Even if it was happening on a large scale, with balanced numbers from all racial groups, that still wouldn't necessarily mean it had happened, as good as that might be. We should ask ourselves, what does integration really mean?"

A pause in the discussion is common here because they think

this must be a trick question. The concept seemed so simple in "Eyes On The Prize."

"I thought it just meant having different groups together," another student admits.

"Well, based on that definition, some of those Jim Crow lunch counter businesses might have been considered integrated; they employed some blacks and whites."

"OK, then add to that 'coming together', or 'uniting'.

"So integration means different groups becoming united. I think I can agree with that. Now, what would you say being united really means? How do people who are united feel about each other?" I ask.

"Let's see, the words that come to mind are respect, caring, stuff like that. They appreciate each other."

"Yes, exactly. And they treat each other equally, but not necessarily the same. This is a very crucial point that hasn't been understood by those trying to put integration into practice. If people who are coming together don't appreciate their differences, especially when one group of those people is used to being in control of deciding how to do things, then what you really end up having is assimilation. That's what we have gained from the Civil Rights struggle. People of color faced integration on whites' terms. Integration failed because it never happened."

Having explained that statement, the class usually spends a few minutes discussing examples that illustrate the failings of so-called integration. They consider issues such as white flight; the retention of a single, prevailing standard for beauty and behavior that comes out of white culture; the way history has often been taught, by overemphasizing the role of whites in developing this American society, while neglecting that of people of color; the patronizing attitude that just being around white kids in school was better education for blacks; and the equally condescending view that all blacks are terrible victims who need whites' help to succeed.

For some kids it is difficult to accept that these ideas have played a part in a process they were trained to see as wholly good. And their reluctance serves to lead us directly into the statement where I claim that racial hatred was not the most important or pernicious aspect of racism. When they think carefully about the arrogance inherent in the points mentioned above, they come to see the destructiveness that can occur without conscious hatred involved at all. A new focus is turned toward the subtle or subconscious forms of racial prejudice that are triggered by superiority and suspicion.

This is the discussion a number of kids have been waiting for all year. They are the ones who kept wanting to cut to the chase and connect all the study of history to what ails our current society. Of course, the importance of the foundation we laid over the course of the year doesn't elude them. They understand cause and effect. But, in the backs of their minds, I think many of them would like to be able to say with confidence that the whole problem was solved in the 1960s. I understand that feeling, because it is easier to accept. Looking beyond the tangible, obvious manifestations of racism, makes finding a solution more complicated and challenging because they realize they can't avoid looking at themselves as part of the problem.

I find it useful to share examples, often personal ones, of how a subconscious sense of superiority operates in whites. I do the same for suspicion among people of color, though I can't speak from experience in that case. Most of these kids inevitably identify with these illustrations of how deeply influenced all of us are by prevalent racial images, stereotypes and myths. In turn, they are able to reflect on their experiences and honestly question their own racial prejudices. Here is a sample of my approach:

"The event that I want to share with you to show what I mean by this subconscious sense of superiority took place at the aquarium downtown a number of years ago. It was my first time there and it was rather crowded, being that it was a Friday night. We had just arrived, my wife and I and my one son at the time, and as we were taking our coats off and planning where to start our visit, I looked up and noticed a young African-American man with his daughter looking at a tropical fish tank. He was carefully reading to her and teaching her about these beautiful fish. As I observed him, the thought that went through my mind was, 'How unusual to see a black man enjoying something intellectual.' I immediately realized what I had done and felt terrible about it. It had happened so quickly; there was no time to control such a perception. And it would never help to deny that it was pure racial prejudice."

Often the first person to respond to this anecdote relates a similar experience.

"That reminds me of the times I have seen young black men driving B.M.W.'s, or whatever, and I assume they're drug dealers. I get so upset for letting myself think that."

"Well, that raises a good point. We don't really let ourselves think that way. We are influenced by everything around us; it is impossible not to be. All the images of black men in the media as criminals, drug dealers, uneducated, etc., create stereotypes that infect our thinking. If that is the main picture we get, it fuels a sense of superiority for whites and inferiority for blacks. Imagine what could happen if the only images seen of black men in the media were of doctors, lawyers and businessmen."

"I agree with what you're saying and it's really hard to deal with," someone else adds. "As a black person in this society I have found myself with those same kinds of feelings about other blacks. I know in those cases it wasn't about me feeling inferior personally, but it was still sort of like inferiority, because I made assumptions about my own ethnic group as being lower. I wouldn't have done that about whites."

"That's another good point," I comment. "And I know plenty of African-Americans who can share specific examples about how they face the same thing you're going through. I understand why you say it's tough to deal with, because I always sense feelings of shame in the people who tell these stories. But, I don't think we should feel ashamed. Responsible for fixing it, but not ashamed. We are products of our society; we didn't ask to become racially prejudiced.

"Think about this example. It helps us see how it is all related to logical reactions. We know there is a huge interest in basketball among many black men in this country; so much so that they work very hard at it and some succeed tremendously. You could say their self-esteem is very high for being basketball players. Why? Because the dominant images of the best players are always of blacks. It says to them, 'This is something you can be.' So these expectations are fulfilled; the best young players continue to be mostly black, and it isn't because they are better than others by nature. They believe they are supposed to be great at it, so they are motivated to work hard."

"OK, you've given some pretty good examples of how this stuff works, and you mentioned responsibility," someone else says. "What is your responsibility for changing that superiority you described?"

"You are right to focus on how to fix yourself. You can't just stop at observing your failures. I think the main thing to do is what I call ACTIVELY PURSUE RACIAL UNITY. That means go out of your way to interact with people of different 'racial groups.' Seems to me this is the only way to dispel the myths and stereotypes that affect our thinking. When you get to know somebody well as an individual, it becomes harder to stereotype him or her. Our history has given us so many faulty reasons to separate. Now we have to break that cycle of behavior that our history has created and develop a new standard."

This discussion goes on for a while, and I know it becomes a test for some of the white students. I can tell they feel they are being told to shoulder the whole responsibility and they don't like it. I assure them, however, that this is not my intention, and that much work also must be done to address the suspicions people of color harbor; namely, the perception that every action by a white person reflects racial prejudice. Nevertheless, whites have to focus on their own healing because the suspicion is often a reaction to having faced so much superiority in the first place. That doesn't mean we should condone suspicion, but we should understand why it is manifested.

Eventually, the discussion also turns more directly to the question of how the history they have studied relates to these forms of prejudice. I encourage them to think carefully about the relationship between stereotypes from previous eras and those that are prevalent in society today. Few people who know this history would fail to see, for example, the Sambo image alive in the perceptions that led to Rodney King's brutal beating. In those officers' eyes, he was a beast, not a man. This is part of a more general attitude that associates blacks with violence and rage, and this can be traced to the fears that began to develop among whites as early as they first contemplated blacks as freed men. Of course, these social problems do exist in the black community, but for every criminal there are many more hard working people who lead honest, decent lives. We let a fringe element dictate the nature of a whole ethnic group.

From the perspective of African-Americans, the history is also very significant, for the current inferiority and self-hatred clearly doesn't spring from a vacuum. It helps to remember that equality on paper has only existed for a tiny portion of our history as a civilization. And we already know that laws alone don't solve the problem. In all the work the students did over the course of the year on the history of racism in the United States, it was always clear how every development reinforced a notion of blacks' inferiority. It is foolish to imagine that suddenly, just in this last generation, the effects of this process would disappear. The causes and symptoms may be more subtle, especially for someone who is ignorant of our history, but they do exist. These points, coupled with the recognition that superiority and inferiority depend upon each other, make it quite difficult to deny history's influence on the present.

In many respects, all these studies undertaken during their eighth grade school year are meant to prepare them for a culminating experience in the form of a race relations conference. We invite students from about ten other area middle schools to attend the day long event.

In the morning, the kids usually listen to a keynote address by either one speaker or a panel of adults. The purpose here is to set the tone for the dialogue by defining terms like race, racism, prejudice and bigotry, and to establish ground rules for dealing with such difficult issues. We find that this eliminates one of the main obstacles to meaningful exchange, because people who talk to each other about race often subscribe to different definitions and therefore accomplish very little.

This is followed by break-out sessions where the kids are put into diverse groups of about twenty, including members from each school in attendance. For facilitation, two teachers are present, but not as instructors. They simply serve to guide the flow of discussion. Later in the day, these small groups reform to respond to further issues raised by a video presentation.

The last session involves a panel of high school students from most of the schools in attendance. All of these older kids get a chance to speak briefly about their experiences dealing with racial prejudice, especially within the campus environment. Then the kids in the audience have plenty of time to raise questions.

Since we started holding this event in 1992, I have been impressed with how knowledgeable our students prove to be. They emerge as leaders in discussion because they have studied historical background in great detail all year long. Most of their peers in the other schools have a completely different curriculum in eighth grade social studies. But another reason they stand out is that they can speak clearly and persuasively about how pervasive racial prejudice remains today, while many of the kids from the other schools come to the event wondering why the conference is even being held. Sometimes, as in the case of one of my discussion groups, a student will openly express concern that Friends School must be having considerable racial tension on campus to need such a conference.

"I'm not sure why we're here today anyway. Did something happen to cause this event? We don't have these problems at my school," reported one white girl at the beginning of our first discussion.

I knew a number of kids had thoughts to share on this point, but since we had just begun and they were being typically shy, I responded first.

"You'll hear some very different claims from yours today,

maybe even from fellow students at your own school. Generally, though, consider the idea that there are more reasons to hold an event like this than just to solve a crisis. Keep your question in mind and see if you can answer it yourself by the end of the day."

By the time the last discussion session came around, all the kids had been exposed to a variety of concerns. It seemed that our goal of raising their awareness of how pernicious and entrenched racial prejudice is in our society had been achieved.

Shortly before our group broke up for the day, my co-facilitator turned to the girl who earlier had expressed confusion about the need for such a conference to ask how she now felt about her original view.

"I definitely came to understand that just because I didn't see the problem didn't mean it wasn't there. I know now that I have to look at myself because there are many subtle ways you can be part of the problem without realizing it."

This closing point served as a wonderful summary for the event. In fact, a newspaper reporter who sat in on our session quoted her in his article that came out the next day.

With only a few weeks of school left and final exams impending, my instruction on the history of racism is essentially complete. Though I do wonder to what extent this work has reached every student, I am encouraged by many positive signs. Most of them stem from the nature of the adolescent age group, for these kids tend to be rather unselfconscious and honest about their feelings. And they are quite eager to address solutions to moral problems. When they become convinced that racism is a thriving epidemic in our society, requiring constant struggle from everyone to overcome, and that it is a major barrier to achieving peace, they become significant, potential agents for change. By setting in motion this personal process at such a young age, I can take comfort that when they become independent adults, they will likely desire to truly live according to the principle of the oneness of humanity, thereby shedding a worn out, warped view of reality.

Chapter 6

School and the Child of Color

by LeNise Jackson-Gaertner

This chapter represents the passionate views of a writer, a social activist, who has lived the very issues which she addresses. Her father was seriously injured by police in a case of mistaken identity. She and her children have been the target of the disease of racism. Through this, she has gained penetrating insights into how racism has affected her fellow citizens, and how integration has failed to produce a truly multicutural society. Ed.

I started the organization, "Mothers for Race Unity and Equality", after my father's racial beating, an incident which still hurts and haunts me to this day. I must explain what happened to my father, because it was the catalyst for my investigation of education's role in establishing change for better race relations. My children are of African-European-American ethnic background ages, seven to fifteen. My youngest sons are twins, and after their birth (April 6, 1987), my father, like any proud grandfather, was excited and wanted to see them. So he came out to see us with a five-pound box of See's candy, baby toys, and flowers. After several hours he and my youngest sister decided to head back home to Los Angeles.

On April 10, 1987, my father who was sixty-seven years old, was attacked by the Pomona SWAT Team. My father had previously suffered from a heart condition and kidney failure that caused him to have to wear a kidney apparatus. My father had to stop in

Pomona with my sister so she could pick up some mail from her ex-roommate's house. The Pomona Police SWAT Team ordered him to get out of the car for what the police later called a case of mistaken identity. My father, a retired Los Angeles sheriff's deputy, had served twenty-eight years in law enforcement. On that night, the Pomona Police SWAT Team was looking for "a black male robbery suspect" approximately twenty-five years of age. The SWAT team pulled his car over and ordered my father, Woodrow, out of the car. The officers told him to walk backward toward them. Walking backwards in the dark of night would be a difficult task for a young man let alone my father, who had a serious heart condition. The officers beat my father, hurled him up into the air, and body-slammed him to the ground. He was cursed at and handcuffed. His kidney dialysis apparatus, implanted in his body, had by that time become dislodged. These officers injured my father both physically and emotionally.

My parents had tried all their life to protect our family from racism, and it still came to my family's doorstep every day. The beating of my father subsequently resulted in my mother and I both taking care of him for over a year. This was all a reminder that racism is more than being called names and being insulted all of your life. Racism is life-threatening. I decided that something had to be done and I had to do it.

These officers were people who had certain preconceived ideas about African-American people because of their upbringing and education. As a mother and an activist, I have committed my life to eradicating racism for the sake of my children, and ultimately all children. It was my way of working against existing bigotry, hatred, and ignorance. I decided to do this by directly confronting educational institutions about their miseducation of, and racial attitudes against, African-American children. As an African-American woman, and mother, I clearly understand the tragedy of racism and its oppression, but not from a textbook study course or a class in ethnic studies. My authority and expertise regarding racism come directly from my life experience of being black in America and working against those elements and peoples who chose to oppress.

The police officers who attacked my father came from the community. The team's racial misconceptions, stereotypes and aggressive behavior toward my father, as an African-American, adult male, are not unique to the police. They are no different from anyone else in American institutions, with one exception; they have the power and authority to arrest, hurt, or kill with few if any questions asked. In looking at my children, especially my sons, I wondered what would happen to them as young black men because of racism. Upon reflection, clearly, the violent occurrences between the races are inevitable, given the lack of value placed on African-American people's lives in this country, and the refusal by European-Americans to coexist with African-Americans as equals. I see public education as the only tool to educate children in large numbers across America away from racial misconception and cultural intolerance. This means there must be a complete overhaul, and an honest assessment of the current public school system's approach to teaching children of color and also European-American children. The educational system must address in a straight forward manner its responsibility to re-educate the child and average citizen towards racial unity.

Racism and ethnic deprivation are pumped through the public school systems like poison through a body, making that body anemic, sick and weakened. I am not the only African-American parent who is aware of this happening. In fact, I want to scream every time I think about what our schools are doing to the children of color. The schools in America are slowly coming under scrutiny by most parents of color because they do not trust the intentions and attitudes of the faculty, who are almost entirely European-Americans. History has recorded a constant conflict between blacks and whites in America's schools and communities, so the fact that European-Americans run the schools in such large numbers raises legitimate questions and concern among African-American parents regarding their children's education. This is important because most white teachers don't understand most black kids. This condition exists because most teachers don't live in black neighborhoods.

The racial socialization brought about by "white racism" affects the interaction between whites and people of color in every stratum of society, and certainly this includes public schools. Public education has its own place in history when it comes to racial problems and segregation as seen in the past and the present for African-American students. One can easily trace the forced segregation of American children of color in schools up to the late 1970s by the European-American communities. This segregation was a common form of social humiliation for people of color. European-Americans used both state and federal laws to their advantage in promoting racial ideas of separation as being a morally correct agenda for America's multi-ethnic society.

This decision to segregate children was not done with the consultation or agreement of people of color. African-Americans, Native Americans, Latinos and Asians worked, served and died in the military, and paid taxes. These same people of color had no say in the policies of schools run by the local, state or federal governments. The European-Americans were determined to control and keep schools segregated even if it meant racial violence and the closing of public schools indefinitely.

The thought of desegregation resulted in the National Guard being called out to stop the violence of European-American citizens, parents and students against African-American children for years in this country. The desegregation of schools was such a volatile issue between European-Americans and African-Americans in particular that leaders from both ethnic groups predicted it would cause unbridled violence and civil unrest. The 1950s' desegregation case of the Little Rock Nine in Arkansas is a vivid reminder of how steadfast European-Americans were as an ethnic group in maintaining segregation. President Eisenhower had to request federal troops to protect the nine African-American students going to school in Little Rock once the Supreme Court overturned the segregation laws. As recently as 1994, an Alabama high-school principal was suspended with pay because he told all the students at the school assembly that he would not permit any interracial couples to attend the school prom. Student ReVonda Bowen, who is interracial, confronted the principal. She asked him what he thought about her parents. ReVonda's parents are an interracial couple. Principal Hulond Humphries told ReVonda Bowen that her parents, an African-American woman and a European-American man, had made a "mistake" by marrying and having children. Hulond Humphries received overwhelming support from members of the European-American community in Wedowee, Alabama. Principal Humphries received no penalties, pay losses, or probation. He was reinstated. Yet, in the light of all this, public school officials and teachers seem puzzled at the open resistance and growing interest of African-American parents in an Afrocentric curriculum and segregated schools for their children. The answer is simple. Integration did not protect African-American children and other children of color from ethnic negation, emotional racial problems and certain academic failure. This was all a self fulfilling prophecy of integration.

My own children, from the time they entered school as young as five years old, have and continue to be called "niggers" every day by European-American children who attend their schools. Their teachers have told me that they don't know how to stop the children in class from saying racially inappropriate things to each other. My children's European-American teachers loved telling me, as an African-American woman, that "black kids call other black kids nigger", which justified their own lack of effort and inability to resolve this problem. First of all, why would any European-American teacher think that under the current educational system, and the generally racist atmosphere in society, that African-American children would be exempt from internalizing a hatred of self and call themselves niggers. After all, African-Americans have been systematically taught by the schools and this society for generations that they were invisible, and not valued as a people.

The practice in schools of depriving African-American students of a positive view of their ethnic history has caused a form of ethnic negation in these children. Ethnic negation is taught through destroying an ethnic group's perception of its history, and its image of itself in society. When ethnic negation takes hold of the child it forces the student to dislike and negate his own ethnic group. This ethnic negation process is especially painful for African-American children who are on the losing end because their European-American teachers see no importance in these children's culture and history. Children of color are forced through a maze of academic processes that never give proper and full consideration to who they are as people, culturally or historically. So, as a result, many African-American parents see a link between racism and the negative emotional and psychological conditioning of their children by public schools. I, as an African-American mother, feel as though my children have been brainwashed when it comes to the interpretations of who they are as persons of color from the perspective of their teachers.

The public school's educational practices have given the European-Americans, as an ethnic group in America, the power and socialization tools to shape the minds and attitudes of an entire multiethnic society. Since all children are required to attend school, they are socialized in their relationships as ethnic groups one to another at a very young age. Racial, social, and economic prejudice in school creates attitudes and supports a racist behavior among American citizens that is pervasive. Educators and parents must take a stand against racism, disrespect for culture, and the segregation of people in schools and society.

The environment of public schools is culturally and racially dominated by European-American teachers and administrators who still need to face and confront their own racial feelings and beliefs toward African-American people. How can teachers who do not want intimate contact with African-Americans effectively teach children of that ethnic background? If European-American teachers were asked if they would voluntarily live in an African-American neighborhood, and have their children marry or form intimate friendships with African-Americans, in equal numbers to their

European-American friends, the answer would probably be no. European-American teachers and administrators hold most of the high-level jobs in public schools. People of color, on the other hand, are over-represented in non-administrative positions. African-Americans and Latinos racially dominate jobs in the school cafeteria, clerical, food service, janitorial, and maintenance positions. I have not heard any protest from the European-American community to change the fact that people of color do not hold positions that can generate change in their educational fate. Although European-Americans may be the largest population in some communities, institutionalized racism in schools is the only way to explain the fact that they dominate high level positions in schools even where they are an ethnic minority in a community of color.

The child of color is totally unprepared to deal with an institution run by an all European-American staff which has not looked closely at racism and its effect on that child. School is the first encounter the child has with the larger society on a daily basis. Imagine what children of color must think when they see that the only positions that people who look like them hold are caretaker and menial positions which are supervised by European-Americans. How on earth does this model equity and fair treatment to those children of color? Educational institutions must work to understand the racism and social factors connected with the school environment – and they have not. Clearly, assistance must be forthcoming from people of color as parents and individuals so that schools will be encouraged to make adjustments in hiring and training teachers and designing social science curriculum and activities.

Understanding the impact of racism in schools and how it affects young people in society is not the only concern of this chapter. A hundred books, videos and new reports have been written about African-Americans being at risk in schools across America. Nonetheless, very few academics and others choose to look at who is benefiting from racism or examine the state of mind and spirit of its perpetrators. An examination of the perpetrators of racism can be politically costly in institutions of learning for anyone who wants to remain a part of these institutions. The pressing question for me as a mother, when I began my work with schools, was why are Americans across racial lines so committed to diminishing the status of African-Americans? Why was it so hard for people to see African-Americans as human beings and equal contributors to American society and the world? The idea of African-Americans' inferiority and devalued status seems to flourish among all ethnic groups including African-Americans themselves. Some would argue that the negative treatment received by African-Americans comes from established patterns of white supremacy and unrelenting racism. The long history of slavery, racial inequities, unemployment and political disenfranchisement resulted in poor treatment and harsh conditions for African-American people. The issue is much more complex than these historically cited conclusions. Institutionalized racism in the public education system is the oil that keeps the machine of racism going in America. Systematic racism operates in education with no barriers, and targets primarily African-American children like a virus or germ breaking down the child's emotional, intellectual and social well-being, with no accountable parties in the educational system to blame.

African-Americans receive negative racial profiles in schools. This has a direct bearing of their ability to thrive in our society. African-Americans' lacking a proper education results in unemployment, a poor self-image, a large prison population, and broken homes. Obviously, something is wrong with the educational system's attempt to educate African-American children and give them a fighting chance at a successful life. There is no Horatio Alger story of pulling oneself up by the boot straps when the straps are cut and the shoes removed from these children by the educational system from the beginning of their academic life. Many Americans believe that the schools aren't perfect, but if a student, no matter of what race, works hard at his or her studies, education will provide some sort of prosperity. The African-American parent attempts to pass on the promises of prosperity to his child that "if he studies and works hard, he can accomplish his goals and travel through society as he wishes." The African-American child goes into school believing his abilities, intelligence and qualifications will serve as standards to be judged by. Unfortunately, many African-American youths enter schools and colleges unprepared emotionally and mentally for their encounter with institutionalized racism at every turn. Children continue to be trained in schools and in homes to accept racism as a normal part of everyday African-American life. It's as if racism is a part of the American culture. The African-American families whether they are poor, wealthy, middle-class, light-skinned or dark-skinned, all have in common being a victim of racism to a greater or lesser degree. African-American parents understand that they are raising children in a society and schools, that, although integrated, still view African-Americans as second-class citizens. African-American parents are unable to impart to their children and young adults the depressing and irrational consequences that they and their children face because of racism, and that the enmity produced from racism puts their very existence in question.

Education should have helped by now to establish the African-American population as an equal partner with the European-Americans – but it has not. When African-American children go to school, naturally these children have the same eagerness to learn as any child. Yet the African-American child soon becomes the victim of a covert type of racism designed to end his hunger and enthusiasm to learn. This racism comes from a place where parents least expect, the public schools. An examination of why the system has failed these African-American children shows they have been set up to commit academic suicide . They have been given the gun and the bullets by a neglectful society and inadequate educational system. This harmful journey starts in public schools for these children as young as eight years old, according to some studies. Harry Morgan (1980) wrote that when blacks enter first grade, the stories they create express positive feelings about themselves in schooling situations, but by the second grade, students' stories express negative imagery of the teacher and school environment, and by the third grade the overall feeling expressed by students is that of cynicism. In other words, upon entering school primary grades, black children's enthusiasm and eager interest is evident; however, by third grade the liveliness and interest are gone, replaced by passivity and apathy. Primary grades presented a more nurturing environment than intermediate or upper grades. In early childhood education, much of the activity is child-teacher centered and child-interactive. In primary grades, black students progress and thrive at the same rate as their white counterparts until "the third grade syndrome." By the third grade, most black children drop out of school psychologically.

Parents of color must require that public schools explain and be accountable for why these children commit academic suicide at the early age of eight. The question is not only how these children of color end their educational lives through academic suicide, but who loads the gun with bullets of hopelessness? Public schools for the most part have created a classroom atmosphere that has led to failure and frustration for African-American children. To complicate matters, children of other ethnic groups learn very quickly that African-American children are struggling both academically and emotionally. The confidence of African-American children is undermined in their social relationship with other ethnic groups. This makes children of color especially vulnerable.

Here is an example of how frustration in African-American children builds in schools over time. The example I will use is a school where European-American children are treated with the same disregard African-American children experience every day. Imagine a school that European-American children have attended for nine years; 95 percent of the teaching staff is African-American from kindergarten through junior high. When they enter high school these European-American children are taught by predominantly African-American males. This school system's social studies curriculum would concentrate primarily on the contributions, culture, courage, conquest and intellectual achievements of African and African-American male heros. However, for one week in

February, the school district proclaims European-American history week. European-American history week is celebrated to boost European-American children's self-esteem and to pacify their parents. The school would give recognition to European-American people as an ethnic group by pointing out how they excel in sports, comedy and music. John F. Kennedy would be the only European-American male figure discussed in this school and district as an ethnic hero for twenty years. The children would even march in a parade celebrating Kennedy's birthday. There would be no mention of European contributions to the world. European-American children would be told they are a minority group that comes from the Third World, that Europeans and their descendants as an ethnic group started out in America as slaves; that they were backward, barbaric, mentally ill-equipped people who were taken from Europe for their own good. The slave population came from Europe, they would learn, a continent that was made up of savages who were ignorant, and practiced pagan religions. These European-American children would be told that this was why the Africans and African-Americans conquered them–to save Europeans from themselves. And in the end the European-American male children are disproportionately expelled from schools in the district in high numbers when compared to other ethnic groups.

Considering what I have described above–how enthusiastically would European-American children approach learning? Would European-American children's self esteem be high under these educational conditions? This example, I feel, illustrates how different and inferior the kind of education most African-American children receive compared to what European-American children receive. The educational system has been used against African-Americans because they still are not equated as an important part of humanity. America's public schools have sustained, developed, and promoted learning primarily for the advancement of European-American males. This focus by schools on the European-American male, when examined, is an historical fact. The public school system's refusal to provide culturally relative materials, or place equal value on the needs of children of color, has caused these children to mentally and intellectually retreat, cutting themselves off emotionally from the learning process.

The outcome of steadfast refusal on the part of public schools to be "pro people of color" has caused teachers to teach racial superiority and inferiority in direct and subtle ways to the students. Learning institutions currently replicate the ideas of European-Americans resulting in Eurocentric racial hierarchy and a forced acculturation of people of color toward Eurocentric values and heroism. Here is an example: My daughter in fifth grade was given a list called by her teachers the twelve most important people and world events. All these people and events on this list focused on the accomplishments of European-American males. The teacher told my child to pick a person or event from that list for her social studies report. My daughter came home frustrated. She pointed out to me that on the list there were no women or persons of color. My daughter explained, "If I don't do the assignment my teacher will give me a bad grade and will say I'm making too much of the fact that women and people of color are not represented on the list." I called the teacher up and explained my daughter's frustration, telling the teacher that the world could not be encapsulated by the achievement of white males only. After this conversation about my daughter's social studies report, the teacher admitted that she had never thought about the effect this kind of lesson could have on a female child or child of color. I also explained how the habitual ignoring by an authority figure like a teacher of an African-American female child's gender and the achievements of her ethnic group can have a mentally paralyzing effect upon the child. The social studies report incident in fifth grade caused my daughter to see no direct or relevant use for studying social studies other than to pass with a decent grade.

This is a clear example of one of the bullets given to African American children by the public schools to help them in committing academic suicide. The teacher's lesson plan and curriculum were approved by the school officials. The school officials knew they had children of color in their classrooms, but this had no bearing on the lessons to be taught to these children of color. The children of color at my daughter's school outnumber European-American students by 80 percent. Recent studies have shown that female students in general are not working to their full capacity, primarily for the same reasons as children of African-American descent.

School officials see no real need to change their staffing policy, teaching methods or curriculum despite racial problems in schools. School administrators care little about the emotional despair suffered and academic failure of students of color. Public school teachers will not deal with the fact that all human beings want to know that they came from people and place worth remembering.

School officials argue that they have changed the curriculum and applications of learning. Recently, I was asked to talk to a fifth grade class in Riverside, California. The school had students from all ethnic backgrounds. I asked the students to tell me what they knew of African people. The students who were mostly European-American were the most eager to respond to the question. The students told me that Africans put large cups in their lips, dance, wear jewelry and little clothing, if any. When I asked them about Native Americans they told me Native Americans wove baskets, danced, and wore jewelry. The African-American students held their heads down and said nothing about African people, Africa or its contribution to the world. These children knew nothing other than the stereotypes and racial interpretations they have learned in schools. These stereotypes come from a mind-set that is evident in a conversation I had with a school principal not long ago. I asked the European-American principal, who runs a multiethnic elementary school, about recent attempts to emphasize the history of ethnic groups by promoting cultural awareness. The principal replied, "Do you mean real history, or the history of minorities and women.?" As the principal went on to explain her comment, we evidently had different interpretations of history. From the principal's Eurocentric perspective, she thought the history of women and what she believed to be minority people was somehow not as real or important as the history of European-Americans. American school children, if asked to speak or write about the African, Native American, or Asian civilizations, repeat the stereotypes of their teachers and parents. Public school children, no matter what their ethnicity, can talk and write positively about European-American history and European civilization. Children's hands will immediately go up in that classroom with enthusiasm when the discussion is about European-American or European history. Students of color, however, are not eager to answer questions about their culture because somewhere in their delicate young psyche they realize they are learning negative stereotypes, nothing about their ethnic groups' contributions to the world, and that they are not valued by the school or society.

Children see teachers as surrogate parents since they interact and control the child's life for at least six to seven hours a day, with the consent of the child's parents. A child of color who views his teacher as a surrogate parent and sees him as exemplifying racist behavior may feel a need to rebel.

The National Coalition of Advocates for Students in 1989 reported that African-American male students are twice as likely to receive corporal punishment and to be suspended as white male students. The American Council of Education reported in February of 1991 that only 55 percent of Latino students will graduate from high school, and that only 3 percent of Latinos in America hold bachelor's degrees. The Associated Press reported in December of 1990 that nearly half the nation's black children live in poverty. These statistics regarding the treatment and productivity of children of color can be traced to their experience in school. The trouble is that most educators aren't aware of this condition, and the crippling of children of color goes on.

REFFERENCE

Morgan, Harry (1980). "How Schools Fail Black Children." *Social Policy*, Jan.-Feb., pp 49-54.

Chapter 7

Taking a Closer Look at Self-Esteem, and How to Strengthen It in Children of Color

by Bernie Streets

In this chapter, an industrialist turned child-care center director, brings to light the challenges uniquely experienced by African-American children in the United States. These challenges greatly influence these young people's self-worth and self-esteem. The author believes that specific things can be done to stimulate and develop self-esteem in children of color, and suggests where exactly the responsibility rests for building and strengthening it. The author believes that all teachers, educators and parents have a responsibility for lovingly training and preparing children to grow up and thrive in a setting which has not overcome its racism. Ed.

A man must be at home somewhere before
he can feel at home everywhere.
– Dr. Howard Thurman,
African-American theologian and philosopher

As a young child, I used to look forward to Mondays. Monday was the one day of the week when we "colored" folks could use the Public Natatorium, a beautiful indoor swimming pool that was owned and operated by the city and funded by local taxes. We could swim until ten at night. Then, after we left, the pool would be drained, cleaned, and refilled for the white people, who used it from

Tuesday through Sunday.

Prior to 1937, this pool was open to whites only. However, during that year the city decided to levy an increased tax to cover necessary repairs and general maintenance of the pool. My father objected vigorously to this tax increase on the grounds that African-American citizens were excluded from its use and, as a consequence, many refused to pay the tax. The town was filled with many immigrants from various countries throughout Europe. Many were not yet United States citizens and spoke no English, but, nevertheless, were welcome to swim in the pool during the "white" time. How would you feel if this happened to you? What would it do to your own sense of proper dignity or value – your self-esteem? As a child, I did not think so much about it, so I could not react. I just liked to swim. However, the attitude behind the pool "cleaning" was offensive to all the African-American adults who were aware of the policy–and also to me when I was old enough to understand what was going on. I began to sense that exclusion and separation were not right. It was absolutely un-American in my mind. Somehow, it made me begin to feel "different," that I did not quite fit in with the majority of people who, by accident of birth, were born white.

Attitudes and perceptions! From early on, even before American Negro slavery, the European had formed very negative attitudes and perceptions, not only about black people, but about all people of color. Armed with self-pronounced "biblical evidence," rationalization, and a firm conviction in a supposed "divine" right of discovery to dominate the world on behalf of "White Christian Civilization", the white European felt justified in viewing the dark-skinned African as inferior, not a true human, and slavery as a "blessing" to the "black savage" (Frazier 1957; Wood 1990). And, as the various European peoples made contact with the colored peoples of the world for the purpose of conquering and exploiting them, the white collective belief of racial superiority and people-of-color inferiority developed gradually over hundreds of years. So, it is not too difficult to understand and realize why many white Americans –

descendents of those Europeans who held such racist views and through the centuries passed them on to their progeny – subconsciously harbor negative feelings, attitudes, and all sorts of spurious notions about people of color. More about this later as it affects young children.

There is not a single person, regardless of skin color, who has not been dealt blows to his self-esteem. We receive challenges to our sense of personal dignity and value all the time. None of us is immune from having these challenges test the very strength, durability, and degree of pride we have in ourselves. Sounds like we all share the same plight, doesn't it? Not exactly. There are some added challenges and tests that people of color uniquely experience in these United States, associated with racism, discrimination, and unequal opportunity and privilege that compound the problem for them, and most notably for African-Americans.

How does all of this affect the youngsters, and particularly their sense of self-worth and self-esteem? How does one develop and maintain a sense of well-being, self-esteem, and pride when you are "told" in so many ways that you are not as good as whites, when almost everything you are allowed to do is controlled and dictated by whites? On the other hand, why have many African-American people managed to persevere and go on in spite of these things? You cannot buy self-esteem. So, where does a youngster of color get it, and, more importantly perhaps, how can he hold onto it?

These are questions that will be addressed in the commentary that follows. In addition, I will share some thoughts and opinions about certain conditions and aspects of self-esteem. In this process, the following items must be mentioned and commented upon: certain factors that produce a sense of low self-esteem in children of color; effects and results of lowered self-esteem; and some examples of behavioral reactions youngsters might develop to things that tend to lower self-esteem. Next, my aim will be to describe and discuss the things that can be done to stimulate and develop self-esteem in children of color, and to suggest where exactly the responsibility rests for building and strengthening self-esteem in the youngster, and how to do it. Some discussion regarding the latter will concern what a teacher can and ought to do. In the process of discussing these various items, I will draw upon personal and family experiences, wherever appropriate, to dramatize a situation or illustrate a condition or feature.

CAUSES AND EFFECTS OF LOW SELF-ESTEEM

Racism has been and still is one of the most pronounced causes of low self-esteem in people of color. It is both a cause in itself and a contributing factor, or catalyst, for other causes which I will mention shortly. Racism is a highly infectious social and spiritual disease that has plagued African-Americans for nearly four centuries. Many people confuse and equate the term "racism" with "prejudice." Racism, in fact, contains the element of prejudice, but also includes the possession of economic, social, and political power by one group over another. In our country, it is the whites who possess and use the "power" to control and maintain advantage over people of color. Rejection and oppression are byproducts of racism which have affected black people over the years in numerous ways and have taken many forms — some quite obvious and others not so obvious, but subtle in nature. Whatever form it may take, the victims are forced to handle the situation as best they can, and often times the anger and shame racism begets are directed inwardly.

My great-grandparents, when they were slaves, had to confront white racism and oppression with the self-survival tactic of extreme docility and servitude. It was the overt form of racism that they experienced, and, whenever they did, it was usually violent. Survival was ever contingent upon out-thinking, out-guessing, out-foxing, and over-placating "the man." They hated having to exist like this. They hated having to feel less than human.

My grandparents were born during the Reconstruction Period and, as "free" people had to face the ever-present, continuous flow of white rejection, segregation, discrimination, and fear of death from hate groups such as the Ku Klux Klan. So-called equal protection under the law to them was merely an abstract ideal, not reality.

My parents were born during the aftermath years of the "Separate but Equal" doctrine which represented one of the most emotionally devastating and debilitating periods for African-Americans. And, in 1933, I came along. I was nearing the end of my junior year in college when the United States Supreme Court, on May 17, 1954, in the case of Brown v. The Board of Education, declared that segregation in education was unconstitutional, thereby overturning the Plessy v. Ferguson case of 1896 which established "separate but equal" as law.

Whatever form racism takes, and whenever or wherever it occurs, believe me, it tears you apart. You hurt, and the tendency is to look at yourself and wonder, "Is there something wrong with me?" During the last fifty years or so, we have witnessed the enactment of nearly a thousand pieces of civil rights legislation, executive orders, and judicial decisions just to grant African-Americans the same constitutional rights that white people have. Circumvention of the laws has been a successful ploy by numerous whites who tenaciously hold onto biased notions and myths about African Americans that were created during the enslavement of blacks. Such negative racial views appear to have served psychological, social, and functional needs for many white people, and today they still find them too difficult to relinquish. So where does that leave the African-American child? Presently, the black youngster is made to feel and believe he is inferior to whites and that his life is not viewed highly or even of any consequence by white society.

So many white people have been taught to see racism only in terms of individual, overt acts of violence, cruelty, and maliciousness. They have not seen or realized how "invisible systems" have conferred dominance upon their own group — and that this is a feature of racism. Racism is a condition which, as everyone knows, puts people of color at a disadvantage. A corollary aspect of it, however, is "white privilege" which puts white people at an advantage and, hence, confers dominance upon them. This insidious aspect of racism is the feature most white people have been taught not to see or recognize. Those who have seem wary of acknowledging it.

Therefore, whites, via racism, receive and enjoy unearned privilege and advantage, as well as conferred dominance and have been conditioned not to think about these benefits. Peggy McIntosh of Wellesley College has identified some of what she terms "the daily effects" of privilege in her life as a white person, and put together a long list of conditions upon which she can rely. To cite a few: while shopping she can be reasonably certain that she will not be followed or harassed by a sales person; when using checks, credit cards, or cash she can count on her skin color not working against her as being financially reliable; she can be very certain of purchasing or renting housing in an area which she can afford and would want to reside; she can be certain, if apprehended by a police officer, that she has not been singled out because of her race; and so on. There are things that many white people take for granted. Yet, these things are very evident to people of color who know full well about the "hidden" systems of white advantage. Care to venture an opinion about what this awareness of unearned white advantage and conferred dominance can do to a person of color's self-esteem?

Hundreds of years have begotten a condition of relative social, economic, and political impotence for people of color. Overt and subtle practices of discrimination, insult, humiliation, and the denial of many fundamental rights and opportunity insidiously continue to strike blows at the very soul and spirit of people of color.

For example, schools! Those places of presumed enlightenment whose primary mission is to expand young people's minds and horizons and to educate them so they will be able to function in this world and live their lives productively. Some by design and some through neglect and ignorance proceeded to "educate" youngsters over the years by choosing to not include, or totally dismiss altogether, any contributions by people of color to our society, while strongly emphasizing the economic, political, and technical/scientific accomplishments of whites.

I remember quite vividly how United States history, for example, was presented in my classes in elementary, junior high, and high school. It was based on the various European immigrants' experiences in America, it romanticized war, and the textbook authors tended to take great poetic license in editorializing and rationalizing not only the inevitability but the right of white expansion and acquisition of Native American lands. American Negro slavery never, to my recollection, was denounced as being patently evil, and the period in which it took place was somehow glamorized and described from a white point of view. Holidays then were based on white history and white male leaders. Today, for the most part, it appears to be the same.

No one really wins in the game of life when bias and racism function as "referees." It does not take young children very long to recognize that color differences are associated with power and privilege. They learn much about the differences and similarities among people through observation. In addition, they learn by receiving and taking in both verbal and non-verbal messages about these differences. Hence, our children's developing senses of self and others are greatly influenced by racism.

I have learned a couple of basic things from working with young children. The first is, never underestimate their ability to perceive the negative information and messages around them; and, the second is to never underestimate the potential of that information and those messages to do them harm. With children of color, it is not necessarily a lacking or diminished personal identity, per se, that engenders feelings of lowered self-esteem. I believe too often youngsters are confused and disoriented about how and where they fit into their overall ethnic group, be it African-American, Native American, Hispanic, or Asian. For example, certain research findings on the impact of racism on black children's identity development interestingly have indicated that the personal identity of those children studied equaled or surpassed that of white children, whereas their "reference group orientation" tended to be low (Cross 1985). Reference group orientation includes ethnic awareness, knowledge, esteem, ideology, and appreciation.

Relative to this, I can remember occasions as a child, youth, and even adult when I almost automatically experienced feelings of shame, not about anything I did, but shame for being a part of the black race, my reference group, which seemed to be so despised. I was victimized by so much negative information out there about black people. This feeling of shame, this effect on me, was actually racism internalized. It was forcing me to accept and agree to my own group's plight and oppression.

Just a few words about reaction formations that often occur in children of color who live in a society such as ours, which finds numerous ways to attack and imperil their self-esteem.

There are those out there who view it as their duty to report on and point out aggressive behavior by students of color. Too often, they imply that bad behavior is a "natural characteristic" of these students. Hence, they presume the non-white student to be the real problem. Many of these reporters seem to be unaware of or unconcerned about the hidden system of privilege whites possess in society in general, and in the schools in particular. If, indeed, the educational system is one which tends to intensify feelings of inferiority, then why be surprised by the behavioral reactions. Should the system keep reminding a youngster that he is perceived as inferior, he might react aggressively. No one really enjoys feeling inferior. So many children of color try to hide this feeling from themselves and others. But, once reminded of it by some source outside, the youngster will resist, and sometimes with physical force. Just turn back the calendar one hundred and forty years and you would observe that the journalistic forebears of these present-day reporters were saying the same thing — only it was about the immigrant Irish children, who were viewed, along with their parents, by society as inferior and of bad behavior.

In a society that continually threatens the self-esteem and self-image of children of color, these youngsters have managed over time to adapt to conditions. For example, African-American youngsters, forced to live in two worlds of culture – the majority culture and their own minority culture – have conditioned themselves to stifle or hold in their aggression when around white people, yet liberally express it with fellow African-Americans. This is viewed by some as a therapeutic emotional release; however, it sometimes finds its expression in a violent way towards other blacks.

Children of color also have managed through the years to use various self-preservation tactics to approach a sense of well-being in an intolerant, often unfriendly, society. For example, in the chapter "America and the Black Child," in their book, *Raising Black Children*, Drs. James Comer of Yale University and Alvin Poussaint of Harvard University state that African-American children

> ...have had to learn to be practical as well as cunning. They have had to learn how to win some sort of acceptance from belligerent whites. Black children have often assumed the responsibilities and burdens of adulthood at a very early age. Many have had little of what we call a childhood. In the black world, adolescence starts early in life, and unlike most white youngsters, many black children do not enjoy the luxury of a period of playtime and learning which extends into their late teens. (Comer and Poussaint, p. 11)

WAYS TO STIMULATE AND ENHANCE SELF-ESTEEM

In a nutshell, self-esteem refers to how the youngster responds emotionally to himself. If self-esteem is high, the emotional reaction is positive. If there is low self-esteem, the emotional reaction is negative. Self-esteem – along with self-awareness, self-image, self-concept, and self-determination – is one of the vital components which constitute the total sense of self, or identity. So, in actuality, confidence, gratifying relationships with others, and happiness all depend on a positive sense of self. A youngster's development of a healthy sense of self, then, can be undermined by rejection, injustice, extreme criticism, disrespectful treatment, absence of humor, lack of knowledge, and unnecessary punishment on the part of people in his life. These types of things occur all too often with children of color. Therefore, it seems only logical that the way to generate and strengthen a positive sense of self in youngsters is to have the influences in their lives do exactly the opposite. Those influences are the child's parents and relatives, community members, the educational system, religious institutions, government, and society as a whole. Sounds pretty pat – not to mention downright idealistic – doesn't it? Well, let's get right down to some "nitty-gritty" stuff, certain ways that are basic and practical, and other ways which require a personal – nay, spiritual – transformation to a higher level of understanding and accepting human diversity.

Basic Way Number One: Good Child Rearing Practices, or Let's Get Mom, Dad, the Family and Friends in on the Act

As Comer and Poussaint (1992) incitefully point out, the element that is most fundamental and essential in raising strong, secure children is none other than good child rearing practices, in which love, care, support, and training are the basic ingredients, and a good feeling about oneself, self-confidence, ethnic pride, and even some assertiveness become the finished product. And, you know, a child doesn't have to be in a home of substantial means and comfort to have all this, as long as the parents, in particular, and other family members create a loving and caring atmosphere in which the youngster can feel secure and learn from them positive things from their culture, human virtues, and ways to adapt in a positive manner to an ever-changing world.

As a child growing up, I was very blessed and truly fortunate because I received plenty of love, care, support, and encouragement from my whole family - parents, grandparents, great-grandparents, aunts, uncles, cousins, not to mention the African-American community, for the most part. There never was a moment when I didn't feel "special" in my family. I know my first notions of myself as a person had a lot to do with how my parents, family members, and others responded to me. I really lucked out in this regard because my relationships with the truly important folks in my life were very good. For the life of me, I can't remember as a child too many times when I didn't feel good about myself.

I learned an awful lot from my family members – especially about their life experiences – from slavery to the present time. Knowing what they did to overcome bigotry, discrimination, and the like in a society that viewed them as interlopers to be scorned and merely tolerated, while they courageously made something honorable out of their lives with dignity and real class was, and is, to me a continual source of inspiration, admiration, and pride. They were very real examples of esteem.

My grandfather, Taylor Streets, used to tell me, "The bigger the test, the bigger the victory." We affectionately called him, "Paw," and sometimes, "Good Lord Paw," because whenever he became excited, or when something happened or surprised him, he'd yell, "Good Lord!" I never, ever heard him utter a profane word. He had a little over one year of formal education, but he had a "doctorate" in character and values. I don't know how any person could have been more caring and loving to me than he was. His every moment with me was filled with love and attention. He taught without lecturing; he taught by example. Children are not born with values. Values and attitudes are acquired through learning, and fundamentally through being with adults who model them. If we adults don't model them, the kids will have a very difficult time in acquiring them without conflict.

Two memories of Paw Streets stand out in my mind which demonstrate how his "modeling" of certain human values and virtues was an act of his love for me. The first was a lesson in trustworthiness and responsibility. Paw worked for the Pennsylvania Railroad as a baggage handler. It was hard work, yet he never complained. I would visit him and my grandmother often.

On occasions when payday fell on his day off, he would take me with him to pick up his pay. After cashing his check, he would immediately go to the electric company to pay the bill, then to the gas company and other places to pay bills. After the bills were paid, he'd smile and say, "Boy, that makes me feel good! Want a treat?" Then, he'd take me to a sweet shop or ice cream parlor for a special treat. I once asked him, "Paw, why do you feel good when you have to pay bills?" "Because," he said, "it's a good feeling I have inside when I settle my debts." Then he said, "If you receive something from someone which you agreed to pay for and you don't, that makes you a real lowdown person, and there's nothing worse than a cheating, lowdown person."

The second memory concerns the time I discovered how good a baseball player Paw had been, how he had been a powerful "submarine" ball pitcher and had organized a team of African-American all stars who played numerous white teams and occasionally a white all-star team of professional big-league players. Here is where one of my training sessions on humility, forgiveness, and not hating began. Remember, in my grandfather's day – not to mention in my father's day – "colored" baseball players were not allowed to play in the big leagues.

My grandfather's team usually won whenever they played the various semi-professional teams in and around Indiana, Ohio, Illinois, and Kentucky. There were many occasions when they had to let the white team win, or be beaten and run out of town, or perhaps even killed. For eight innings my grandfather's team would be way ahead of the other team, then in the ninth inning let the other team score enough runs to win. This was part of the white man's, "Nigger you can play but you can't win," philosophy at that time.

Against the professional all-star big leaguers, Paw's team won more games than it lost. When I found out about this, I became so angry, started spewing out my disgust for those white people, and felt so frustrated because I couldn't turn back time and make it right. I screamed at my grandfather, "They let all of those white foreigners into our country, and they were allowed to play baseball even when they couldn't speak English well!" I was very angry, speaking impulsively, and my energy was being vented and wasted negatively. Here is where his love and an important part of my training came in. He put his hand on my shoulder, then rubbed my head, and said: "Boy, don't have any regrets about not having been allowed to play big league baseball because of being a Negro. That's the hand I was dealt. I loved baseball. Still do. And, I had fun playing the way I had to. But you remember this: it's enough for me to know I was good enough to play big-league ball, even if I couldn't. Anyway," he continued with a big smile of satisfaction on his face, "Jackie (Robinson), Campy (Roy Campanella), Larry (Doby), and Newk (Don Newcombe) showed them real good that we could play baseball. And when they take the field, in my mind, I'm right there with them." As you can see, that day I learned a valuable lesson. My grandfather showed me the mature way he directed his own emotional energy about an injustice: not to those who offended him, but to his own proper sense of worth, identity, and good feeling about himself. No doubt about it. Paw's sense of self-esteem was intact.

There were in these days, and are now, many African-American children who are unknowledgeable about their own cultural heritage and history. They don't quite know exactly where they fit in as a people. On the other hand, Native Americans, for the most part, are aware of their cultural heritage. They were not stripped of it as were African-Americans. Both groups, to be sure, have been wounded by racism. However, with African-Americans part of this wound had to do with an impaired black identity and a diminished or absent feeling of self-esteem. I don't believe I'm as wounded as many of my fellow African-Americans, for a number of reasons. The first is this: the child rearing practices of my entire family greatly strengthened and enhanced my primary identity as a good and able person. As a result, the task of assuming a positive African-American identity became so much easier.

The second reason is that my parents were educated people, and knowledgeable in black history. From them and their vast resource materials on this, I learned many specific facts and details about the rich history and contributions of black people. Also from them, but particularly from my grandparents and great-grandparents, I heard and learned many things about United States history and various events as they lived and experienced them.

Reason number three is that my light skin color allowed me a certain degree of anonymity. I didn't stand out in a crowd of white people and, therefore, could come and go without too much fear or stress. However, once they determined who I was, some would react civilly, but guarded. Others, you guessed it, would treat me as if I had the plague. Strange as it sounds, I was always prepared for these reactions. You see, my parents and other family members carefully trained me for occasions such as these. They knew they had to protect and look out for my psychological well-being. So, I was gently and carefully told the types of reactions I might possibly receive, as well as dignified and honorable ways to handle rejection, from whites in whatever form it took.

All of these things I've mentioned also were done with my own children. Starting when they were infants, they were showered with lots of love and care. Later, training was added. Love, care, attention, and training were the basic materials used to assist them in developing strong, positive feelings about themselves. This was the way we reasoned that they would be able to form a durable, lasting sense of self and self-esteem even while growing up in a racist society. Think about it! We can't always change racist thinking and actions in others. Nonetheless, we certainly can lovingly train and prepare our children for growing up and thriving in a racist setting while still holding onto positive feelings about themselves.

Personal evidence which verifies this was beautifully demonstrated by my daughter Karen when she was a seventh grade student. A very precocious child, Karen walked and talked at a very early age. She was read to continually by us, her grandparents, and one of her great-grandmothers. So, early on, she appreciated the written word, and by the time she was four years old, Karen was very conversant in the English language. By the age of five she was writing stories and poetry. Well, once for an English class assignment, Karen wrote and submitted an essay. On the following day, as the teacher was passing out the graded essays, every student except Karen received his paper. The teacher commented that the class did fairly well and heaped praise upon several of the white students for writing outstanding essays. At the end of class, the teacher called Karen to her desk and told her that the essay was "so good" that she must have copied it from another source – a book or from someone else. In other words, the teacher accused her of plagiarism. The teacher's exact words were, "Well, it's so good, honey, I'm sure you couldn't have written this on your own."

Of the twenty to twenty-five children in the class, Karen was the only student of color and the only one whose writing ability not only was questioned but flatly disbelieved by the teacher. A coincidence? Not hardly! This teacher likely had expectations that most of the white children could and would do well; she obviously had the expectation that Karen could not and would not write an exceptional paper. In addition to being degrading and insulting, the teacher's accusation was a harsh assault on Karen's capability, sense of worth, and esteem. The teacher never considered the possibility that Karen was talented, nor did she make even the slightest attempt to verify that Karen did her own work. Karen perceived the comments as insulting, but reacted most admirably. First of all, she recognized the racial implication. Secondly, she knew that she had personally composed and written the essay without anyone's help. So, armed with this truth and filled with self-confidence, Karen pushed aside her hurt and embarrassment and channeled her anger and disgust into a very positive, assertive way. She challenged the teacher to give her a topic, and she would write another essay right on the spot in the teacher's presence. This was done, the paper was excellent, the teacher apologized profusely, Karen was vindicated, and I was so proud of her. It was shortly after that when I decided to run for and was selected as the first African-American on the Niles Township, Michigan, Board of Education.

Earlier, I had posed the question as to why so many African-American people managed to persevere, obtain an education, and go on in spite of racist hurdles encountered along the way. Like many others, Karen had the unified, inexhaustible support of her family, and through her own inner strength she had refused to accept racist restrictions. The courage she had shown by directly confronting her English teacher very dramatically demonstrated the direct relationship between one's self-value and personal achievement. Karen's concept of herself was so firmly intact that day, her confidence high, that she had no doubts whatsoever that she could prove her teacher wrong. Karen's success here reinforced her self-concept and strengthened her self-esteem, and this made it so much easier for her to take on new challenges and continue to develop her talents. Continue she did! Karen went on to graduate with distinction from one of the finest, Mount Holyoke College, with her degree in English and political science.

Basic Way Number Two: The Teacher as a Facilitator in Enhancing the Student's Self-Esteem

I firmly believe that the teacher's primary purpose, if not moral obligation, must be to promote and facilitate the development of every child's human potential. Each child has capacity and potential to do something, to be someone. Unfortunately, our educational systems – insensitive to the conditions of many students of color and entrenched in pedagogical rigidity while harboring preconceived notions that African-Americans, Native Americans, and Hispanics are by nature intellectually inferior to whites – continue to provide all the educational best they can to white students and heedlessly dismiss the rest as not really worthy of too much attention. It is very difficult for students of color to reach the heights of their potential when, literally thousands of these youngsters have been shunted into "special" classes. Nathan Rutstein (1992) has termed this as being placed "... in the poor quality track, which is the academic landfill, where the system's human garbage is flung". (p.180)

Let me take a moment here to share a story of how one perceptive, sensitive, caring and courageous teacher saved a girl of color from the "academic landfill."

Chuck Smith and I met as students at Indiana University in the early 1950s. Getting the opportunity to receive a college education wasn't easy for Chuck. He was from a large African-American family from East Chicago, Indiana, located in the heart of the steel mill area of northwestern Indiana. Chuck was several years older than the rest of us because he had to work in the steel mills after high school while attending classes part-time at the Indiana University Extension Center in nearby Gary. Chuck always had a burning desire to be a teacher. His parents and family, though poor, were rich in love and support. Chuck knew what he wanted, and had charted a path towards his goal with strong determination. He was a person of very high self-esteem and confidence. He had an amazing Shakespearean voice – powerful, resonant, convincing. It was always fun to observe white folks' reactions whenever they heard Chuck speak. I really think Chuck was born well versed in English grammar and the art of elocution.

During his senior year, Chuck was given his practice teaching assignment in an elementary school in one of the cities near his home town. The classroom to which he was assigned was second grade, and he was told by the teacher, his supervisor, that many of the children were of low ability, low potential, or "educationally impaired." In that class was twelve-year-old Maria, a shy and frightened Hispanic girl who had been given the latter classification, and was, more or less, written off as someone to be kept in school somewhere until she reached age sixteen, at which time she would probably quit school.

Chuck was shocked, and wondered why a twelve-year-old was still in second grade with a roomful of seven and eight year olds. He noticed that the teacher just let Maria fend for herself and go through the motions of doing in-class assignments. According to the teacher,

Maria and others like her were simply a waste of time and effort, so she spent the major part of her time with the students (mostly white) that she believed were more deserving of her teaching efforts. Chuck decided to work with Maria. He discovered that she was very intuitive, had exceptionally good eye/hand coordination, but his biggest discovery was that, in trying to understand what she was reading, Maria was first attempting to translate the English words into Spanish because her comprehension of English word meanings was not very good. Until Chuck appeared on the scene, nobody had even noticed this. When Chuck presented her with readings in Spanish and tested her, she did very well. He talked to the teacher and principal about getting Maria tested and into an English language tutorial program. They said no! Money was not available. So, out of his own pocket and unbeknown to school officials, Chuck paid to have Maria tested. The tests revealed that she was of exceptionally high intelligence. Chuck then managed to get her a grant to attend a special private school for gifted children.

Maria soared like an eagle! She ultimately went to college, graduated with honors, and did not stop until she had received her Ph.D. Thank heavens for Chuck Smith's coming into Maria's life. Her potential was realized. This does not mean that all children of color would be like Maria. That's not the point. It is the teacher's duty to be a positive force in helping each child reach the highest level her or his natural talents will allow.

Most definitely, the teacher who has his act together first has to understand what human potential is, what the wound of inferiority does to a student of color, and how to reach and "make blossom" those students who typically exhibit a pattern of learning that leans more towards intuitiveness rather than reasoning. Here, it is important to be flexible and knowledgeable enough to use lots of visual materials and information. Once the overall picture is observed, the student can begin to ponder and handle the component parts. This offers another approach to the development of the process of logic.

I am most emphatically opposed to the practice of arbitrarily tracking or grouping youngsters by ability, as so many school systems do. Primarily, I do not like this practice because it labels the student, and labels exert a tremendous impact upon the child's potential. Children discover very rapidly whether they are in the bright, average, or below average (i.e., "dumb") tracks. So, once knowing what track he is in, why wouldn't the quality and level of the child be affected in some way? Chances are good that self-fulfilling prophecy will become harsh reality in the child who has feelings of inferiority, a low self-concept, and poor self-esteem. Once labeled and put into a "special" category, the youngster's ill feelings about himself become strengthened and even more entrenched in the psyche. Why wouldn't a child act out in some way, for no one wants to be perceived as being not worthy, not up to par, "different."

For the life of me, why do we so-called human beings get so riled up over other people and things that are "different?" Why does "different" have to be perceived as something objectionable, disgusting, or bad? The teacher who is "with it" is able to see the beauty of, and gems of possibility latent in, the term "different." When the teacher fully understands that a true human being is one who exhibits values and virtues, is of service to others, and sees no contradiction between unity and diversity, and then stresses the importance of these to her or his students, then and only then will those children be able to grasp and appreciate more readily the positive connotation of differences. Children realize that there are differences in abilities among themselves. What they haven't been taught is how to accept and respect differences.

The teacher who successfully can engender and strengthen feelings of esteem in her or his students and assists them in acquiring virtues, social skills, and positive ways to deal with differences will most assuredly experience a significant rise in harmony and learning in a classroom of children who come from varying ethnic groups, backgrounds and abilities.

All too often, teachers become more involved with providing busy work for the students, and provide little or no time for stimulating the students' desire to learn, think, and be curious about things. This is tantamount to "giving up" on the youngsters. It is such a tragedy when teachers give up on their students, and this happens time and time again with students of color. The result is that they become, as Rutstein has termed it, "undereducated." He states, "...most young Americans are undereducated...because they have been underestimated. And underestimation is the result of teachers being unable to draw out the potential of their students, and something even more basic than that – not believing that all of their students can succeed. When a teacher constantly manifests faith in his students, they begin to believe they can succeed. Conversely, when a teacher expects a student to fail, he usually fails. And that confidence-shattering message is usually transmitted non-verbally." (pp. 146-147)

I recently spoke at an area high school. I had been invited to speak on the topic of prejudice and the historical development of racism. This was part of a week-long program on ethnic and cultural diversity. The first group of students I addressed was a sociology class of junior and senior level students. The teacher was very upbeat and expressed how very proud she was of this class. She told me the students were all college-bound, fast-track young people – all "good kids." These students were polite, happy, attentive, energetic and very enthusiastic souls. They were receptive to what I had to say. Lots of questions. Enjoyable! As the bell sounded, ending the class period, the students graciously expressed their thanks as they filed out of the room to their next class. Some even stopped to ask more questions. Hold onto this picture!

As I walked down the hall to find the next classroom, I wondered if this group of students would be like those to whom I had just spoken. I soon found out. The teacher greeted me and introduced herself. I asked what subject was being taught. This, too, was a sociology class. That was all I wanted to know. However, she then held her hand next to her mouth, so the students entering the room could not hear, and stated that this was a low track class. Continuing, she added, "These kids come from blue collar families and are not expected to go to college." Continuing further, she said, "I hope we don't have any disturbances or problems with them. I hope they behave and listen to you." For a brief moment, I felt nervous. Then, thought to myself, "Dismiss what you've just heard and give these young people a chance."

There they were, a room full of teenagers – all seated quietly, all somber, all blank-faced, and all emotionlessly staring at me. I sensed that many were in pain emotionally and more than likely would have preferred to be somewhere other that in that class. They reminded me of scared animals, poised and waiting to react to something frightening or threatening. That was when I decided to drastically change my approach from that used with the first group.

Leaving all my notes and materials on the podium the teacher had set up for me, I walked around it and leisurely plopped myself down on top of the teacher's desk. I wanted to let these young people know I really cared about them. Somehow, I wanted to boost their confidence and, even though I would talk about prejudice and racism, I wanted to show how bias and pre-conceived notions about people can stifle initiative and seriously affect one's human potential. Warmly, I smiled and expressed my gratitude for being allowed to meet with them and share some information, thoughts, ideas, and opinions. While doing this, I purposely made eye contact with each of the students. In my heart were warm feelings of compassion and brotherly love for them, and I wanted them to sense that.

Instead of merely focusing on the nature of prejudice, the development of racism, and the resulting evil effects they have on people, their attention was drawn instead to understanding what a human being is. We focused on those attributes, qualities, and virtues that distinguish a true human being and how racism and prejudice can thwart their development in everyone – the victim and oppressor alike. The students were admonished to challenge everything I said, and were told not to be ashamed or dismayed if they disagreed with anything that was mentioned. My wish for them was only to listen, consider, and ponder what was being said and independently search for truth to corroborate or disprove. Shortly thereafter, some degree of relaxation became obvious and I could tell that their defensive stances began to soften somewhat. Faces heretofore devoid of expression began to convey some reaction. At that point, I knew some interest or curiosity had been evoked in them. Now, I really began to perk up and was happy that they were beginning to react. I was moved to say:

"I want you to know that you all are very special. Every one of you is unique, and in this whole world there is nobody exactly like you. I know deep in my heart that each of you has the ability and capacity to do something, and probably better than anyone else can. The big job is to find out what exactly that is. But, whatever that something is, if you find and use it to serve and help your fellow human beings – and do it with honesty, love, care, and dedication – you most certainly will be a true success. It does not matter whether one goes to college or not, becomes a tradesperson or not, is a ditch digger or not. Whatever you choose to do is valuable and important if you exhibit the virtues and values of a true human being.

"You know, the world is in a mess. My generation and others before it have chosen to let the wound of racism spread. We have been consumed by it. I'm asking you to break the cycle of hate, prejudice, and racism. You are very important to us. Look beyond your own race and identify yourselves with the human race. Become a true human being."

Examples were given of how several individuals responded to and overcame other people's low expectations and opinions of them and went on to succeed in life. I related some of the experiences my parents, my children, and I had in school, and the young people listened very intently.

The class ended too soon for me. This seemed to be a different group from that which I saw at the beginning of class. As the students filed by on their way out of the room to their next class, they nodded approvingly. Their faces had a mellower look. They knew I cared. We had connected.

After all the students had departed, I told the teacher that I thoroughly enjoyed the young people. She looked surprised and exclaimed, "Oh?" I said, "Yes, we connected and they were with me all the way." She said, "But, they didn't talk much." "Not with their mouths," I said, "but with their hearts." She thought about that for a moment. I continued. "I believe that many of those young people were able to get a quick glimpse at their true selves, that maybe they could be something – and they liked it! The more they perceive and understand themselves, the better they will be able to manifest more self-esteem, confidence and inner strength." She stood quietly for a moment, thinking. Then, she smiled. We had connected.

Involvement! A real teacher has to be committed to educating the whole child. To just concentrate solely on the intellect in today's small world is not enough. The teacher has to be a facilitator in stimulating the spiritual or moral aspect of the child's education. Therefore, it not only seems logical to prepare youngsters for getting along in this "shrinking" world by focusing on those attributes which constitute a good person, it is practical. Further, it is quite reasonable that educating all youngsters to be kind, compassionate, truthful, honest, fair, courteous, and trustworthy, for example, is a sure way to foster and strengthen self-esteem. The development and demonstration of virtues in children provide them balance and stability, and, if this aspect dominates their consciousness, they will be able to attain their true stations as human beings. All students are winners and empowered emotionally when they mirror forth virtues and values and have a positive understanding of the oneness of humankind principle and an appreciation of human diversity.

Thus, a truly responsible teacher strives to develop the students' human potential and, at the same time, works to develop their learning skills. In order to effectively accomplish this, today's teachers have to operate and function within a moral education framework. As Noguchi et al (1992) have observed, this period of humankind's passage into the age of maturity and inevitable movement towards a world civilization which will embody the principle of unity in diversity calls for a new kind of person. This new kind of person will, on a personal level, have to be directed and pointed towards the development of his true potential: achieving those qualities, values, and virtues that every human being should possess, plus those talents and capacities that are individually unique. And since a person cannot develop qualities, values, virtues, and talents in isolation, these, on a social level, have to be focused upon and directed towards the benefit and welfare of others. This, then, is the twofold purpose of moral education, and it is motivated by a desire for knowledge and truth about oneself, human nature, and the world around us. (pp.4-6) All students can benefit from this approach, and all can maintain a sense of worth and self-esteem.

Teachers never should underestimate the effect their words, attitudes, expressions, and body language have on the children they teach. Teachers, in fact, do represent a persuasive force in a youngster's life, so one prejudiced statement, no matter whether uttered innocently or on purpose, can negatively affect or exert some influence on a student, irrespective of what the student's ethnic background is. Let me cite an example.

An incident occurred one day when my daughter, Karen, was in a fourth grade history class. In the context of discussing the contributions of various groups of people in American history, the teacher proceeded to proudly glorify the accomplishments of whites, while at the same time telling the class that the Native American people were barbaric, uncivilized, and in essence had been deterrents to progress. He kept referring to them as "savages." It was obvious to the youngsters that he held absolutely no regard or respect for the Native American people he was talking about.

Karen, like many African-Americans, also has Native American lineage, and she was offended and hurt by his remarks. She knew the teacher was wrong, for she had been taught about Native Americans at home. Therefore, she rejected what the teacher said and recognized that he was prejudiced. What was worse, perhaps, was how some of the white children after class were laughing and talking about the "savages."

No sooner had the school bus dropped her off in front of the house, Karen hurried to tell her mother, Pauline, what had happened in class. Pauline said, "Karen, get in the car. We're going back to your school. I want to have some words with Mr. ___, because what he said to you and the other children was wrong and improper, and I'm very angry.

Return to school they did! Taking Karen by the hand, Pauline stormed into the teacher's room and said she wanted to talk to him seriously about what he had said in class about Native Americans. She told him his comments were prejudicial, inaccurate, and revealed his lack of knowledge about Native American people. In addition, she told him she was angry and offended that he had said these things in front of her daughter and her classmates. Pauline then said that she expected him to rectify the damage by apologizing to the class, and that if he did not she would take further action by going to the principal and the school board. Deeply shaken and embarrassed, the teacher apologized to Karen and Pauline, and in class the following day he told the students he was wrong and apologized to them. Karen was pleased. She felt good and was so proud of her mother. She later told me, "Even though Mom was short and small, she looked mighty that day when she was talking to Mr.___." Whether the teacher was truly repentant, only he and The Great Spirit really know. The point is, this teacher's inane, clearly inappropriate remarks were heard by a classroom of impressionable children, two of whom had Indian ancestry. No doubt the teacher was oblivious to the fact that one of the boys in the class was a Native American. Care to guess how he must have felt when he heard the teacher's remarks, what effect it had on his self-esteem?

The effective teacher of today's generation of young people must possess a belief in the innate nobility of humankind, that all human beings have been created noble. Such a conviction is central to self-knowledge. Should the teacher get this idea over to his students, and they hold onto it firmly, their power and ability to transform their own characters for the better would be significantly enhanced, not to mention their self -esteem. In my mind, there is no doubt whatsoever that a teacher can positively influence a student's self-esteem and sense of worth. When the teacher is truly committed to those same human values and virtues she or he is trying to develop in the students – has sound and reasonable expectations for learning, is respectful, unbiased and impartial – chances are good that children of color will have good feelings about themselves and will be successful in their studies. When the teacher positively acknowledges children's ethnic backgrounds or color, shows respect for their culture and history, interacts comfortably and positively with their parents, this will be observed by the youngsters and will help them greatly in developing a concept of who they are and how they feel about themselves. All of this has to do with respectful, concerned, and loving treatment. Again, I call your attention to the observations of Drs. Comer and Poussaint (1992) that children's overall feelings of self-concept are greatly influenced by the way they are treated by the important people in their lives, and this includes teachers. Furthermore, poor performance is very often a result of poor treatment. So, if the youngster receives poor treatment from the teacher, not only is learning adversely affected, but how then can the student ever hope to succeed? Success and accomplishment really do boost one's self-esteem, and every small victory gradually improves the self-concept and thereby minimizes one's fear of failure.

Related to this is what Dr. Robert White (1959) of Harvard University terms the acquisition of competence. He uses the word, "competence", in a broad biological sense rather than in its limited everyday meaning. His view of this concept of competence regarding humans is in reference to their capacity to interact effectively with their environment. This interactive ability, he claims, slowly and sequentially is "attained through prolonged feats of learning." (p. 297) He argues that it is necessary to view competence as a motivational concept, as opposed to the more traditional practice of looking at various kinds of behavior using theories strictly based upon organic drives. He claims that all behaviors have a common biological significance and, therefore, the behavior that leads a child to its effective development of grasping, crawling, walking, focal attention, perception, memory, thinking, language, and curiosity, to name a few, is not due to a "general overflow of energy." Rather, "It is directed, selective, and persistent, and it is continued not because it serves primary drives, which indeed it cannot serve until it is almost perfected, but because it satisfies an intrinsic need to deal with the environment." (p. 318).

So, a big challenge that children of color face is one of dealing with their environment. Certainly, when the environment is racist or racially comfortable, these youngsters are confronted with unique types of self-esteem threatening nuances white children do not have to handle. Therefore, for many children of color, dealing with their environment really becomes the most fundamental element in motivation. A hostile setting does not enhance one's motivation. Without motivation, one's desire to learn is greatly diminished, and the mind tends to shut down and is more concerned with "fight" and "flight." This is why the teacher has to provide an educational environment that will foster human virtues, promote acceptance of diversity, and facilitate and enhance feelings of security, understanding, warmth, love, and respect.

WHAT'S IT ALL ABOUT, WHERE DO WE GO FROM HERE?

A fact of life is that advances in science and technology have made this planet Earth small. Diverse peoples have been brought together because distance and time mean nothing now with our modern means of transportation and communication. The peoples of the world are truly interdependent. As such, we can no longer continue to dwell on differences and superficial factors without suffering terribly destructive consequences. The big task today is that of achieving global unity, and this calls for us humans to make a basic change in the way we relate to each other. And that includes how we relate to and teach our children, how we work to strengthen their sense of worth and esteem.

Children of color, like all children, are trying to figure out who they are and what their place is in this world. When our children – all of our children, irrespective of ethnic background – learn and understand what a true human being is, recognize the nobility of all humankind, earnestly develop a consciousness of the organic oneness of the human race, and start to feel a kinship with all people, then the self-esteem of humanity collectively will skyrocket.

A parting comment. The term "race" is a mythical word that has been unscientifically used to categorize human beings. Black people are not black, white people are not white, red people are not red, and yellow people are not yellow. Everyone on earth is, in fact, a person of color. It's only a matter of degree, because, the truth is, we are all really different shades of a single protein, called melanin.

References

Comer, James P., and Alvin E. Poussaint (1992). *Raising Black Children.* New York: Penguin Books.

Cross, W.E. (1985) "Black Identity: Rediscovering the Distinctions Between Personal Identity and Reference Group Orientations." In M.B. Spencer.

G. K. Brookins, and W.R. Allen (Eds.) (1985) *Beginnings: The Social and Affective Development of Black Children.* Hillsdale, N.J.: Erlbaum, pp. 155-172.

Frazier, E. Franklin (1957). *Race and Culture Contacts in the Modern World.* Boston: Beacon Press.

Noguchi, Lori McLaughlin, Holly Hanson, and Paul Lample (1992) *Exploring a Framework For Moral Education.* Riviera Beach, Fla.: Palabra Publications.

Rutstein, Nathan (1992) *Education on Trial.* Oxford: One World Publications, Ltd.

White, Robert W. (1959) "Motivation Reconsidered: The Concept of Competence." In *Psychological Review*, Vol. 66, No. 5, pp. 297-333.

Wood, Forest G. (1990) *The Arrogance of Faith: Christianity and Race in America From the Colonial Era to the Twentieth Century.* New York: Alfred A. Knopf.

Chapter 8

Why Many Students of Color Have Trouble Learning in Schools

by Nathan Rutstein

Racism causes immense unconscious damage to people of color. Because teachers do not understand, and are unconscious of the effects, they don't realize that they may be exacerbating the problem in their African-American students. The author, a retired professor who has written and lectured extensively on the topic of racism, illumines through examples some of the occurrences which cause students of color to perform poorly in educational settings. Ed.

Sadly, most teachers of good will aren't aware of the difficulties and pain most students of color endure in the classroom. If they were, I'm sure they would want to change the learning environment in their schools, and find new ways of reaching and teaching African-American, American Indian and Latino children.

School dropout statistics remain consistently high among students of color. So does mediocre to poor classroom performance. To social psychologist Claude Steele (1992), this condition is no surprise. He points out, for example, that when black children enter the existing school systems they enter with two fears – the fear of being devalued and the fear of lacking the ability to succeed. Also, educational psychologist Harry Morgan's (1980) studies show that by the third grade most black students drop out psychologically.

Does this mean that African-American children are innately less intelligent than European-American children? No. It means that

America's educators are not aware of the real causes of the American black child's educational dilemma. The authors of the *Bell Curve Wars* (Fraser 1995) completely miss this point. Creating an appealing school environment is the key. But, in order to create the appropriate classroom environment, teachers need to know the real emotional condition of their students. Otherwise, considerable unintentional harm can be done to them. And, I contend, this is happening to thousands of students of color every day across America. To gain an accurate diagnosis of the average black child's state of mind, it is necessary to delve into the past.

After a thorough exploration of how racism came about in America, I realized that most of the descendants of American slaves are wounded. This, however, doesn't mean they are inherently less intelligent than others. It isn't a physical wound, but rather an emotional condition. The wound is a lack of confidence, a lack of self-esteem, feelings of repressed inferiority and self-hatred. Acknowledging that you possess the wound isn't easy, for no one wants to admit to suffering from feelings of inferiority or not liking oneself. That's why falling into denial is a very human reflex.

For most people, denial is a carefully concealed mental maneuver that springs from a sense of shame. You can see why many whites of good will are in denial when it comes to dealing with their race prejudice. They can distinguish between what is right and wrong. Intellectually they know it is wrong to have negative feelings toward people of color, and, when those feelings surface, shame forces most of them to immediately repress those feelings and convince themselves that they are race prejudice-free.

While teaching at Springfield Technical Community College in Massachusetts, I was able to identify at least four forms of denial among my black and Latino students. The most apparent one was the "tough guy" posture. This form of denial was designed to keep their enemies from recognizing the fear, hopelessness, and insecurities beneath their veneer of toughness. The second form of denial was something they picked up from white folks; and that was the flaunting of their material possessions. It was their way of telling the world that everything is OK, that they are "making it." And perhaps the most psychologically harmful forms of denial were the other two: pretending that everything is OK when deep down you know it isn't, thus forcing yourself to live a lie. And then there's the blowing up of a small victory in one's life, like a small job promotion. A fantasy is created that you force yourself to believe is the truth. And those intimate friends you share your "good news" with want to embrace the fantasy as the truth as well, for it is a way of feeling good for a few moments in what is normally a life of misery. These forms of denial are harmful, because the further one drifts away from reality the more unhealthy you are from a mental health standpoint.

The deep-seated sense of inferiority that plagues most African-Americans was highlighted in the late 1940s in a famous study conducted by Drs. Kenneth and Mamie Clark — both accomplished psychologists and blacks themselves.

They tested scores of black three- to seven-year-olds in a number of Northern and Southern cities and towns. All were exposed to white and black dolls. The child was told: (1) "Give me the doll you like to play with," or " the doll you like the best," (2) "Give me the doll that is the nice doll," (3) "Give me the doll that looks bad," (4) "Give me the doll that is a nice color." The great majority of black children preferred the white doll and rejected the black doll.

About forty years later – in 1988 – the same test was given to black children of the same age group. Despite a greater effort to acquaint blacks with their heritage, despite ongoing "Black is Beautiful" campaigns, the test results were the same as for the one given in the late 1940s.

Refusing to consciously acknowledge the problem forestalls solving it. Living with a lie can create emotional havoc. When there's a strong impulse to escape, drugs, alcohol, and sexual promiscuity have great appeal. The bad behavior in school, so often equated with black and Latino students, is usually an assault on an institution that heightens feelings of inferiority. No sane person likes the feeling, he wants to get rid of it; when he can't, he tries to hide it from himself and others. And when he's reminded of it by an outside force, he resists the attempt, sometimes violently.

Educational administrators and teachers should be aware of those feelings and how they come into being, as well as know how to eradicate them in the human beings they are charged with educating. Sadly, that kind of sensitivity and knowledge is not forthcoming in our school systems. There may be individual administrators and teachers who have that ability, but are afraid to tackle the problem without the support of the school system hierarchy.

The problem, which is the direct result of racism, is real, and unless it is dealt with, those who are plagued by it will never experience true freedom and will continue to wear the brand of a social outcast, a stigma that engenders anger and rage. Even people who seem very secure and independent are struggling with the problem. A number of years ago, a friend of mine who is black revealed to me in a heart-to-heart discussion that he was trying to overcome his deep-rooted feelings of inferiority. To make his point, he said, "When I'm about to enter a train, and I notice the engineer is black, I begin to worry about an accident. I never feel that way when a white man is in the driver's seat." My friend felt that way even though he was driving a bus for a living.

At a meeting of educators at the college where I taught in the fall of 1989, the chancellor of the Massachusetts Regents of Higher Education, Dr. Franklyn Jenifer – a black – shared an incident with the audience that demonstrated that he was afflicted, too.

"I had to get to an important conference in Philadelphia and bad weather had grounded all of the regular airlines in Boston," he said.

"The only planes flying were the small propeller-driven aircraft. So I led my party to one of the feeder lines and waited for the pilot. When he arrived, I noticed my white colleagues felt uneasy, and so did I. In fact, I had an urge to flee. And all because the pilot was black. Had he been white, I would have felt more secure. I had no control over the feelings that possessed me. It didn't matter that I was black myself, held an important position in society and had earned a doctorate degree."

While people like Dr. Jenifer can talk openly about such feelings, most can't, especially young men and women. And I can understand why. Yet, they need to overcome their feelings of inferiority.

Several years ago, I gained some insight as to how those feelings of inferiority are reinforced in the classroom of a predominately white school. I was engaged in a campaign to end racial discrimination in a nearby high school. Our group had gathered most of the black and Latino students together in a local home. We wanted to know from them how race prejudice was manifested in the high school. At first they were hesitant to talk, because they were afraid that the teachers and the white students would view them as troublemakers if they shared their honest feelings with our group. They wanted desperately to fit in, to be accepted by all of the student body and faculty. Finally, a young black man, who had transferred to the high school from a predominately black school in Cleveland, spoke first. What he had to say broke down the reserve of the other students.

The young man — his voice trembling — said that in Cleveland he had been an "A" student in science and mathematics. He wanted to be an electrical engineer, an inventor. In fact, he had won several awards for the electrical gadgets he had invented in Ohio. Eager to make his mark in his new school, which had an excellent academic reputation, he decided to work harder than usual. But, deep down, he was scared, because he had never attended a predominately white school. He wasn't sure that he would be accepted as an equal.

And he wasn't. Not in an overt manner. For example, he wondered why the teacher rarely called on him in class when he felt he knew the answer to her question. But I understood why the teacher ignored him most of the time; she had lower expectations of him because of his skin color and the fact that he attended a predominately black school. To avoid embarrassing the boy, the teacher didn't call on him. She probably felt he didn't belong in the college prep track.

He was made to feel different, because he often found whites staring at him, as if he were permanently sullied. He felt rejected. Oh, teachers and students said hello, but he wasn't encouraged to mingle with them. Feeling isolated, he grew inward-directed, and preoccupied with time, often glancing at the clock on the wall. The sound of the period ending bell was the source of relief from the psychological oppression he was experiencing. He sensed that staying in the classroom was destroying him. But he couldn't quit, because he had made a commitment to his mother that he would do his best in the new school. When he tried to confide in her about his troubles, she urged him to try harder. But trying harder didn't help. He was too emotionally upset to absorb the teacher's lessons. After a while he found himself unable to reason, and his grades began to fall. That had never happened to him before.

The young man began to cry when he revealed that he had been dropped from the school's college preparatory track, and placed in a track for "dummies." Of course, he knew what that meant — his dream of becoming an electrical engineer would never be realized. He had been psychologically murdered. And those who committed the crime, are, to this day, unaware of what they had done to a fellow human being. Tragically, what happened to the young man is happening to thousands of other African-American, Latino, and American Indian students at this moment – at the hands of teachers who mean well, who want to do the right thing, but who are unaware of the "wound."

Several months later, I learned why that young man failed to realize his career dream, why he wanted to flee the classroom and why he lost his ability to reason effectively in school. While in Hawaii, I learned of the work being done by Kenneth Yamamoto (Rutstein, 1993), who had been trying to find out why there was such a high incidence of school dropout among native Hawaiian youth. The desire to flee the classroom, he pointed out, is a Pavlovian reflex. When a student suffering from feelings of inferiority enters the classroom, the classroom turns into a factory for failure. Not wanting to experience defeat again, he wants to flee.

But Dr. Yamamoto added that a student's negative feelings of self also shuts down the brain's cerebral cortex, which is the seat of thought; and the medulla oblongata, which sparks human survival emotions, takes over, creating in the student a desire to flee or fight.

Those who want to fight are angry; their inner voice often cries out: "I don't know what's happening to me; I can't think here. I know I'm not a dummy. The teacher doesn't understand how I really feel; and I can't explain my feelings to her. And I know what the teacher is going to do to me. It's unfair."

The teacher, unable to hear the inner voice of the desperate student, can only respond to the frightening outward expression of the child, and, for reasons of self defense, brands the student a "behavioral problem." And the student is tracked in a special class for either slow learners or the emotionally upset. The student carries that stigma throughout his school days until he comes to a crossroads, where he must choose between two paths. At one path, the branded student acquiesces to the educators' evaluation of himself and acknowledges to himself and others that he is, indeed, a dummy, and spends the rest of his life looking for ways to dull the pain. Our cities are packed with men and women who have chosen that path.

Those who choose the other path actively resist the educators' evaluation of themselves; but they resist with the seeds of doubt planted in them, causing internal conflict. They fight the establishment. Some fight with such intensity they get in trouble with the law. So it doesn't surprise me that about 25 percent of African-American males between twenty and twenty-nine are either in jail, parole, or on probation; that more than 50 percent of the inmates in Alaska's penitentiary are American Indians.

Those students who want to flee either drop out physically or psychologically from school. The latter continue to attend classes, prodded by their parents to continually try harder. Sadly, these well meaning parents, who feel that a good education will help their children find success in life, are unaware of their child's cerebral cortex shutting down. Tracked as slow learners, the students often graduate having difficulty reading their diplomas. Worse yet, they are unequipped to land a job in an economy that is becoming more and more high-tech. Sadly the authors of *The Bell Curve* fail to take into account these views.

Simply telling students that they aren't inferior doesn't work. While they may on the surface nod in the affirmative, deep down their doubts dominate. In order to make headway, they need to prove to themselves that they aren't inferior beings. This can be done; but to do it, a complete change in teaching approach and classroom learning environment is required. In my book *Education on Trial* (Rutstein 1992), I describe what I did at Springfield Technical Community College to help students replace their feelings of inferiority with a sense of self worth and respect. As they felt better about themselves their grades improved. When I started our program, less than 25 percent of our students went onto four -year colleges. By the time I retired, close to 80 percent went on to pursue a bachelor's degree.

Most European-American teachers and administrators have little understanding of what students of color, even those who get good grades, must endure in school. When Iris, a young African-American woman, graduated near the top of her high school class, she turned down a full scholarship to Harvard University to attend Hampton University, a predominately black college. Her parents, both white-collar, college-educated professionals, supported her decision and were willing to pay the tuition.

Thinking that Iris had made the wrong decision, I tried hard to persuade her to take Harvard's offer. "A degree from Harvard is like a key to success," I said.

"Mr. Rutstein," she replied, "I can no longer attend a predominately white school. I don't have the energy to do what I have been forced to do for the past twelve years – and that is to live in both the black and white worlds. It is hard enough to live in one world these days. In this country there is no place for someone like me to live and work simply as a human being. I'm forced to make a choice, and I've chosen the black world because I feel more comfortable there. Frankly, I'm tired of girding myself to be someone I am not, in order to get a good grade. I'm tired of being psychologically whipped. I'm going to college where I can be myself."

Unlike Iris, most African-American, American Indian and Latino children don't have college-educated parents, providing consistent wise academic counseling. What they must endure each day is, I suspect, far more painful that what Iris had to endure.

References

Fraser, Steven (Ed) (1995). *The Bell Curve Wars.* New York: Basic Books.

Morgan, Harry (1980). "How Schools Fail Black Children". *Social Policy,* Jan-Feb.

Rutstein, Nathan (1992). *Education on Trial.* Oxford, U.K.: One World Press.

Steele, Claude M. (1992). "Race and the Schooling of Black Children". *The Atlantic.* April.

Chapter 9

Advice for Teachers on Racism and Oneness

by Barbara Hacker

The author, a primary school teacher, writes about the critical responsibility of teachers for helping to eradicate the disease of racism. She believes passionately that teachers can make a difference, and she writes of how teachers can, and must, believe in their ability to inspire students. The author offers a format which can help teachers learn about the disease of racism and help their students do the same. Ed.

True education is not something that's given to or done to students, but a process that happens within them. The teacher's role is to draw out the potentialities and skills latent within the student and offer road maps and keys to unlock the wonders of the world and the student's own talents. Many have tried to capture this difference in the conception of the role by avoiding the word "teacher" completely, preferring "director/directress" or "guide" instead. This idea of the role implies that the teacher must also be a learner, someone a little further along the path who can lead and guide, and, most importantly, excite and inspire.

Knowing where there is to go suggests to me awareness of the possibilities in two broad areas. One is content, the what and who there is to know, with knowing implying respect. I recall a presentation given by a young man from a children's museum to a group of young people. His subject, and quite obviously his love, was whales. He told the children he wanted them to know and respect whales, and they couldn't do one without the other. He then proceeded to ignite in his audience the love and respect he had for these wondrous creatures. He had a great knowledge, but he shared much more than facts. I know he awakened in me a profound respect for the place of these animals in creation, a sense of responsibility to protect them and to learn more about them that has stayed with me. He knew some place there was to go, and he took us there.

Another, perhaps more important, area of knowing where there is to go, involves knowing and respecting human beings. A personal exploration of what it means to be human, the nature of human potentialities, how humans develop and learn, the purpose of life. How people develop physically, emotionally, intellectually, socially and spiritually seems an essential prerequisite for serving as a guide for someone else's becoming all he can be.

Teachers, of course, can't know everything and can't arrive at some point of ultimate development before they begin their work. What does seem essential is that they be active learners, continually expanding the content areas in which they have knowledge, and which allows them to be continually involved in their personal growth and transformation. I've done an exercise with many adults, especially those wanting to be teachers. They simply reflected back on those adults who played the most memorable roles in their education and development, both positively and negatively, wrote them down, then shared these memories for the group to analyze what helped and hindered. For example, in my own case, I have a wealth of positive memories of fourth grade. I remember specific content areas about which I became excited, a sense of empowerment and esteem that I could write poetry because of the teacher's encouragement that included sending my work to a literary magazine, and an indelible mental image of her hands as she worked with me in physical closeness. Yet, I have absolutely no memories of fifth grade except for putting on a radio play during the two weeks we had a student teacher! The fourth grade teacher continually re-arranged the room, filled the environment with interesting things and initiated projects. Her interest in me extended beyond my leaving her class. Later she was picked to teach in a lab school at a school of education. The fifth grade teacher sat us in rows and taught strictly from the texts. The difference seems to be in the teachers and who they were as living, learning, loving and growing individuals.

The particular content areas in which individual teachers have a love, knowledge and expertise can vary, as will their personal paths toward inner growth. There is one area, however, that I have come to believe is critical for all teachers in America to become knowledgeable in, regardless of their age, ethnic background, grade level and subject area, or where and who they teach. That is to understand the disease of racism and the principle it violates—the oneness of humanity, simply because it is, I believe, the most vital and challenging issue affecting our country, and because it affects all of us, regardless of our background, whether born and raised in the U.S. or an immigrant to this society. Of all the challenges facing this country, realizing our unity as a people, eradicating the disease of racism that has threatened the life, hearts and minds of all of us, and healing the wounds in all of us seems the most critical first step in solving the other challenges. All Americans must play a role, but for those charged with guiding the next generations, the responsibility is especially great.

In 1973, sitting on the porch of an old farmhouse in South Carolina, site of the alternative school where a group of poor but dedicated individuals were striving to make education happen for a diverse group of kids, I wrote down what at that point I saw as my lifetime goals. They have never changed, and over the ups and downs of the subsequent twenty years have served to bring me back to focus. Among them were to learn all I could about children in all their many aspects, doing all I could to promote true education, and to do all in my power to overcome racism. Setting those goals as a young teacher was for me an important act, affirming the power of the individual to make a difference.

One of the most disturbing characteristics I observe as

widespread in society is a sense of powerlessness, of individuals feeling controlled by events and institutions and forces beyond themselves. Yet, all around us are examples of people whose stories can inspire us as to the power of individuals. For teachers, developing and maintaining the belief that they can make a difference is crucial, not only to their success as teachers, but as a gift they can pass on to their students. When we hear the stories of teachers like Jaime Escalante, the California math teacher who guided so many of his largely Latino high school students to success on advance placement math exams, or Houston elementary principle Thaddeus Lott, who led his teachers and African-American students to high levels of achievement, the defeatist and racist elements of our society assume they have cheated. If these children are achieving, they claim, something must be wrong. To me, they are the example of what the power of individual educators can do. As badly as we need educational reform, and more money and changes in our schools of education, it is my conviction that it is still the individual teacher's belief in his power to effect change and his ability to believe in and inspire students that will be the means to real changes in our schools and in our society.

In recent years, in addition to my work with young children, I've helped to develop a learning format for adults that assists them to learn about the disease of racism. It helps them to understand how racism has impacted them personally and aids them to begin to heal the hurts that pile one upon another, affecting perceptions, ability to think clearly and creatively, hindering further development and affecting interpersonal relationships. A few have peeked in and rejected the journey. Many have fully partcipated and left with a new awareness and sense of personal empowerment that they can effect change within their sphere of influence. Others have been very inspired, continuing the journey on their own. I see people going out like ripples in a pond to touch others. These ordinary people are to me the real change agents in America. I saw a bumper sticker that summarizes this conviction: "If the people lead, the leaders will follow."

If teachers across America could arise and make the personal commitment to do something about racism, beginning with their own selves, their eventual impact would, I believe, be tremendous. Even the first tentative steps will bring new awareness that can instantly affect the teacher in the classroom. As the teacher's growth continues, the young people will increasingly be the benefactors.

Ability to participate in a workshop such as the one my group created is not what is most crucial. An individual can start the process alone. After all, we created the workshop with information gleaned from many sources because we as individuals wanted to grow and learn and change. The process we went through in creating the program is more important than any particular idea or concept. The workshop continues to evolve as we grow and learn more. Some of the principles we've discovered, and how they particularly apply to teachers, may be helpful.

First, accept that it is OK to talk about racism. Cherry, my partner in facilitating workshops, often remarks, "For whites, the word racism is like yelling 'Fire!' in a crowded theater. They panic and want to flee." The reason, I believe, is that most know how deeply wrong racism is. They especially think of the most blatant forms like the KKK and don't want to be associated with them. And they fear finding the disease hidden within themselves, many carrying shame and guilt and painful early memories of their early indoctrination to racism.

People of color, we often find, have protected themselves by saying and believing that they were not that affected by racism, only to have something later in the workshop stimulate memories of deep pain. Typical was a vivacious middle aged woman who was eager to participate, but in introductions shared that she felt she had personally not been that affected. Later, as we watched an historical film and the image appeared of a lynched black man hanging from a tree, she was filled with deep, convulsive grief. My able partner held her in support, but allowed the tears to flow, knowing that releasing the hurts is the key to healing. This friend later shared with the group how she had happened on such a scene as a young child.

No adult talked to her about it or allowed her to speak her horror and pain or ask her questions. The pain of that experience had been buried inside of her for years, utilizing a great deal of her energy to keep itself hidden.

The key to being able to talk about racism is for people to make "I" statements, speaking of their own feelings and experiences, and agreeing not to judge or in any way comment upon another's sharing. Learning to really listen to others without the need to react is the balancing skill.

Students can learn to speak about racism in a productive manner if given the protection of guidelines for how they will share and how they will listen, and the trust that the guidelines will be enforced for all. Cherry and I were invited to speak to a diverse college class on aspects of racism. The night before, we received a call from the teaching assistant warning us that he had tried at the last class meeting to lead a discussion on racism and everyone, black, white, Asian and Latino had exploded with anger and many walked out. We began our session by setting up the parameters or guidelines for how we would share, and the same group of students had a worthwhile experience, many individuals sharing, who, the teachers later reported, had never spoken before in class. We gave them a printed set of guidelines to hold in front of them, which we read and explained, including: sharing is voluntary; we want to create a safe, loving and respectful atmosphere; and sharing is about one's own feelings, experiences and perceptions. The guidelines also contained prohibitions against cross-talking, an emphasis on the importance of feelings and the statement that it is OK to see things differently. The fact that we facilitated as an interracial team is also an important factor in creating safety. Racism is a reality in America, and we must sweep it out from under the rug and deal with it, but in a way that creates safety for all involved. Teachers can play an invaluable role by instituting such sessions, and learning and teaching the skills that create safety.

A second major principle is that a lot has been written about the nature of prejudice and racism, the many ways in which it is manifested, how it is transmitted and perpetuated, and even the stages that individuals go through in overcoming its effects. This knowledge is not held by the average person in the street, however, and even highly educated people can be woefully ignorant on this subject. By seeking out this information from books, research articles and knowledgeable individuals, and incorporating it into our workshops, we experienced that coming to grasp the nature of the disease was a critical factor in increasing people's awareness of themselves and their society and increasing their ability to act in a meaningful way. Everyone needs this body of knowledge. People of good will are, in fact, craving it. Knowledge like this sets people free and empowers them to do things they would have never thought possible. If teachers could thoroughly digest this information, how they react to and teach their students who are caught up in this web of racism would change, and the knowledge they could pass on to their students would be perhaps the most valuable gift they could give them.

A third important principle is that we all have prejudices. The very nature of a prejudice is that it is based on ignorance, a falsehood or an over-generalization that we cling to, often with emotional commitment. We come by having these prejudices, often quite innocently, by the information and impressions that bombard us daily from our families and associates, the media, things we observe and only partially understand. To understand the nature of prejudice and commit to discovering it in ourselves and then ridding ourselves of it, creates a freedom to get on with the business of growth without being bound up in guilt and denial.

A corollary of the concept that we all have prejudices is the idea that it really is OK to make mistakes, and that mistakes are opportunities for learning and growing. So often in our educational tradition teachers have been set up as gods, or at least authority figures, not to be challenged. I have a vivid memory of my first grade teacher accusing me of an offense I never could have done. The humiliation was awful. When a few minutes later I saw something that explained how the "crime" had taken place quite accidentally, with no one to blame, I couldn't tell the teacher for fear of her anger at having her error exposed. I recall how clear my understanding of the situation was, and how trapped and pained I felt. This was the first of many "educational" experiences where the truth was hidden to protect the authority of the teacher. Thankfully, I learned fairly early in my life as a teacher the glorious, freeing feeling of being able to admit mistakes to children and apologize. Its an exercise I try to repeat regularly. How powerful it could be if teachers across America, regardless of age group or subject area, could teach the nature of prejudice, and both embody and teach the principle that mistakes are opportunities to learn and to grow. Classes (including the teacher) could have regular sharing sessions on prejudices they have recognized and mistakes they've made, and how, of course, they've grown from the experience. What more valuable life lesson could there be?

A fourth key principle in starting this journey of overcoming racism is the recognition that we have all been miseducated. The facts and concepts we've been given, especially about our history, are frequently erroneous. A major problem is what was omitted. History has been taught to us largely from a white, European perspective. The history, civilizations, and contributions of people from other parts of the world, and of Native Americans, have been ignored or given cursory treatment such that it makes a statement about how they were regarded. Young children largely take in this information uncritically, especially when they've never been taught to ask questions. I remember sitting in my sixth grade classroom staring at a map in my social studies text and wondering why we never learned about Asia, Africa or South America, but I never voiced my questions aloud. As a college student studying Afro-American history, I wondered why the material I was learning wasn't covered in my U.S. history classes. Black History Month was instituted as an impetus for people to learn about some of the events and people that had been neglected by our general history books, and it has done much good. It is past time now for us to realize that this is **all** of our history, not to be relegated solely to one month a year, but to be incorporated in a substantial, meaningful way into the social studies and history curriculum taught throughout the year.

Part of the difficulty, I think, is in the history as mythology many of us received as young children: the prim, immaculate, starched and pressed Pilgrims who made friends with the Indians and lived happily ever after; the Columbus who in 1492 "sailed the ocean blue" to prove to the unbelieving masses that the world was round and "discovered" America; the numerous poems and stories about Washington and Lincoln that are either patently false or far from the essence of who these presidents were. All too often, teachers of the very young repeat ceremoniously the mythology they were given. These images are hard to erase from children's minds even as later teachers might attempt to build a more complete picture of history.

Even the very young can begin to learn a more truthful, if simplified, history. My five- and six-year-old students know of Columbus's voyage, but they also know that most educated people in Europe did not think the earth was flat by that time, and that there is evidence that others from the Eastern Hemisphere, particularly northern Europe and Africa, had already visited in the West and that there were people already there with cultures and civilizations who Columbus mistakenly called Indians. This leads to a discussion of native peoples today (many children think Indians existed only in the past in the heyday of the cowboy), and why some might prefer to be called by their tribal names instead of Indians, which recalls Columbus's mistake. We talk about what "discover" means, and little of what the encounter was really like. The children themselves realized that the 500th anniversary of that event was something to learn about and think about, but not celebrate. Children of this age can readily begin to understand these concepts, and they can be building blocks upon which a more developed and thoughtful history can be built. It is not our fault that most of us were miseducated in this respect, but it does become our responsibility to reeducate ourselves when we recognize that there is another side to the story. It is important for all Americans to go through this process, but especially for teachers, who have the opportunity of interrupting the cycle of misinformation. It is not necessary to be an expert, but to keep an open mind and keep learning. The reading of one new book can start the process.

Related to the study of history is the need we all have, and especially children, for heroes and heroines. Not only do children need facts, but they need to be inspired. There are heroes and heroines of every heritage, people whose lives can inspire us to a higher conception of human possibilities. Children of all backgrounds need role models of all backgrounds. For children of color, who have all too often not been taught the stories of great people who look like them, it is critical. It is also critical for European-American children to know, that in addition to the achievers of their heritage to which they've been widely exposed, there have always been people of their heritage who saw things clearly, worked to overcome the injustice of slavery and segregation and even gave their lives in the struggle.

These heroes and heroines don't need to be presented as perfect people, but ordinary people just like us, who did extraordinary things. It starts with a teacher being excited by a life he has discovered and sharing it with students. Hopefully it continues as a regular and anticipated part of the school experience. Older students have a continuing need to be read to by adults and they can also read to each other or dramatize the stories they discover. Elementary age children are especially interested, developmentally, in issues of fairness, and are eager to learn of the struggle for civil rights that has been a constant major theme throughout American history. Even my five-and six-year-olds know what a biography is. We read their own biographies, prepared as a family project on their birthdays. They can understand stories read to them beyond the level they can read themselves, and this "stretches" them in many ways. When written stories are too far beyond their level of comprehension, the teacher can retell the story in his own words, an experience they love.

The deep response of children has fed my desire as a teacher to continue sharing biographies. After concluding a "chapter-a-day" book about Harriet Tubman there was great appreciation among the children and her name came up in their own conversations months after the book had been returned to the library. Once, in a discussion of virtues, a child brought up incidents from the life of Harriet Tubman and appropriately identified the virtues she embodied. In learning to write the letter upper case "H," another child asked that I spell Harriet so he could practice by writing her name! One five-year-old boy approached me with stars in his eyes, and said he wished I'd read the story of Harriet Tubman every day. I arranged for him to take the book home. Another child was especially captivated by the story of James Weldon Johnson. After reading his biography, I taught the children the Black National Anthem and we discussed what the words meant. This became Charlie's favorite song and his request at every group singing session. In another class at the end of the year I found a six-year-old furiously writing something. When I inquired he explained that he was copying the words to "Let there be peace on earth and let it begin with me..." which we had learned six months before. He explained that his new teacher might not have the words to that song and he never wanted to forget them. Hopefully, these memories of early schooling will stay with these children as indelibly as my images of humiliation and fear.

One of the ways that I have come to understand that racism is perpetuated is through a cycle of oppression. When as children we are treated in an oppressive manner, we are not respected, we are physically or verbally abused, our voices are not heard and our need to make responsible choices not nurtured, we tend to treat others less powerful than ourselves in the same manner. Of course, it is not inevitable, but it is a tendency. The degree to which we are exposed to this kind of treatment, combined with our personalities and life circumstances can mitigate or strengthen our chances of falling into this cycle.

In America, much of the prevailing attitude toward children has incorporated what I would consider forms of abuse that are so widely accepted as to be considered normal. All too often, schools have become an institutional vehicle for perpetuating this cycle. When children are made to sit still and be quiet for extended periods of time, isolated from people older and younger than themselves, their every activity directed by an adult, their desire to question and think for themselves thwarted or even punished, their mistakes ridiculed and their desire to cooperate often branded as cheating, a frustration builds that all too often turns outward and treats others in the same way. The higher order characteristics of human beings—intelligent thought, an inquiring and creative mind, the urge toward self-perfection and mastery, the urge toward movement and manipulation, the urge to communicate—to understand and be understood, the desire to aid and cooperate, are thwarted and buried rather than being nurtured and developed. What this type of education is really about is control.

Having experienced a controlling education myself, as a young person I vehemently did not want to be a teacher. I was disappointed when, as a college urban studies major, I was given a field placement in an urban elementary school. My experience in that school confirmed my stand against teaching, though I loved the children and the dedicated first-year teacher I'd been assigned to assist. I have many painful images of that experience: the school nurse who came in to check heads for lice, finding success with a shy little girl who though poor, was walked to school each day by her mother, neatly combed and dressed and ready to learn. In a loud and contemptuous voice the nurse commented on the filthiness of this family and what a bad and neglectful mother the child had. Then there was the conference the teacher sent me to between the white principal and the African-American mother of a child I had been tutoring. Not only was my positive input about the child not heard, but the mother was treated in the most patronizing manner I had ever witnessed, the child repeatedly referred to as "little Johnny" rather than the two full given names his family and teachers used, and his fate seemed decided by this woman who didn't even know him. I'll never forget the face of a little girl "promoted" out of our class to a teacher known for her strict and rigid approach to teaching. All the child's joy was gone, and she looked at us with pleading eyes and didn't say a word. On another occasion, I questioned the principal as to why she continued the old practice of having the children line up each day to enter the school at separate entrances for boys and girls. She snapped a reply: "It's just a matter of convenience. If we had more white children we could line them up black and white." I was horrified. The result of my questioning such things was an evaluation that said I had a problem with authority.

I don't know if that first-year teacher survived the system, but she changed my life by encouraging me to observe at a local Montessori school. It was a profound, soul-stirring experience that showed me the education of children did not have to be as I had experienced it. I subsequently studied this approach and have been learning and teaching ever since. While the Montessori environment has given me tools and methods which have assisted me in overcoming the cycle of oppression in my own schooling, it is *still something I have to struggle with on a personal level.* I have known Montessori trained teachers who had not escaped the cycle though perhaps intellectually they wanted to, and I have known traditionally trained teachers who have created healthful learning environments within their classes. The bottom line is that it is an inner struggle for each individual teacher to reach a level of personal growth and confidence that he is able to create a learning environment in which personal dignity and respect are affirmed for all students, and the higher human capacities of virtuousness, cooperation, thinking, questioning, and personal initiative are nurtured despite the forces of habit and institutional patterns that try to thwart the efforts. If this cycle is to be broken in society, then it must be broken in our schools. While the way teachers are trained and the kinds of support and encouragement they get from administrators and school systems is terribly important, the primary battle must be waged in the hearts, minds and wills of individual teachers.

Two of the most important concepts for teachers to understand in fulfilling a commitment to act on racism are the concepts of unaware racism and internalized racism. Unaware racism is when individuals with good hearts, and often the best of intentions, do and say things that are hurtful and insensitive to people of another group. They may sense by the reaction they get that they did something wrong, but not know what it is, or they may be oblivious to the wound they have caused. For the targets, these unaware acts make up a "here we go again" pattern of experience that can be, at the least, exhausting to handle. For example, assuming that all African-Americans like the same things and think the same way; assuming that those with non-European features or names are foreigners and don't belong; or offering assistance when it has not been requested and is not needed. Teachers are as prone to these unaware gestures as others. A young African-American woman I know is a doctoral candidate at a major university, her area of study, Shakespeare. One of her professors, never having had an African-American student in this specialty, made assumptions about her and offered her assistance clearly beyond what was offered to other students. The assumption that she would need help and the patronizing way in which it was offered were hurtful and frustrating. On the elementary level, a friend recently observed her daughter's class where the teacher repeatedly called on only white children. She observed that the African-American students whose hands were in the air were ignored and eventually began to doodle and tune out.

It is imperative that teachers become aware of the typical unaware behaviors. Sometimes, when European-Americans are confronted by this concept, they become fearful and want to retreat from all contact with people of color because they are fearful of making mistakes. The most healthy response is just the opposite. When people are sincerely working on the issue and striving to embody the principle that mistakes are opportunities for learning and forgiving, they are more easily forgiven and helped along in the process. It is the arrogance of not trying that is hard to take.

The second critical concept for educators to begin to learn is internalized racism. It is the result of a group of people targeted by racism, systematically, over a long period of time, from all around them hearing stereotypes about people like themselves, and the message that they are inferior and cannot achieve, and their coming to believe or internalize those stereotypes and messages. The tragic result is varying degrees of loss of self-esteem, from the lingering internal doubts of a high achiever to the total giving up and chilling out of an individual addicted to drugs. It leads to individuals not only limiting their own potential, but also sabotaging the success of others in their group, and even to the extreme of hatred and destruction of others who look like themselves. It is at the root of a teacher of color placing a ceiling on students of color, while having higher expectations for white students. It is the root cause of students putting down the leadership or academic success of those in their own group. Of course, the root cause of it all is the racist, negative message endemic in our society. It is a deeply painful and sensitive subject, best dealt with in support groups within the targeted population, but it is essential for all teachers of all backgrounds to understand so they can grasp what is happening to their students and avoid further racist interpretations of the behaviors they might observe among their students—seeing these behaviors as confirmations of inferiority, rather than what they are, the tragic consequences of living in a society infected with racism.

All these aberrations must be looked at and understood by teachers if they are to be forces for healing. At the same time, however, we must not lose sight of the principle they have violated—that we are one people. It has always been our reality that we are one human family. Humanity as a whole has just not recognized that fact. Race is an erroneous concept, used by anthropologists when science was at the describe and categorize stage of its development, abandoned when evidence of our common ancestry and continual intermixing was better understood. Recognition of the truth of this principle requires more than brotherhood, more than tolerance, more than multicultural awareness. We are one human species, with wonderfully diverse expressions of that humanity. If teachers can internalize this concept and transmit it to their students it can become the secure anchoring point from which the aberrations, the painful history can be examined. For younger students the knowledge of this principle can be the vaccine that inoculates against the more painful results of racism. When they know who they are, human beings of nobility and dignity, with vast potential for achievement, related to every other human being, the instinct to oppress and the mechanisms by which people are oppressed will be transcended. When there is change in human hearts, institutions will follow. First, teachers must know who they are, their personal growth and centeredness communicating to students even without words. Beyond modeling, however, the principle of the oneness of humanity can be communicated at every level and in every subject area—the biology of oneness in science class, our common human themes in literature, the realities of the different branches of our family in geography, history or social studies, our universality in art and music. Even the history of math leads to an appreciation of our oneness, and computation skills can be used to illustrate how we are all at least fiftieth cousins. The concept is really quite simple and many of these things are being taught already. The consciousness of the overriding principle and its implications by the teacher and sharing it with students is what is important. For example, I learned in biology about blood types shared by all humans, and that genes, not blood, transmitted hereditary characteristics, but no one ever took it a step further and used this knowledge to knock down prevailing racial concepts. The ways and means of sharing this basic principle of oneness are as numerous as the individual teachers and subject areas to which children are exposed.

Another step individual teachers can take in acting on a commitment to fight racism is to contradict the pattern in our society of separation between groups. Along with misinformation about each other as a major factor in keeping racism going stands the separation that has kept us from correcting that information by firsthand experience. Where we live, work, shop, party, study or sit in the cafeteria is just part of the picture. It is not enough to say you have friends of a different heritage because you work together or attend the same school. Do you go to each other's homes, keep each other's children, confide over coffee around the kitchen table? Meaningful relationships between people of historically separated groups must be built with the care any friendship deserves, plus often requiring an extra measure of effort, tact, wisdom and patience. A long history of hurtful experiences can make people suspicious and reluctant to trust. Fear of making mistakes and inadvertently offending can make people hesitant. For everyone, the need to step out of one's comfort zone and habits of life requires conscious effort. Initial rejection might have to be overcome, but the effort is so worthwhile! Friendships thus formed between individuals, based on respect and sincerity, nurtured with the skills of nonjudgmental listening, can become powerful bonds and resources for mutual support and healing.

An image comes to mind of a poster I had years ago featuring a disheveled teacher, after a long day's work, surrounded by the inevitable paraphernalia creative teachers scrounge, haul and utilize to create magical experiences in their classrooms. Across the bottom were the words, NOBODY EVER SAID IT WAS GOING TO BE EASY. To add to the already overburdened teachers the task of overcoming the centuries old, endemic disease of racism in America may seem a bit too much. But rather than a sentence this is an invitation—to a process that gives so much meaning, understanding, power for transformation, and hope. And the process begins, quite simply, with the individual teacher arising to make a commitment. The subsequent steps will be as varied as the teachers of America and the situations in which they work. The first step takes place inside of us. This is a step we all have the capacity to take. Much is depending on our willingness to arise.

Chapter 10

Prejudice-free Schools: A Vision of the Future

by Donald T. Streets

The author writes of the important role of the principal in changing attitudes and creating a climate which can transform schools into prejudice-free environments. The author, himself an elementary school principal, believes that racism finds institutional expression through a school's overall philosophy, the beliefs of its teachers, its curriculum, and through other administrative structures which come together to create the school culture. All of these are examined by the writer as he suggests that schools can be transformed into places where students can become prejudice-free. Ed.

The year was 1920, the place, a freshman social studies class at Logansport High School in Logansport, Indiana. As was the custom with all of his classes, the social studies teacher asked his students what they wanted to pursue as a vocation or profession upon graduation. Each student, in turn, responded accordingly, based on his hopes and aspirations. The class comprised white youngsters with one exception–a young black student, who responded when asked the question, "I, sir, want to become a dentist." Although his parents had not completed grade school, they nevertheless knew the importance of a sound education, especially in creating opportunity, and had already begun encouraging their son to aim high academically. He chose dentistry after having worked in a local dentist's office after school and on weekends. Though his work was custodial, his job exposed him to an occupational possibility his ancestors never allowed themselves to dream of, which led to the decision at the young age of twelve that this was what he wanted to be — a dentist. That dream was further reinforced by an insistent mother who was the driving force behind his desire to excel academically. With her encouragement, he strove to do his best, knowing that a strong academic record was imperative if he had any hope of reaching his dream. And that was why he responded to his teacher's question with great confidence, "I, sir, am going to become a dentist."

The unanticipated reply he received shocked him to the core. The entire class was stunned as well: "No! It's the railroad yards for your kind," his teacher curtly retorted. With this one devastating statement his teacher shattered his dream of fulfilling his life's ambition, and underscored the all too familiar message his racist society had been telling him and all other young people of color their entire lives, that opportunity in America is not so much a function of one's hopes, aspirations, ability, and effort as it is a function of one's race, economic status, ethnicity, gender, and social caste. Moreover, educators, as key personnel in the largest formal institution for socializing the oncoming generation, occupy a very key and hence crucial role in determining the extent to which any young person gains access to the world of opportunity. They serve as gatekeepers to advancement because of the roles they play in influencing who can or cannot get through.

That this cruel response from the teacher was also in the presence of his classmates exacerbated the humilation and enormous devastation he already felt. The choice for this young man at this juncture was simple: either accept the shattering of his dream and the resultant decimation of hope so cruelly imposed upon him, or reject it with the determination that his dream might be recaptured and protected from any further assault. Something deep within him would not allow acceptance of the fate his teacher had prescribed for him. With an anger and indignation that startled his classmates and even surprised himself, he sprang to his feet and charged towards his teacher, who made a speedy exit. The young man literally chased his teacher out of the school and down the street. Having gained a head start, the teacher outdistanced the student until the young man was able to regain control of himself, and repress his personal sense of violation, anger, and pain.

The student, of course, was expelled. Before he could be reinstated his parents were required to meet with the principal, with the assurance that their son would not do such a thing again–a capitulation to racism only too familiar to the powerless. They knew unequivocally that a conciliatory posture on their part was necessary if there was any hope of getting their son back in school.

This was not an isolated episode; rather, it represents but one of countless others of a similar nature that have taken place, and continue to occur. It exemplifies both prejudice and racism: prejudice on the part of the teacher who believed that blacks are inferior, and therefore ill-suited for and unworthy of positions which require a college education, and racism on the part of the principal who shared and supported the teacher's prejudice through the power he wields because of his position.

Prejudice is an emotional commitment to a falsehood that prevails in spite of evidence to the contrary. Despite the fact that this teacher had taught many outstanding students of color, he allowed race to be the determining factor in his judgment as to whether a black student should aspire to a college education, not his scholarship and industry. Racism is prejudice with a power component. When the position that one holds in an institution allows one to bring to bear the power of that institution to repress or oppress an individual because of race, gender, religion, ethnicity, or cultural heritage, then he is a racist. This is why racism is so much more destructive and so much more crippling than prejudice.

Racism finds institutional expression in our schools through the following avenues: the overall philosophy of the institution; the beliefs of those who promote it, particularly with respect to how students are viewed; the types of curricula to which students are exposed; the quality and nature of the instruction, staffing, classroom placements; and, the school climate and culture.

THE SCHOOL'S PHILOSOPHY

Most schools do not have an explicit philosophy. But they all have implicit philosophies as reflected in the attitudes and actions of the staff and the choices they make in terms of curricula, advisement, and instructional strategies. These attitudes and actions, to a large extent, are a reflection of the attitudes and values of the building administrator. Therefore, to eliminate prejudice and racism in a school, the place to begin is with the principal. What values that person holds and the leadership direction he chooses can make a significant difference in the moral tone of that institution.

ADVICE FOR THE PRINCIPAL

The starting point for a school principal who chooses to eliminate prejudice and racism is to first look at himself. Everyone has prejudices, to be sure. If culture, indeed, is the ubiquitous educator of mankind, and if, indeed, each culture tends to reflect some degree of self-preference (politically, we call it nationalism), then one's own attitudes and values have consciously or unconsciously been shaped by those biases. Identifying one's own prejudices, therefore, can be difficult because our cultural biases become blinders that prevent us from being aware of them. Consequently, one's first task is to become aware of one's own prejudices by carefully and systematically peeling back those cultural blinders. Because of the close relationship of culture to one's own attitudes, values, character, and personality, one must leave the comfort sphere of one's own reference group and establish meaningful relationships with others whose feedback will shed light on our attitudes, for it is next to impossible to rid oneself of prejudices against a particular group without meaningful exposure to that group.

Seeking friendship with individuals of diverse backgrounds is essential for school administrators. By doing so, they create opportunities to learn how to function well socially within the context of that diversity, and to model it for others. As trust builds, one can expect more direct feedback on how one is doing. One can even request it. Through this process, one can refine one's sensibilities. As one progresses in this process, a reciprocal response is likely to be forthcoming from one's associates. I firmly believe that one can never learn too much about how not to be prejudiced. How one goes about doing this is crucial. It would be annoying to a minority individual for one to use his newly found liberalism as an excuse to intrude socially.

Most people function within settings that include individuals of diverse backgrounds in a natural way. Seize those opportunities to share experiences and to interact. For those who do not normally encounter minority individuals during the course of the day, there are organizations and service projects of diverse membership in which one can become involved. If you are representative of a majority, then expect that you may have blinders to the myriad ways in which you may be inclined to wield power and unconsciously convey an air of superiority and a patronizing attitude. Also, don't be surprised if the individuals of other races, cultures, and nationalities with whom you wish to establish closer and more meaningful relationships may initially respond to your overtures of friendship and goodwill with suspicion, and may even question your motivation and sincerity. Both of these responses are rather typical when effort is initiated to establish a closer relationship of trust between individuals of divergent backgrounds, races, cultures, nationalities, and classes, especially those with long histories of estrangement ,and, in some cases, outright antagonism and hostility. No matter how awkward, uncomfortable, or clumsy the approach, those whose motives are pure, and whose hearts are in the effort and who are committed and persevere will eventually succeed.

Concomitant with the internal exploration of making the effort to rid oneself of prejudice is the need to reconsider how one views others. One way to do this is to ask, "Do I ascribe limitations to anyone because of race, gender, social status, culture, religion, or economic status?" If one does, then that prescription of limitation in one's attitude, one's behavior, consciously or unconsciously, will be picked up in no time by the victim. Victim is a strong word; but I use it intentionally, deliberately, because the effect of this prescription of limitation is oppressive. There is an old adage in education which states that the teacher's minimum expectation is the student's maximum. I've seen this truism borne out over and over again during the thirty-seven years I've been in the field of education. Schools often convey prescriptions of limitation based on race, gender, ethnicity, social status, economic status, IQ, and achievement test results. Only in rare instances is the prescription of limitation rejected by the victim, as was the case with the young person who wanted to become a dentist. Most succumb to the intolerable weight of it because it induces uncertainty as one contemplates the future. We are uncertain at times because of the myriad unknowns we face as we grow and develop. Confidence is easily undermined by excessive criticism, ridicule, sarcasm, and, as mentioned earlier, prescriptions of limitation, which, in turn, destroy hope. This is why educators must become masters of encouragement–not insincere spouters of platitudes and phony hype–but agents of encouragement in helping students to shape noble and ambitious self-ideals towards which to aspire. They must also become effective facilitators in helping students to realize their dreams through skillful guidance, instruction, and support.

Rather than prescribing limitations to others, educators, and especially principals, should view each student as a repository of limitless potentialities. This position is the most tenable one philosophically, and it is supported by science as well. Science has not been able to identify limits to human potential. Quite the contrary, science has demonstrated that the actualization of potential creates further potential. One should therefore view others in an open-ended fashion, as possessing an infinitude of potentialities awaiting actualization. What better premise to base the definition and role of education on than this one. In so doing, education will have defined its ultimate purpose–to facilitate the actualization of human potential at an optimum rate. Students and staff who view themselves in this way will surely sense it, and, therefore, feel impelled to adopt and reach for that ideal. This is what hope is made of – belief in the possibility of something better. With hope there is motivation. With motivation one feels energized and empowered. Just as racism is the most endemic suppressor of human potential, belief in the unlimited potential of all peoples as a social value and ideal, coupled with the conviction that humanity is one, is the most powerful force for the releasing of human potential. It defines our purpose from which everything springs.

To illustrate this very crucial relationship of self-definition and purpose to the actualization of potential, I am reminded of the story about the family who won a refrigerator. There was one problem, however, they didn't know what its purpose was. So they put the refrigerator on their porch and kept their boots in it. It served that purpose very well, to be sure. But here is the catch–because they didn't know the purpose for which the refrigerator was created, they were put out of touch with its essential reality, and hence were unable to draw out its full potential. When one prescribes limitations to another in spite of the fact that human potential is limitless, one is therefore out of touch with the reality of that person, and therefore unable to draw out his or her full potential.

From history we know that when the Roman soldiers moved their forces into the region now called the the British Isles, one of Julius Caesar's generals sent word back begging him not to ask that any of the indigenous population be brought back as slaves, because they were considered hopelessly uneducable; retarded beyond redemption; and, therefore, would only be a social and economic drain on the Roman system. And yet, the descendants of this "retarded" population years later created the British Commonwealth with some of the finest minds the world has known, and institutions that are among the most outstanding in the world today. This fact stands as historical evidence of the limitless potential latent within humanity. A perusal of the histories of all the great civilizations shows the enormous capacity for accomplishment present in all societies. For the individual, the key factor is belief in oneself. This belief does not come automatically. Research on self-perception and self-concept reveals that how one defines oneself is largely shaped by the kinds of messages one receives from one's society. This is why the philosophy of the school should convey the ideal of limitless potential, and why the administrator as an educational leader must not only include a clear articulation of that ideal, he or she must also ensure the translation of this philosophy into the purpose, policies, objectives and operations of the school.

CHANGING THE SCHOOL

It is well known that the best way to change a school is to change the direction of its leadership. Although possessing less power than in former years, the principal still has a considerable amount. Through effective leadership, the principal can wield great influence in shaping the priorities of the school. A leader who makes rooting out prejudice and racism a top priority can have a transforming effect on the school. Adopting this goal will not be easy because in most schools prejudice and racism are evidenced on a daily basis in the interactions with and among students, with their parents, and with staff. Consequently, one doesn't have to conjure up hypothetical examples in the abstract to deal with, as real opportunities abound should one choose to address them. The most common occurrences of prejudice among students are racial slurs and put-downs. Young students often don't know exactly what the slurs mean, other than that they inflict great pain on the victims, usually triggering responses of humiliation, or anger and retaliations. This is why racial slurs are so destructive. And the harm goes both ways. For the victim, there is the indignity of being ridiculed and condemned for something over which that person has no control. For the perpetrator, the slur has the dehumanizing effect of reinforcing an erroneous belief and an attitude of superiority in defiance of the reality that the minority individuals who are its victims may very well be – as is often the case – brighter, more talented, more accomplished, more articulate, more sought out by others than the racist, and with better character.

Occasionally one encounters racist comments directly from parents, or indirectly through their attitudes or requests, which may have been made under some other pretext. Regarding racist comments directly expressed, a forthright response, using tact and courtesy, is usually the best approach. Showing that one does not share the racist views lets the parents know that they haven't found implicit support. This kind of approach allows one to present an alternative perspective. This hopefully and advisedly must be done with utmost kindness and sincerity, without a tinge of condescension or evidence of a patronizing attitude. This approach tends to be effective with what I call unconscious racist comments. For the aggressive racist who knows that he is asserting a racist position, who is belligerent and unyielding, a more confrontational approach is needed. But saying something to the effect that racist comments are not appreciated, and that continued use will result in the termination of the conversation, almost always is enough. Again, this should not be done in a self-righteous or condescending manner. What is important is to convey that you don't share that view, are bothered by it, and hence will not give ear to it.

Prejudice which manifests itself indirectly is much harder to deal with. In a recent situation, some parents asked that their children be excused from a set of activities which involved learning about African cultures through dance. I asked to meet with them to discuss their request. When they arrived, I asked if I might know their reason They said that the activity teaches their children to worship a false god. I asked, "How did you come to that conclusion?" The mother replied that on the first day, as she was observing the dance lesson, she asked the teacher, an African-American trained in African dance and African cultures, what the dance symbolized. He indicated that when the children pointed to the ground, the movement symbolized recognition of mother earth, and when they pointed upward, the movement symbolized acknowledgement of God. My question then was, "What is objectionable about that?" She said, "Their god is a false god." I could have dropped the matter at that point and merely honored their request, in accordance with district policy. Instead, I decided to engage them in a dialogue, hoping that I might offer an alternative perspective for them to at least consider.

Continuing, I said, "Would you have objected had the children been asked to do the jankaa dance?" They said with a slight tone of objection, "Is this an Indian dance?" "No," I said, "this is a Finnish folk dance which comes from the Finnish culture. They said, "Oh, that would be all right." I said, "How about the polka?" "That would be fine, too," they said.

I then said, "The African dances are very much like the jankaa and the polka in that they are folk dances which have evolved from particular cultures, just as the jankaa and the polka evolved from particular cultures." Unconvinced by my rationale, they persisted in their belief that the African dance still would be unacceptable to them. At this point, they explained that they were born-again Christians, hence any other theological or religious point of view was wrong. In response to this disclosure I asked, "What would be the likelihood of your family being Christian, let alone your own particular denomination, had you been born in Tibet or China? In all probability you would be Buddhists as that is the predominant religion of those areas." They weren't sure. I further explained, "Most people do not profess membership in a particular religion based on conscious choice, but rather based on the culture of their geographical region.

"Geography and culture are the main determinants of one's religion, i.e. belief system. Therefore, how can one say that his religion is right and all of the others are wrong based on the accident of geography and culture? One can rightly say this religion is right for me. Everyone has the right to this position. But to then go further and say because it is right for me, then it must be right for everyone else is prejudicial. Moreover, participating in the art forms arising from other cultures does not affect one's basic religious beliefs. One can, however, learn a great deal about other cultures by participating in their art forms."

I can't say that we reached accord on this issue. The parents persisted in their request, which I honored, stating my regret that their children would miss a wonderful opportunity to be exposed to a different culture through the arts. However, we all had an opportunity to state our positions and hear each other out, and through the juxtaposition of our differing views the prospects for a clearer understanding on both our parts was at least attempted and explored. I have often thought about the interchange I had with these parents, and have the feeling that they very likely may have done so as well. In all cases of this matter it is important to avoid, if at all possible, placing the child in between the differing views of parents, on the one hand, and the school, on the other. But, in some situations, accord between home and school may not be achieved. One then has to trust that the child will be able to take a reasonable position with which he is comfortable, based on an understanding of the issue.

THE CURRICULUM

The school's curriculum represents another area to be addressed in dealing with prejudice and racism. Most states determine particular aspects of the curriculum content and the minimum amount of time to be spent on each part. Most curriculum areas required by the state are not controversial; however, as with sex education, there are other areas which are. Because of religious or philosophical beliefs some communities, for example, take exception to certain parts of the science curriculum. For some, this is an area of great controversy. Everyone's opinion cannot be honored. Furthermore, curriculum decisions should not be solely based on opinion. Parents and other community members certainly have the right to air their views regarding any aspect of the educational program, and forums for doing so should be provided.

Their ideas are important. However, the school district has an obligation to establish a broad and inclusive process for developing and continually upgrading the curriculum and its content for accuracy, balance, relevance, comprehensiveness, depth, and direction. Once this process has been honored, the school board has the final say on what then is taught. Once the school district has decided upon the curriculum, the role of the administrator is more one of helping parents to understand why the curriculum is what it is.

I anticipate the time will come in the not too distant future, that states, in response to social unrest due to the harmful effects of racism, will require schools to develop and implement a curriculum dealing with prejudice and racism. If we were only able to accurately assess the toll prejudice and racism have taken on our society, it very well may rank above heart disease, cancer, crime, suicide, and AIDS, as the greatest threat to our well-being.

Each state has its own school system, and within each state there are many school districts with considerable autonomy in developing their curricula. Yet, these curricula across the nation are remarkably similar due largely to tradition, the influence of various professional education organizations, and the common elements contained in the various textbooks for each subject or discipline. Many educators believe that our curricula are textbook driven–teachers tend to teach what is in the text. Educators who want to take an active posture in dealing with prejudice and racism see this as presenting a particular problem, because even a cursory glance at social studies textbooks, for example, reveals that they have failed to recognize and, therefore, acknowledge many of the contributions of minorities and women. Moreover, those events in history which have involved the mistreatment of minorities and cannot easily be omitted have been "sanitized" of their racist realities, cleaned up and made out to be far less heinous, vicious and inhumane. These include the treatment of the institution of slavery in America, reputed to be the cruelest, most dehumanizing, and hence most devastating of any in the recorded history of mankind; the incarceration of the Japanese during World War II and the confiscation of their property; the segregation of society along racial, ethnic, and religious lines, with its attendant lack of equal opportunity, its humiliation, and its unequal treatment before the law; the exploitation of the garment workers in clothing industry sweatshops in which Latino and Asian employees are subjected to long hours of labor for less than minimum wage, and the atrocious treatment of Native Americans involving genocide and exile to reservations.

Rather than having a textbook-driven curriculum, the principal and staff need to develop a curriculum that acknowledges the legitimate contributions of all who have been a part of this nation's history, beginning with the indigenous population whose rich history and culture predate Columbus's journey, and the other early explorers, down to the courageous efforts of those who participated in the civil rights movement, and more recently the women's movement. *Indian Givers* and *Native Roots: How the Indians Enriched America* by Jack Weatherford are extraordinary compendia of the contributions to Western Civilization made by Indians of North America, Central America, and South America. In similar fashion, *Historical and Cultural Atlas of African Americans* by Thomas R. Frazier chronicles the history and enormous contributions made by African-Americans, beginning with their first arrival on these shores. One of the most horrid legacies of the modern age is the Holocaust. Everyone must know of this outrageous atrocity, because it, indeed, did take place, because our collective moral psyches have been damaged by it, and because we must learn from it so that it shall never be repeated.

DIVERSITY IN THE SCHOOL AND IN THE CLASSROOM

Hardly anyone would take exception to the observation that society worldwide is changing with increasing rapidity. As recently as one-hundred years ago most people could expect to live their entire lifetimes within a radius of less than ten miles from where they were born. Today, families are scattered all over the nation, and in some cases, all over the world. Through advances in modern technology and through political and economical networking, and because of innumerable wars accompanied by the uprooting of countless numbers of individuals forced to seek refuge in other lands, and because of the voluntary relocation of many due to family ties, jobs, or just plain adventure and curiosity, humanity throughout the globe has become more connected and the areas in which they have settled increasingly pluralistic. The world indeed has become one geographically, politically, economically, and socially.

There is no great social problem that any longer can be exclusively identified with one country. Environmental problems (global warming, deforestation which alters weather conditions worldwide, acid rain, depletion, and contamination of topsoil, air pollution, toxic waste, to mention but a few), and health problems (AIDS, hunger, tuberculosis, cancer, multiple sclerosis, heart disease, genetic damage due to substance abuse and environmental toxicity, crime and violence, nuclear stockpiling, and more), do not honor national boundaries.

In spite of this rapid movement towards an increasingly diverse society, nowhere has there been the kind of startling success to which we can point as a model. And yet, survival on this planet is dependent upon our succeeding. In other words, we have no choice, because the alternative to succeeding in what undoubtedly has become the greatest sociological experiment in the history of mankind is annihilation, either through widespread disease, political chaos accompanied by wars and terrorist activities, economic collapse, and/or the destruction of the earth's capacity to serve as the host organism for what has become its worst parasite--man. This is not doomsday prophesying: this is reality, and we are at the crossroads of these two alternatives. We can expect the diversity in society to increase, because, as divergent populations continue to intermix, a variety of new permutations will inevitably emerge alongside existing ones. Herein lies the challenge, and, hence, opportunity for educators.

Rather than allowing our schools, heedless of the consequences, to acceed to society's attempts to maintain segregation through overt and de facto means, why not see the creation of diverse classrooms and schools as a critical and therefore indispensable dynamic in the education of our children. Along with the skills of reading, math, language, science, and social studies, students could learn about the backgrounds, beliefs, customs, values and traditions of others from their teachers and classsmates of different races, religions, cultures, and economic levels. Through this process each would learn better how to relate to diversity in a positive manner, and hopefully find a common and universally viable basis for respecting one another.

Putting diverse elements together in and of itself is not enough to ensure that a better understanding and closer ties will result. If that were the case, then the United States would be among the most successful countries due to the extensive travel of tourists and the international deployment of military personnel. The more homogeneous a group the less likely it is that there will be conflicts related to culture, values, biases, and predilections, and, at the same time, fewer opportunities for learning about different peoples and the acquisition of those skills and attitudes required in order to relate to them. But opportunities alone to rub elbows with people of various backgrounds will not accomplish the level of unity required for the promotion of fairness, justice, and opportunity for all citizens. Basic to success in this regard is the unequivocal recognition of the fundamental oneness of humankind. Once this fact is recognized and acknowledged, then one has the basis for understanding those variations which derive from the influences of culture, ethnicity, one's character, and one's personality. The luxury of racial, cultural, ethnic and economic isolation is vanishing as the world gets smaller and its population becomes more mobile. One can expect one's neighborhood, town, city or village, workplace, and the public facilities therein to be increasingly more diverse. The person who knows how to relate well to that diversity and appreciate it will be able to negotiate all aspects of living much more easily and effectively than one who only knows his own kind.

Irrespective of race, culture, ethnicity, nationality or degree of affluence, I have yet to encounter a people who do not value fairness and justice, courtesy and manners, service and cooperation, kindliness and affection, mercy and compassion, and respect for and deference to legitimate authority. But neither children nor adults can learn to relate to others of different backgrounds in abstract. Denmark thought it could, and in the early 1960s prided itself on not being a prejudiced society. One of its film makers even made a movie postulating what Denmark would be like if the Danes were prejudiced. Now that Denmark has become a pluralistic society, all of the ugly elements of racism are surfacing, largely against Middle Easterners who have sought and been given political asylum in Denmark.

Rather than the current definition of cultural disadvantage based on perceived deficiencies in the tools of learning, a better definition would be one based on the perceived inability to relate to diversity, for it is this condition that will render one maladapted to one's changing environment, and therefore less sought after in the marketplace as a prospective employee, less qualified to function in the service fields, and definitely more of a social liability because of the lack of intercultural, interracial, interethnic, and, hence, interpersonal skills.

Again, just putting people together, is not enough. Teachers, once properly trained through pre-service and in-service opportunities, need to be encouraged to mediate the relationship between and among students. Skill in mediating relationships rarely comes naturally. Ongoing in-service sessions are needed to instruct teachers on how to identify the manifestations of prejudice and how to assist students to overcome acting in this cruel manner. This can be achieved by instituting an Institute for the Healing of Racism in one's school. More on the IHR in some of the forthcoming chapters. Considerable research and other related information can be provided teachers about moral development in students, about stages in the development of moral reasoning and development in the acquisition of moral values, and, finally, how all contribute to character development and the structuring of personal identity. Identity formation doesn't take place haphazardly or by fluke: one's identity is structured in an ordered way through countless interactions. In other words, identity formation is a process which is learned and is not necessarily associated exclusively with any particular set of religious beliefs. It is induced largely from the prevailing values which make up one's social environment. Values, which form the structure of identity, can also be explicitly taught.

Most keenly in the earlier years of education (pre-school through sixth grade), and then later during the dramatic restructuring of the personality during adolescence, children go through sensitive periods in the process of forming their values and character, during which time they are particularly susceptible to negative influences and receptive to positive influences. The kinds of beliefs they induce from experience about others can lead either to an understanding or misunderstanding of them. This is why the process needs to be guided by teachers and administrators who are sensitive to behavior which might be racist in nature so that the conclusions students draw from their experiences, both directly and vicariously, are not based on inconclusive data or error which can lead to stereotyping and prejudice. Because prejudice and racism are sealed by high emotion, reprimand exclusive of a discussion of why is insufficient. Youngsters need shared experiences that are positive both in deed as well as feeling. Collaborative efforts to serve others is one good way to accomplish this.

Both sports and the arts provide wonderful opportunities for individuals to collaborate in a positive way. I am reminded of a concert that took place at Carnegie Hall some years ago in which an outstanding cellist was scheduled to perform. At the last minute, the cellist was taken ill and a substitute had to perform in his place. The audience was shocked, disappointed, and annoyed, as well, when they learned that this world-renowned cellist was not going to be performing. They were even more upset when it was announced that his replacement was a sixteen-year-old person. And when he walked on stage to assume his place to perform, the audience gasped in horror, for in their eyes not only was he practically a child, he was also black. Ordinarily, New York audiences are highly disciplined. However, the mumblings that preceded the director's downbeat were most disconcerting to the orchestra, and would have been unsettling to the most experienced performer. Yet, this young man launched into the first number with a ferocity and virtuosity that would have stunned the severest critic. The audience immediately became spellbound by what they were experiencing. Any preconceived notions related to age and race were instantly swept away as his fingers searched up and down the strings with a flurry and precision that seemed too fast and too precise and, of course, too beautiful to be possible. Their hearts were touched and their minds stunned by the sheer artistry and excellence of his performance. After this sterling performance, anyone in that audience harboring prejudice against blacks was transformed, at least for the moment, by the aesthetic infusion of reality registered in bold relief against any prejudice notion previously held. The word aesthetic, tracing it back to its original Greek root, means just the opposite of anesthetic. An anesthetic deadens or takes away feeling or pain. Aesthetic means literally that which gives feeling. The emotional component–hate–which accompanies prejudice can, indeed, through exposure to a powerful aesthetic experience, be replaced by respect, admiration, and, yes, even love. Therefore, the arts should be fully exploited educationally in rooting out prejudice and racism.

CONCLUSION

Within a very few years we will be entering the twenty-first century. The close of the twentieth century undoubtedly will be accompanied by undreamed of advances in science and technology as well as unprecedented problems and challenges on practically all levels. A recurring theme running through practically all of those challenges is mankind's failure so far to find a permanent and just foundation for the establishment of world peace. And yet there seems to be competing forces released in the world, leading us toward the prospects of either resolution or disaster. The destiny of mankind hangs in the balance, awaiting solutions. Belief in the ability of most of the traditional social institutions to make a difference has waned, with one notable exception – our schools.

Perhaps this, in part, is why the schools are criticized so severely for their shortcomings. Educators, and most particularly, school principals, rather than despairing because of being under siege, should take this universal concern both as a wake-up call and an opportunity to draw upon the talents latent within this vital institution to transform it into the vibrant social force required in this modern age, and redirect the energies and potential of a disillusioned humanity toward progress and greater opportunity. Fundamental to doing so involves finding a cure, once and for all, for the major malady which has plagued mankind since time immemorial, and which precludes moving ahead.

Should we succeed in this endeavor, we will have eliminated this virulent disease, racism, which has so completely infected humanity, stifling progress and crippling efforts toward the advancement of social evolution so desperately needed on this planet. Addressing this social and spiritual ill can brook no further delay. Courageous and insightful leaders are called for who are willing to make the elimination of prejudice and racism top priority as an institutional goal toward which all efforts would be directed by the school as they shape the identities and values of the next generation. When that day comes, the student who tells his teachers, "I, sir, want to become a dentist!" will receive the full support and encouragement of his teachers and school, something denied my father so many years ago.

Chapter 11

Healing Racism: Education's Role

by Brian Aull, Barbara Hacker, Robert Postlewaite, Nathan Rutstein and Tod Rutstein

The authors of this chapter feel that racism is at the heart of many of America's problems, and that educators should play a major part in efforts to eliminate it. The writers, whose professional interests range from electrical engineering to teaching, feel that integrating the principle of the oneness of the human family into the school system would serve as a vaccine against racism. They offer a definition of the concept of oneness, and suggest strategies by which a theory of oneness can be integrated into the school curriculum. Ed.

We all know that racism is a serious problem in America. What was started in the 1960s has not been completed–not by a long shot. The racial flare-ups on college campuses, in inner cities, in high schools, and even in elementary schools across our nation–all are evidence that much needs to be done before we can experience ethnic harmony.

Because we are confronted with a complex and deeply rooted problem, there are no quick-fix remedies. The roots of racism go back to the institution of slavery and the use of white supremacy theories to justify this institution. Although primarily directed against blacks, the legacy of these theories includes prejudice against other people of color and ethnic groups, as well. You cannot expect to eradicate overnight a social poison that has had nearly 400 years to spread through the human root system of America. Even our federal government is at a loss in dealing with a problem that is rapidly evolving into a full-blown national crisis.

In many ways the black-white situation is worse today than in the 1960s. According to the 1988 Committee on Cities report, the polarization between these communities is much more pronounced now than in the sixties. "There is greater despair, less hope and less opportunity to escape from poverty and misery" among blacks now than in the sixties. An underclass has emerged that is growing in size and anger. Cut off from the mainstream of America, it has created its own set of mores, laws, and economies, one of which–drugs–has caught the attention of the nation's leadership, because its poisonous tentacles are infecting the mainstream of the nation.

Why have we made no substantial progress in eliminating racism? We have failed to get to the core of the problem. Many of us thought that through the long-needed legislation passed in the sixties we had solved the problem. We can, of course, cite the gains made by some blacks in the political, judicial, military, and corporate arenas.

The problem persists because we have avoided addressing it for what it really is–a social disease, virulent and infectious, woven into the moral and spiritual fabric of society, passed from parents to children, from one generation to another, for over three centuries. The civil rights laws failed to thwart the growth of the cancer of racism, because they only dealt with two of the disease's symptoms–segregation and discrimination–but not with the disease itself.

Because the disease has not really been dealt with, whites have found ways of circumventing the laws. There has been the white flight to the suburbs, leaving the city schools populated largely by minorities and those few whites that are too poor to flee. The best teachers have also fled to the suburbs, leaving the city schools not only segregated for the most part, but with teachers who lack the training and skills of those who left. In small towns and rural areas, private academies have arisen to block racial integration in education.

Growing up in a community afflicted by even subtle racism fosters an adversarial attitude, an "us versus them" mentality that is acted out on the job, in school, on the playground, and even in church. In time, the attitude becomes a deeply rooted obstacle to attaining real community unity.

The consequences go beyond disrupting social cohesion, however. The United States is undergoing a demographic transition in which an increasingly larger fraction of the work force is made up of minorities and immigrants. By the year 2000, it is estimated, white males will constitute only 15 percent of those entering the work force. The jobs being created today require more education and skill compared to the jobs of previous generations. Racism, which results in the denial of quality education to minorities, will increasingly exacerbate the crisis of human capital, and further jeopardize the economic vitality of the United States.

The "us versus them" attitude fostered by racism also has international consequences. It is carried into political affairs by those who grow up in our society, and ultimately becomes a barrier to world peace. Indeed, many international problems parallel the problems of de facto segregation by race in the communities of America. Addressing the problem of racism is necessary in order for us to live successfully in a multiracial country and a multiracial world.

What is the cause of the disease of racism? The cause is the whites' inherent and at times subconscious feeling of superiority toward blacks and other people of color. Everyone is affected. For example, it creates a sense of inferiority among blacks which inhibits their development and self-empowerment. It also fosters strong feelings of suspicion toward white people, which is difficult to overcome because of the pain blacks have experienced for such a long time. It is such a powerful disease that it has even spawned a prejudice within the black community against those with darker skin. Getting most whites to acknowledge that they are infected by the disease is difficult, because most of them recognize intellectually that racism is bad, and they do not want to be associated with something that is universally recognized as evil. So many white men and women, people of good will, are repressing their true feelings about blacks under the hard shell of denial, a major obstacle to overcoming racism. Cracking open the shell and finally acknowledging the truth can be painful, but in time the pain subsides as progress is made in the healing process. What is important is the recognition of the personal problem, for without that there can be no solution.

Education can play a significant role in curing the disease of racism in America. Since racism is based on the myth of white superiority and nonwhite inferiority, schools can make a conscious effort to expose the deeply entrenched lie that has been embraced as the truth by the great majority of Americans for more that 300 years. To do this, schools must familiarize students with what we refer to as "the oneness of the human family." Because of the magnitude of the problem, this theme should be woven into the school system's curriculum from kindergarten through the twelfth grade, and reflected in every course a child takes for 12 years, even electives such as art, music, home economics, and shop.

This approach will act as a shield against racism. Imagine–kindergartners, black, white, Latino, Asian-American and Native American, learning about the oneness of the human family, learning that their classmates are actually relatives. The seeds of truth will have been planted in five-year-old minds and nourished for the next 12 years. The children will be fortified to repulse the poison of prejudice that they are exposed to in their homes and in the street. They will graduate from high school with hearts free of race prejudice--and their racial wounds healed.

WHAT IS ONENESS?

At first the word "oneness" sounds vague and even a bit strange. In science, however, it is recognized as a reality. Electricity and magnetism, once believed by physicists to be separate forces of nature, manifest an underlying oneness: a changing magnetic field creates an electric field and vice versa, so they are now regarded as aspects of a single force field, the electromagnetic field.

Of course, when realities are first discovered, it often challenges the conventional wisdom of the day. At one time it was believed that the earth was flat, and the most respected scholars could validate this belief through "logical" arguments. This did not alter the reality of the roundness of the earth, however.

The oneness of the human family is a reality whose implications are now being discovered. What does this mean? The reality has three major aspects:

1. The biological relatedness of human beings.

All human beings come from the same ancestral stock. Every person on our planet belongs to the same species. However, we are even closer than this may imply. All humans, without exception, are related to each other. We are at least as close as fiftieth cousins.

2. The common spiritual capacities of all human beings.

Human beings from all cultures and ethnic and geographic origins have the capacity to yearn for transcendence and to be dissatisfied with materialistic ideals. Even scientific materialists are often compelled to recognize an "organizing force" in the universe.

3. The common destiny of all human beings.

The planet earth is a tiny and fragile life support system for the 5 billion people who live on it. (The population will be 10 billion by the middle of the twenty-first century.) It is the only home that the human race has. The preservation of this home and the survival of the human family depend on our coming together.

This "coming together", the achievement of unity, is a social process that stems from the recognition, understanding, and internalization of the reality of oneness. The resulting unity does not mean uniformity, but implies a celebration of diversity, because once the reality of oneness is understood, diversity becomes an asset rather than an obstacle.

Unity in diversity appears superficially to be a contradiction of terms, but in fact is an integral aspect of reality. The universe operates on the principle of unity in diversity. It is as real as the law of gravity, and is manifested in every level of life, even among look-alikes. A sandy beach, for example, may appear from the boardwalk as a grey- or beige-colored mass. When we scoop up a handful of sand and examine each grain, however, we find that each one has its own particular size and shape. We discover upon close scrutiny, that among a bed of red roses some flowers have more petals, are shorter or taller and are in different stages of maturity. The same is true among animals, not only in physique, but in temperament as well.

Imagine what life would be like if every rock were the same size, weight, color and shape; if all vegetables tasted alike; if every flower had the same scent; and every person thought, walked, and felt the same way. Uniformity would turn life into a prison made of mirrors and inhabited by robots.

Another way of understanding unity in diversity is through analogy to the human body or any complex organism. The organs are extremely different from each other, each performing a unique function that the others cannot perform. Yet this diversity is the very basis of a coordinated and healthful life system for the organism. In this sense, diversity is a prerequisite to achieving a whole that is more than a sum of parts.

Many thinkers have recognized the reality of oneness and understood its implications for the development of human society, including paleontologist Richard Leaky:

> We are one species, one people. Every individual on this earth is a member of "homo sapiens sapiens," and the geographical variations we see among peoples are simply biological nuances on the basic theme. The human capacity for culture permits its elaboration in widely different and colorful ways. The often very deep differences between those cultures should not be seen as divisions between people. Instead, cultures should be interpreted for what they really are: the ultimate declaration of belonging to the human species (Leakey and Lewing 1977).

ONENESS: A BIOLOGICAL REALITY

The oneness of the human family is not only a spiritual reality, but a biological reality as well. Anthropology, physiology, psychology recognize only one human species, albeit infinitely varied in the secondary aspects of life. In particular, the insights of genetics and population science show that the human race is indeed a single species–a family in the literal sense of the word. This reinforces the spiritual truth of oneness, and also points to practical ways in which it can be incorporated into science curricula. We indicate four such points:

1. Humanity meets the scientific criteria for a single species.

What do biologists mean by the word "species"? The genetic information that an organism inherits is like an "instruction book" that tells the organism how to construct the proteins and other substances that compose it. A gene can be thought of as a "page" of the instruction book. Two organisms belong to the same species when there is a one-to-one correspondence between the "pages" of their genetic instruction books, and they could exchange corresponding "pages" and still have a viable genetic code. Sexual reproduction involves many such exchanges; therefore, two sexually reproducing organisms of the same species can generally mate and produce fertile and viable offspring.

James King, (1981) professor of microbiology at New York University School of Medicine, cites studies of interracial offspring in order to make the point that "no better example of the biological species than man could be found." Several extensive studies of hybrid population have been made and they show no evidence for reduction in viability, fertility, or functional efficiency in the first, second, or later generations of hybrids between unlike human populations. These studies include one on Dutch-Hottentot hybrids in South Africa made more than sixty years ago, one made in the 1920s on the descendants of the mutineers of the Bounty, and an elaborate study of 179,000 babies of mixed Caucasian-Oriental-Polynesian descent born in Hawaii between 1948 and 1958. (King pp. 136-37)

2. The genetic differences among human beings are slight compared to the differences that differentiate humans from any other species.

Our differences are trival in a biological sense. In fact, geneticists estimate the variations in genetic make up regarding racial differences occupy only about 0.01 percent of our genes. And those differences exists for practical reasons. They help certain groups adapt effectively to their environments (Rensberger 1994). King (1981) states that when the measurements of protein differences within the human species are compared with those between ape and human, the latter are from twenty-five to sixty times as great as any difference between two human populations, and neither Caucasians, black Africans, nor Japanese are any nearer to the chimpanzee that either of the others.

3. There are no "pure" races.

The genetic markers that supposedly divide the human species into races represent only a minute fraction of our genetic endowment. The differences between "races" involve a few superficial physical characteristics which have differentiated because of long-term adaptation to different climates. Furthermore, the boundary between different races is not well-defined. No matter how one tries to divide humanity into races, there are always many peoples who do not fit neatly into any of the categories. This is because movement and mixing has always occurred, causing genetic material to pass between widely separated human populations. Richard Lewontin, professor of zoology, biology and population sciences at Harvard comments:

> Anthropologists no longer try to name and define races and subraces, because they recognize that there are no "pure" human groups who have existed since the Creation as separate units. The most striking feature of global human history is the incessant and widespread migration and fusion of groups from different regions. Wholesale migration is not a recent phenomenon brought about by the

> development of airplanes and ships; in fact, an amalgam of the Beaker Folk of the Bronze Age, the Indo-European Celts of the first millennium B.C., the Angles, Saxons, Jutes, and Picts of the first millennium A.D., and, finally, the Vikings and their Parvenu grandchildren, the Normans. . .
>
> Nor is the situation different in the Far East. The Japanese are a mixture of Korean invaders and northern islanders. Even the Australian aborigines, who were regarded as virtually another species by some anthropologists, have large infusions of Papuan and Polynesian ancestry on the eastern and northern coasts of Australia. The notion that there are stable, pure races that only now are in danger of mixing under the influence of modern industrial culture is nonsense (1982).

The four blood types (A, B, AB, and O) are found in all human populations. An Irishman with type A blood can receive a transfusion from a Ugandan with type A blood. In fact, the "races" of humanity do not differ in terms of the presence of absence of certain genes, but only in their frequencies of occurrence. This statement about genetic diversity can be quantitatively validated. One can measure the amount of genetic diversity in a population by answering the question, "If two individuals are picked at random from this population, what is the probability that they will differ in some inherited characteristic, such as blood type?" Lewontin reports a study of genetic diversity using inherited blood groups. The study indicated that of the diversity that exists in the global gene pool, only 6.3 percent is due to differences between traditionally defined major races (Caucasoid, Negroid, etc.), only 8.3 percent comes from differences between nations and tribes within the major races, and 85.4 percent is contributed by differences between individuals within a nation or tribe. He summarizes quite instructively,

> To put the matter crudely, if, after a great cataclysm, only Africans were left alive, the human species would have retained 93 percent of its total genetic variation, although the species as a whole would be darker skinned. If the cataclysm were even more extreme and only the Xhosa people of the southern tip of Africa survived, the human species would still retain 80 percent of its genetic variation. Considered in the context of the evolution of our species, this would be a trivial reduction (1982).

4. There are no superior or inferior races.

The "evidence" for the intellectual superiority of certain races is based on inadequate and culturally biased measures of intelligence, or a failure to account for the fact that children of different racial ancestry often grow up in different environments because of culture and social forces. The few studies in which children of different racial backgrounds grew up in a similar range of environments show no significant racial differences in intelligence. (See, for example, B. Tizard, Nature 247, 316, 1974, for a study of black, white and mixed children raised in an English orphanage.)

THE RECOGNITION OF ONENESS: A PRACTICAL NECESSITY

Just as oneness is a biological as well as a spiritual reality, its recognition is a practical necessity as well as a moral imperative. Ties of transportation, communication, and economic interdependence have made the world a very small neighborhood. Humanity has the technology to make our world uninhabitable in a matter of hours. The realization is growing that the security of one nation cannot be rooted in the insecurity of another, and that the prosperity of one people cannot derive indefinitely from the impoverishment of others.

This is made most apparent by studying the global environment crisis. The greenhouse effect, ozone depletion, air and water pollution, acid rain, soil erosion, salinization, and desertification, deforestation, and depletion of resources are among the threats to the ecosystem that sustains human life and civilization. This crisis has arisen from a very extensive and complex set of interactions among human population growth, economic activity, use of energy and natural resources, and social, cultural, and political forces. The following four points illustrate the practical necessity of oneness.

1. These environmental problems can have extremely serious consequences.

The planet Venus is only 27 percent closer to the sun than we are. Yet the temperatures on its surface exceed 800° F. The reason for this is the greenhouse effect. Certain gases, such as carbon dioxide, trap the heat from the sun, causing the temperatures to be much hotter than they would be otherwise.

The greenhouse gases produced by fossil fuel combustion, agricultural activities, and deforestation are expected by many scientists to cause an unmistakable global warming on earth within the next ten to twenty years. A warming of only a few degrees could endanger a substantial fraction of agricultural production in the Great Plains and Western states. It would also cause melting of polar ice, leading to a rise in sea level that could endanger heavily populated coastal cities.

This is only one example of how serious the repercussions can be when mankind is careless of the planet which sustains life.

2. Environmental problems can cross national boundaries and generations.

Sulfur dioxide emissions in one nation can cause acid rain in another. Indeed, air pollutants can cause global changes in the atmosphere and climate. The hole in the ozone over the Southern Hemisphere, for example, has been caused by chlorofluorocarbons, used primarily in the Northern Hemisphere to make refrigerators, aerosols, and foams. Even if the emission of these gases stopped today, those already in the atmosphere would linger for over a century, continuing to destroy the ozone that screens out dangerous ultraviolet rays from the sun.

3. The pattern of economic growth that made the industrialized West wealthy cannot be sustained, let alone practiced on a global scale.

The traditional understanding of economic growth and industrialization in the West does not take into account the finiteness of the natural environment. Rather, it assumes nature to be an inexhaustible reservoir from which energy and raw materials can be taken and into which wastes can be dumped. Market economics have not reflected the true ecological costs of this economic growth, so that much of the wealth in the industrialized countries is robbed, in a sense, from our descendants. People in the developed countries are beginning to realize the need for efficiency and ecological soundness in the processes of industry and agriculture.

Globally, this new awareness is even more urgently needed. The current population of the world is over 5 billion and is expected to double by the middle of the next century. The industrialized nations constitute one-fifth of the world's population, but are responsible for 70 percent of the energy consumption. If the Third World countries follow a development path that is equally demanding on energy supplies and equally destructive to the environment, the consequences are likely to be disastrous. For example, by the year 2030, Third World industrialization could cause global carbon dioxide emissions to rise to more than double the current level and world stocks of essential raw materials to drop perilously low. Substantial transfers of technology and capital to the developing nations will be required to assist them to make a transition to sustainable development.

4. The global inequities in the distribution of wealth must be dealt with in order to solve the environmental problem.

Trade barriers and massive debt force developing countries to draw heavily from their ecological "bank accounts" in order to survive. These circumstances force these nations to focus on short-term crises rather than long-term planning for a sustainable pattern of development. The ecological destruction that results has global consequences that could be disastrous to the economies of the wealthy nations as well as the poor ones. (For example, rapid deforestation in Brazil contributes to the greenhouse effect, whose economic repercussions in the U.S. are discussed above.)

Thus, the impoverishment of Third World countries could lead to the impoverishment of the wealthy countries. According to William Ruckelshaus, EPA administrator during the Nixon and Reagan administrations, we must realize that the planet is finite and cause our economic systems to account for the environmental costs of production. He also states the following as a central principle of "sustainability consciousness."

> The maintenance of a livable global environment depends on the sustainable development of the entire **human family**. If 80 percent of the members of our species are poor, we cannot hope to live in a world at peace; if the poor nations attempt to improve their lot by the methods we rich have pioneered, the result will eventually be world ecological damage.

A CALL TO ACTION

We all know that educators have a responsibility to help students appreciate the truth, and to inculcate within them not only a yearning to discover more of it, but also the skills needed in the discovery process. Now that the principle of oneness–which always existed–has been discovered, it stands to reason that children in our schools should be exposed to it.

The integration of the "oneness theme" may seem, at first glance, like a Herculean task, for the prevailing educational approach in our schools is greatly influenced by the antiquated mechanistic view of the world. However, that can be altered by the enlightened leadership of a school system's administration or by inspired teachers who appreciate an aspect of reality that hitherto was unknown, and are compelled to share it with their students. In a way, they pioneer a new approach, and their success inspires their colleagues to follow suit.

This is beginning to happen in one Massachusetts elementary school. You walk into the kindergarten classroom of one teacher there, and you are struck by the environment she has created. Pictures and displays around the room reflect the oneness of the human family and our common home, the planet Earth. The environment she creates functions as an aid in carrying out what most established educators would consider a daring approach; she considers the children as family members, and the boys and girls view themselves as belonging to one family. To actualize the law of unity in diversity, she has initiated a program whereby youngsters of different ethnic backgrounds spend weekends in their fellow students' homes, sharing foods, customs, traditions, and games.

Weaving the principle of the oneness of humanity into the K-12 curriculum does not require, at the outset, significant changes in the existing curriculum. Experience bears this out. Educators in the field of peace education, for example, have taken this approach, an approach they refer to as infusion, and found it highly effective.

The Justice/Peace Council in its manual entitled *Infusion: An Approach to Education for Peace and Justice Within the Existing Curriculum*, states, "Infusion implies pouring in something that gives new life or significance to the whole." Dr. Betty Reardon of Columbia University, in commenting on this technique, stated:

> The technique is one that does not require any significant change in the curriculum. What it inspires, however, is a

change in the teacher, providing new lenses for looking at the curriculum so as to see opportunities to raise issues and questions that lead to student reflection on peace and justice concepts. It is primarily a conceptual approach that enables teachers to incorporate "justice and peace concepts, knowledge, skills, attitudes and activities into appropriate segments of the basic content of the curriculum. It consists of matching concepts and skills."

IMPLEMENTATION

In teaching the reality of the oneness of the human family to young children, five aspects of the educational experience should be addressed: the diversity of the classroom community, the educational process, the physical environment in the classroom, curriculum content that promotes a positive experience of human diversity, and curriculum content that deals directly with the phenomena of racism and prejudice.

1. The classroom community

The classroom is a microcosm of the world, and there is no substitute for a diverse classroom community. A teacher who values each of the children as individuals, each with unique gifts, and who values the various cultural backgrounds of the children will naturally encourage the same perspective in the pupils through the course of their daily interactions. Children in such a classroom will interact with each other on a natural and equal basis rather than through stereotypical, prescribed roles. This type of early positive experience of diversity is the single most important step toward counteracting the forces of separation in our society.

The racial integration of the classroom may not be within the power of the individual teacher. However, the integration of the classroom experience is still possible. For example, mutual visits and exchanges between "sister" schools of different racial compositions can be arranged. Children can be taken to plays and dance performances that expose them to other cultures and ethnic groups (e.g., African art or Spanish folk dancing). Private schools can actively recruit minority children who could otherwise not attend. There are many creative ways to promote positive experiences of contact if there is a will to do so.

2. The educational process

Much is communicated to children by the manner in which they are educated, for example, how they are regarded and spoken to by the teacher and how they are allowed to function in the classroom. If the experience of the classroom is one of oppression and rigid, arbitrary control, the pupil will learn to treat others in the same manner.

If we want children not to be racist, we must teach them courtesy and respect for themselves and others, and this begins by treating them with the courtesy and respect that they deserve as human beings. By giving them appropriate freedoms and limits we ensure their development. Children must be taught to take responsibility for themselves, to be independent, to be self-motivated learners, to take care of their environment and to function in a fair, considerate and loving way with peers. They must be in an atmosphere free from intimidation, fear, and humiliation. They must be given an emotionally safe place to feel their feelings and express them. They must see in their environment situations handled in a just and fair manner. Discipline is appropriate, but its goal is to foster cooperation and the development of the children rather than to control the children.

3. The classroom environment

Young children absorb what is around them in a largely unconscious fashion. The classroom itself can, therefore, be used to teach the oneness of the human family. For example, the teacher can use a picture of the planet Earth from space, surrounded by pictures of real people from all over the world with captions telling who they are and what their everyday lives are like. Teachers can use these displays to take their students on "visits" to different cultures, instilling an appreciation both of the diversity of the human family and of the universal desires and aspirations that demonstrate the oneness of the human family. Books, folk music, and other materials in the classroom can also reflect the same message.

4. Human diversity in the curriculum content

Teachers can use their presentation of science, geography, and the arts to foster a knowledge of and love for the human family. A Montessori teacher in Houston, Texas, promotes geographical literacy through a series of globes and puzzle maps. The first globe emphasizes the earth–its land, air, and water–and has no geopolitical boundaries. The next one has the continents painted in different colors and helps the children learn the names of the continents. As each country is studied, the children discuss artifacts from that country or prepare and eat the food of that country. This approach not only leads to geographical and cross-cultural literacy and an appreciation of diversity, but also fosters an understanding of oneness through seeing the universality of the creative human spirit.

5. Prejudice and racism

Once the children have had positive experiences of the oneness of the human family, they can be presented with the facts about slavery, racial injustice, and prejudice. Since they have internalized the reality of oneness through their previous educational experience, learning about the reality of racism will touch them through their sense of justice and arouse their anger. They can then be very clear that the oneness of the human family is the reality, and that prejudice is based on ignorance of that reality. They can then be taught to be agents of change, to help others understand that all people are members of one family.

One way to begin this process is observance of holidays and commemorative periods, such as Martin Luther King's Birthday, Black History Month, Native American Heritage Week, Thanksgiving, Jewish holidays, and Chinese New Year. Each of these occasions can be used to discuss the historical contributions of an individual or ethnic group, the effects of racism directed against an ethnic group, or the story of contact between disparate cultures. This will give children at an early age a frame of reference for examining the prejudice and racial injustice that they will inevitably encounter, and give them the tools to promote justice and foster interracial harmony.

SPECIFIC SUBJECT AREAS

In terms of content, the theme of oneness can be integrated into virtually every subject area. We present a few brief examples.

Science and mathematics

Biology and other sciences that deal directly with the study of human beings and human society are windows that reveal the oneness of the human family. The biological oneness of the human race has already been discussed. The interdependence of peoples has already been illustrated through a discussion of the environmental crisis. These are only two examples; teachers who are excited about the theme of oneness will find ways of integrating it into many other sciences as well.

The history of math and science should give due credit to the great contributions of non-European cultures. The abacus, for example, was invented in the Far East, and the system of numerals used in mathematics comes from Arabia, and is one of the great contributions of Islamic civilization to our technological society.

Many systems that are studied in science exemplify unity in diversity. When a biology class studies the human body, students can gain an appreciation for this principle. A teacher demonstrates how each organ contributes to that whole in an important way, and how diversity is a natural and essential aspect of a whole that is more than a sum of parts.

Many concepts and ideas in math and science are common to seemingly disparate fields. For example, mathematical laws governing bacteria population growth are very similar to those governing lasers. Students should be taught to appreciate such connections and commonalities. This will help them to appreciate the concept of oneness, and enrich their understanding of math and science.

Finally, the methodology of science and the nature of scientific inquiry should be taught. "Scientific evidence" for racist theories are only convincing to those who lack an understanding of the capabilities and limitations of scientific inquiry. Students should understand that deductive reasoning, for example, always operates on a set of assumptions, so that different assumptions lead to different conclusions. The "logic" of a reasoning process does not guarantee the correctness of the conclusions drawn. Students should also understand that the validation of scientific knowledge is inductive, not deductive. As an allegorical example, one's confidence that "all squirrels have tails" is a law of nature is based not on logical proof, but on the fact that, so far, squirrels without tails have not been observed.

History

In the past, the teaching of history has promoted ethnocentrism if not racism among American school pupils. The contributions of blacks and Native Americans to our civilization has not been given due attention. "World" history has emphasized Western civilization, often giving the impression that white Western cultures were always the most advanced. Therefore, careful attention to the history curriculum will have high payoffs in terms of teaching the oneness of the human family.

American blacks, for example, are descendants of people who lived in highly advanced civilizations. They were producing iron when the Europeans were still in the Stone Age. The Kingdom of Ghana, which flourished from the sixth to the eleventh centuries, maintained large towns with skillfully designed buildings. The people of Ghana engaged in elaborate sculpture and metalwork, and were prosperous in commerce. Their trading contact reached as far as Baghdad and Cairo. A complex political structure governed the kingdom, sporting an army of 200,000 men. The Kingdom of Mali produced another outstanding culture. Southern Europeans traveled to Timbuktu, Mali's capital, to study with local scholars. Mali had drugs for surgical anesthesia when European surgeons were still knocking their patients unconscious with mallets. There was a deep belief in God in both kingdoms, and prayer was a common practice.

Art and literature

One example of teaching oneness through art is "Dancing Colors and Singing Buildings," created by Maureen Kushner of New York City. This activity, in her words,

> . . . revolves around the beauty and joy found in the movement of colors and sounds. Many stories, games, songs, poems, plays, dances, and murals were created around this theme. Some depicted conflicts; others showed how to live in harmony. The children were divided into several groups of colorists, designers, composers, conductors, and rhythm makers. They discovered how to create new colors and sounds, and as they mastered their new

skills, they moved on to the next color and sound group. This project encouraged the children to explore the harmonies that exist with colors and sounds as well as to celebrate their differences.

In English classes, the literature read can contribute greatly to the understanding of oneness and the appreciation of diversity. For example, one twelfth grade class in New York City examines the literature of several major ethnic groups in their community. To demonstrate their oneness the unit revolves around universal themes in this literature: family, dreams, and self-discovery.

Over a six-week period, learners examine the historical background of these groups, view films, write analytic essays, personal reflection essays, and creative essays. This generates, among other things an openness to new understanding of different groups, a willingness to identify one's prejudice, and an identification with the universality of ethnic experience, essentially reinforcing the principle of oneness.

MAKING IT WORK

This chapter purposely avoids providing step-by-step directions for promoting the oneness of the human family in the classroom. Each class is different and every teacher has a different style. Teachers should have the freedom to create an approach with which they feel comfortable. What is most important, however, is that the teacher has the will and the commitment to carry out the responsibility to help students understand and internalize the reality of the oneness of the human family.

A committed administration can generate teacher commitment. Usually, when superintendents of schools are enthusiastic about a pedagogical concept, they are able to persuade principals to adopt and vigorously promote the concept in their schools. In order to persuade the teachers to integrate the oneness theme into the curriculum, the principal must emphasize the need. In doing this, it is important to keep in mind that commitment is mainly an emotional response springing from conviction.

Granted, making a commitment will not be easy because it requires an honest appraisal of one's real feelings about race. Many may be reluctant to undertake such an appraisal for fear of what will be discovered. Most teachers and administrators are people of good will who recognize racism as something evil; they do not want to be associated with it in any way. This leads to denial, which is a major stumbling block in the battle to eliminate racism in America.

If teachers understood that racism is a social disease, dealing with it on a personal basis would be less threatening. People are not evil because they have pneumonia; they seek a remedy, apply it, and eventually heal. The disease of racism manifests itself in different ways. Overt bigots who flaunt their racism suffer from an ugly form of the disease. Most teachers, however, do not fall into this category, nor is this the form of racism that we are most concerned with here.

Most white American teachers have been affected by racism in a much more subtle way. Although they may have genuine love for members of another ethnic group, they often harbor a subconscious sense of superiority toward them which manifests itself in a patronizing manner. While they may be unaware of such patterns in their own behavior in classrooms and hallways, the condescension is usually obvious to the victims of racism and rankles blacks, Latino, Native Americans, and Asian Americans. It is this subconscious feeling of superiority on the part of whites, which is part of the dominant American culture, that must be addressed.

When white teachers become acquainted with the gravity of America's racism problem, they will better appreciate the pain, anguish and frustration that the targets of racism feel almost every day of their lives. They will begin to understand that many minority students come to class already afflicted by the fears and uncertainties that plague their parents. The white teachers will feel compelled to devise creative ways of overcoming communications barriers that do not exist between themselves and most white students. By reading and discussing with their peers books such as *Black Like Me, Hidden Wound, To Be One,* and *Healing Racism in America: A Prescription for the Disease* (all authored by college-educated progressive whites from the North and the South), these teachers might be moved to break through the shell of denial and come to grips with their own prejudices.

To help teachers and administrators who are earnestly grappling with their prejudices, the school system could organize and operate an "Institute for the Healing of Racism." It could be opened to parents as well as all school personnel and students. Institutes have been started in many communities throughout the United States. Understanding how racism came into being in America would also help educators develop legitimate empathy for those who are the targets of the social disease. To be able to distinguish between prejudice and racism will also help. Prejudice is an emotional commitment to ignorance, whereas racism is institutionalized race prejudice linked with the establishment and maintenance of political, social and economic power. For example, racism is developed when a government encourages or sanctions a prevailing prejudice toward a particular people in order to dominate and control them and gain something from them (such as cheap labor).

Weaving the oneness of the human family into an existing curriculum is a step beyond the multicultural education approach to combating racism, because it fosters more than tolerance. It can instill in children and youth a sense of universal belonging that can develop into a lasting love for all people.

References

Gould, Stephen Jay (1981). *The Mismeasure of Man*. New York: Norton.

King, James C. (1981). *The Biology of Race.* Berkeley: University of California Press.

Leakey, Richard and Roger Lewin (1977). *Orgins: What New Discoveries Reveal About the Emergence of our Species and its Possible Future.* New York: Dutton.

Lewontin, Richard C. (1982). *Human Diversity.* New York: Scientific American Books, New York, 1982.

Chapter 12

Institutes for the Healing of Racism in Primary and Secondary Schools

by Paul Herron

Institutes for the Healing of Racism exist in over 200 cities across the United States and in Canada. They are built upon the principle that racism can be best dealt with when individuals are given the opportunity to openly and honestly confront their feelings in a systematic process. The author, a neuroscientist, tells how he was able to lead an effort to establish an Institute for the Healing of Racism, and provides guidance as to how one might attempt a similar endeavor within a school setting. Ed.

I started an Institute for the Healing of Racism (IHR) at my children's school with other parents and teachers. Their school, Snowden Elementary and Junior High, is a public school located in Memphis, Tennesee. In this chapter I will describe what we did to establish an IHR at Snowden, and what resulted from the understanding. I will also note some things that hindsight suggests we should have done differently.

Snowden is situated in a racially diverse community; it has a diverse student population and faculty. During the era of officially sanctioned racial segregation, Snowden was an all-European-American school located within an all-European-American neighborhood. Many of the European-American children currently at Snowden have parents and grandparents who went to Snowden. The school has always been considered one of the better schools in the Memphis school system. Some parents who live outside of the school's boundary will give false addresses within the boundary in order to get their children into the school.

The current fear among many parents and teachers is that Snowden is in a state of decline. This expectation for decline has coincided with an increased number of African-American students. With court-ordered integration and "white flight" from the urban center, many white parents have opted for private schools for their children. As a result the student population is now about 75 percent African-American, about 24 percent European-American, and less than 1 percent Asian-American, Native American, or other ethnic origin. Also, more children come from single-parent, lower socioeconomic homes.

Snowden has an optional educational program along with a traditional program. The optional program is designed to provide accelerated and expanded coverage of curricular materials relative to the traditional classes. Many parents and teachers in the school view the optional program as an effort by the Memphis school system to keep European-Americans in the system, both to insure support from European-American voters, and to maintain as much socioeconomic and color diversity as possible.

The optional school program has been a source of division for the community and for teachers and students within the school. Qualifications for the optional program include performance on standardized exams and grades, and conduct, and recommendation by teachers. On the positive side, the optional class that my son is in is about 50 percent African-American and 50 percent European-American, which approximate the racial demographics of the city. Teachers appear to be more enthusiastic about and interested in teaching optional classes.

On the negative side, the optional schools program has contributed to racial segregation within the school. The predominant criteria seem to select for middle-class European-American language skills. Hence, it does not rate fairly for native ability, and thus discriminates against African-Americans. Since the optional starts as early as first grade, performance in kindergarten can largely determine what "track" kids will be on for the rest of their primary and secondary education. The great majority of Snowden's African-American students are in the traditional classes with very few European-American students. Usually, if a European-American child does not qualify for the optional program, he will be withdrawn from the school if the family can afford private school, or find another school. The traditional classes are quickly becoming stereotyped as all African-American, with little academic potential. There is certain amount of elitism bred into the program and a disproportionate amount of the school's resources are allocated to it. The optional program tends to create or exacerbate negative contrasts: white vs. black, middle socioeconomic vs. lower socioeconomic class, and smart vs. not so smart.

Of course, children pick up on these contrasts quickly or are told in explicit terms by teachers and administrators. For example, my son, who entered the second grade at Snowden after we moved here from a small town in the Northeast, was not in the traditional class his first year at Snowden. His teachers told his class that the "smart" students were in the optional classes and the not-so-smart kids were in the regular classes. This view is held by many, if not most, teachers at Snowden. In my conversations with teachers I have heard many variations of this theme. One teacher told me that one of the great racial problems at Snowden was that the principal assigned white teachers to the optional program, and black teachers to the traditional.

Consequently, there are still numerous complaints against and within the school system about fairness, results, and expectations for students of color compared to European-Americans. The city has not completely healed the racial wounds created by the events leading to the death of Dr. Martin Luther King. Almost forty years after the United States Supreme Court's decision on racial integration in the Brown vs. Board of Education of Topeka, Kansas, just about every single administrative act, personal interaction between teachers, and the perception of students' ability to perform are viewed from the perspective of race. It was for these reasons that I believed that an IHR would help Snowden.

Getting an IHR started at Snowden

My first initiative for an IHR was proposed at a group meeting between parents and the principal, and it was turned down by the principal. He viewed it strictly as a traditional racial sensitivity exercise, and he felt that teachers were very weary of such exercises. The usual approach at Snowden to lessen racial tension and create awareness is to have symbolic gestures, infrequent presentations or programs built around Black History Month. The principal proposed as an alternative to my request that parents, one black and one white, come in to talk to the seventh and eighth grade social study class about racially harmony. I explained that such limited efforts were inadequate and that teachers ought to be focused on efforts to lessen racial tension since "fertilizer put into the soil was much more productive in the long run than putting fertilizer on individual plants."

However, (luckily) this principal left at the end of the school year and we had a new principal. I and one other parent, Rev. Tory Mashburn, met with the principal to discuss some of the problems that we believed were prevalent at Snowden. Again, I proposed an IHR, and this time was asked to write a description as to how an IHR would operate. I wrote a description based on the format, intent, and workings of the citywide IHR in Memphis, which borrowed most of its ideas from the Houston, Texas, IHR. My description for a Snowden IHR sat on the principal's desk for weeks. Meanwhile, parents were becoming more and more concerned about racial tensions, attitudes, and behavior at the school. At another meeting with the principal, she agreed that something needed to be done and the idea of an IHR was accepted.

At a subsequent meeting with more parents and the principal we discussed ideas for a name, and promoting it to faculty and parents.

Since everyone in the school seemed so weary of anything that had the name "race" or "racism" attached to it, the IHR was given the name "STARS" which is an acronym for Snowden Takes A Right Stand." It was agreed that I and one other parent would present the idea to teachers at a faculty meeting.

In our environment in Memphis and at Snowden, much as in other cities and places where I have lived in the United States, racism has an omnipotent presence. Everyone will admit that its effect on the human potential and spirit in education is very costly, but individuals will rarely admit to owning any part of it. However, by simple logic, if racism is deeply rooted in our society, every individual is contaminated by it to a degree, much the same way that anyone who lives in a bacterial or viral infested environment is infected by the bacteria or virus. Consequently, IHRs treat racism as a disease. In my experience, this is the most difficult concept for IHR participants to accept. Yet, from our experience thus far, it is an essential threshold of understanding.

When we mention disease, people immediately think of organic dysfunction, such as tissue damage, such as inflammation or loss of an organ. Racism viewed from this perspective is difficult for most people to readily accept. Disease, however, does not necessarily mean these things. It can simply mean "disease," the uncomfortable internal workings of the body and/or spirit. If people can understand it as a "disease," then the healing can begin to take place. Healing can occur because we can understand more precisely how we are affected. At Snowden, on hindsight, I wish that we had spent more time getting this point completely understood and accepted. This makes it easier for people to understand how the disease can be treated.

Many worthwhile efforts have been responsible for many laws and policies to reduce the conscious practice of racism in the United States. Thus, most people know what is legally correct to do. What the IHR at Snowden wants to do is transform peoples' hearts. We believe that, short of transformation of heart, people will still engage in unconscious, deeply ingrained, heart-felt racism.

With these ideas in mind, we introduced STARS to the faculty at a faculty meeting. I explained to the faculty how racially diverse Snowden's faculty and students were, how diversity should be the source of strength rather than the source of disunity. I also stressed that children consciously and subconsciously learn a lot by modeling the behaviors and attitudes of their teachers. I then asked that they take a look around the room and at those they had chosen to sit with at their table. I noted how racially divided the seating was, not only by table. In fact, European-American teachers were sitting on the left side of the room and African-American teachers were sitting on the right. There were a few nervous laughs, but clearly what had generally been considered natural seating choices were greatly motivated by race. I was asked several questions, primarily about format, time, and place. Many seemed interested and all were invited to attend.

The principal format for STARS operation in the beginning was dialogue sessions. The purpose of the dialogue sessions was to provide a forum through discussions and sharing for the transformation of the heart regarding racism. A loosely organized steering committee was formed by ten to twelve parents and teachers. STARS never had the vigorous support of the principal, and as a consequence, teachers did not receive administrative encouragement for participating or being involved.

I was surprised by the large number of teachers and parents who came to the first meeting. We wanted to sit in a circle, and we had to keep widening the circle to accommodate the entry of new people. I facilitated the meeting, and I asked everyone to introduce themselves and to say in one sentence why they were here. Some teachers said they were distressed by the racial tension; some said that they wanted to ease racial tension between students; one parent said that he was saddened about the quality of relationships between kids of different colors, teachers of different colors, and between parents of different colors within the community. An African-American teacher and a European-American teacher said that they had considered starting a dialogue group for students.

At the second meeting, after reading guidelines for sharing, I asked if there were any reflections on last week's discussion. Teachers spoke of acknowledging and of being acknowledged by other teachers of different colors in ways that had not occurred before. It was as if openly talking about color had finally enabled teachers to see friendly colleagues for the first time.

Many participants wanted to get involved in action-oriented programs right away. I encouraged individuals to be patient, to allow time for transformations, so that behaviors would be different and transformed rather than traditional, albeit well-meaning. I believed parents and teachers whose hearts were being transformed by their experience in the dialogue would naturally manifest different behaviors with regard to racial interaction with the school and community.

Both parents and teachers said that they were more hopeful about making progress at Snowden. Some parents and teachers thought of STARS as somewhat of a support group. It allowed all of us to draw on the support of others fighting the same disease. We began to see other people different from ourselves more as human beings, as members of the human family, rather than as "white" or "black." This does not mean that everybody should be "the same", but rather that one should appreciate diversity of experiences, culture, and color. From this transformed state, we were better able to understand how racism degrades the human spirit.

One European-American parent described an encounter she observed while in the principal's office, involving an African-American student. The student had been accused of mischievous behavior. She described the student as unable to make eye contact with the principal and teachers, and exhibiting no confidence or expectations that any sort of defense would help. She described how wrenching it was to observe this child, so completely helpless. She wondered what sort of alien environment would produce such a human being. As the discussion progressed, it became clear that the context of the encounter in the office was an extension of our environment in the community and in the school. We discussed the context of the situation in the office, historical interactions between African-American youths and European-American authority figures, and how the child had probably learned and "internalized" a sense of inferiority and helplessness when in this context. When parents and teachers are touched by experiences like this and these experiences are shared at dialogue sessions, it forces everyone to think about our learning and social environment. We can change the environments by changing our behaviors. Transformed individuals will develop creative responsive behaviors for situations like what was described above. Their transformations enable creative behaviors that are instructive examples for others in the community.

Time went very quickly and we realized at the outset that time would present several logistical problems. First, it would be hard to get teachers back to school frequently if STARS meetings were held at night. Second, if they were held after school, many teachers would have to come late or leave early because of prior commitments, and many parents would not able to attend because of work schedules.

Over the next several months, we used one to two facilitators at each dialogue meeting, trying to match African-American with European-American, parent with teacher, and female with male. We ran exercises, including one I developed called "tell me who you think I am." In this exercise, we separated into groups of twos. We would try to achieve color or gender diversity in each group. Each individual would then say to his partner, "My name is (each gave his name), I live at (address was given)." The facilitator would then instruct each partner to write down the religion, political affiliation, learning, and educational level of his partner. The idea was to get individuals to determine how impressions based on a minimum amount of information can lead to the categorizing of individuals based on stereotypes. Stereotypical perceptions lead to unsubstantiated expectations which determine how we interact with one another.

The subject of stereotypes and expectations kept coming back into the dialogue for the rest of the year. We discussed why stereotypical perceptions are so easily accepted and used. One parent described stereotypes as being consistent with a method of organizing information in the mental file cabinets of our brain. For most things, the mental file cabinet works well. It helps us set up a hierarchy for the storage and retrieval of information — related information in the same drawer and, within each drawer, closely related information and folder and subfolder. It helps us store and retrieve information rapidly. Such a system works well for living in a society where we have to assimilate a tremendous amount of information. As a result, this informational storage system becomes our unconscious habit, that starts very early in life.

As regards racial stereotypes, it was discussed how prejudice and racism distort the way we assimilate information about others. Also, racial and ethnic stereotypes generally do not allow for individual differences or recognitions. One teacher suggested that the constant used of "black students do this..." and "white students do that..." by teachers and parents help harden stereotypes. Many agreed with this insight, but some disagreed as well. One teacher pointed out that culture and race were very closely related, nearly inseparable, and that cultures were different. Some teachers and parents saw these differences as innate rather than learned. One African-American teacher said that "one black student was hanging (socializing) with white students," which was unnatural. The teacher said, "Many black students thought she (the black student) was trying to be white."

One may agree or disagree with what comes out in honest and sincere sharing, such as that described above. I firmly believe that learning and transformation of the heart occurs as a result of honest, sincere feelings that come out in dialogue sessions. We believe that transformation occurs when individuals listen to their own speaking, for it often reveals in complete sentences thoughts and beliefs that lie within, but which were never consciously articulated before. Individuals have an opportunity to examine these beliefs and to integrate information and thoughts shared by others into their beliefs and heartfelt feelings. On hearing the sharing, occasionally I would hear teachers or parents say, "I didn't know that", or, "Is that how that is perceived?"

Some individuals were not able to deal with heartfelt feelings before colleagues. Although we stressed in our guidelines for sharing that what was said in dialogue sessions was confidential, some individuals did not feel enough confidence in their colleagues to openly share. The school has cliques divided along racial lines. Some teachers were openly feuding with one another to the extent that their students were used as pawns in the feuds. A strong administrative presence by the principal that promoted fairness and unity may well have promoted more sharing. We did not get as much support from the principal as we had hoped.

The steering committee met near the end of the first half of the year, and decided to initiate several action-oriented projects. We wanted them to be projects in which students and faculty were not just talked to, but in which they could immerse themselves, and, from the experience, internalize a sense of unity in an environment that was very diverse. We developed what we call the "Harmony Project."

In this project, students were to be given cameras, and asked to take pictures of situations showing racial and ethnic harmony in the school. We selected to participate two fifth-grade classes — one optional class, and one traditional — for a total of sixty-three students. It was a fairly expensive project. Each student would be given a disposable twelve-shot camera. Each camera and its processing came to about nine dollars retail. However, money was not a major problem. Schools in Memphis are typically adopted by neighborhood businesses, community organizations, or churches. One of Snowden's adopters is Evergreen Presbyterian Church, which gave STARS $1,500 for mailing and special projects. I approached Fox Photo for support, and they gave us fifty-seven cameras and the processing of films at cost.

Another parent, a European-American, and I, an African-American, took a camera to each class, and explained the project to the students. I had called the teachers earlier, and they were excited about the project and the educational activities that could be developed from it.

Students were given simple instructions: to take pictures showing racial harmony and unity. If they were unable to find these elements, they were to create examples for photographing. We did rudimentary demonstrations of harmony vs. conflict, but stressed to the students that they were to find their own examples of harmony and unity. We also told them that, after the film was processed and the prints made, each student would select three to five of his photos that he liked best, and that at least one of the photos would be placed on a display board in the school mall. The idea was to stimulate students to think of unity and harmony, and how these qualities can be manifested. We believed that students would find the experience rewarding, and thus engage more in this kind of behavior.

The students were very excited. They volunteered many different examples of unity and harmony as we discussed it with them. The students took to the project with such enthusiasm and energy that the whole school and community were drawn into the excitement. Indeed, the students were revealing to the community examples of harmony and unity that were not regularly seen at Snowden. They were snapping pictures of kids playing together, sitting together, eating together, or simply quietly enjoying being with one another. They took pictures of African-American and European-American kids appearing to be delighted to be encouraged to show friendship, affection, and happiness. They took pictures of European-American and African-American teachers in somewhat exaggerated friendly interactions, with arms around one another, and enjoying each other's company. These behaviors were very different from what I saw in the meeting when we introduced STARS to the whole faculty.

The major newspaper in Memphis, the *Commercial Appeal,* was contacted by someone (I believe an assistant principal) and they reported on it. The story was very positive and had a large photo of an African-American student and European-American students, fourth and fifth graders, engaged in a conscious, but natural, harmonious interaction by playing a simple patty-cake game. The story quoted one student as saying "This is very much fun showing how the races get along together."

Once we got the photos back, a photo from each student was placed on a large bulletin board in the mall. The photos were very nicely displayed by two artists in STARS. The title of the exhibit, "PICTURES OF HARMONY," was embedded in the middle of many excellent photos. Several parents came by. All parents liked the exhibit; in fact, one of them said "This ought to be done every year. This experience has many levels of learning and enjoyment for students." He added that it was very instructive for the faculty, staff and the community at large. I agreed. That was the last major event of our year. We had several more dialogue sessions. The photo exhibit increased attendance at our dialogue sessions.

Conclusions about one and one-half years of an IHR at Snowden

An IHR requires the commitment of teachers, administrators, parents, and community. In an environment, like a school, where there are different levels of interactions, harmony, and unity among and between faculty and administrators is helpful. Also, it is very helpful if the principal strongly supports the IHR and is a leader for unity though our institute achieved most of its goals, it could have been more successful had the school's principal wholeheartedly supported our efforts.

Chapter 13

Institutes for the Healing of Racism on University Campuses

by Denise Gifford

The author, who is vice president for student affairs at the University of Louisville, describes the process of establishing an Institute for the Healing of Racism on a higher level of education than discussed in the previous chapter. She tells how institutes were developed in all residence halls on the Lousiville campus, and provides insights into how the process has succeeded. Especially valuable is her advice on how to avoid pitfalls while the institutes are being organized. Ed.

The University of Louisville is similar to many other large urban campuses. It is located close to the center of downtown Louisville, and has grown markedly in the past fifteen years. Its mission embodies an "urban focus" which relates to its expected interface with the community and peoples of this urban area. The campus population reflects this mission, and boasts approximately 11 percent minority students university-wide, with approximately 32 percent of its residence hall population being composed of minority students. Although there are some international, Hispanic and Southeast Asian students, the largest minority group at the University of Louisville is African-American. The residence halls are the home of almost one-third of the freshman class, and provide the first multiracial social environment experience for many students. As a multicultural environment, the residence halls provide a perfect laboratory for social interaction between persons of different racial groups.

It was with this "laboratory" concept in mind that we first embarked upon the concept of the "Institutes for the Healing of Racism." As in other schools across the country, racial incidents and negative interactions had occurred on campus. One highly publicized incident four years ago involved an African-American student who received racially harassing notes under her door, and, while in her residence hall, was the subject of a direct oral racial epithet from another student. This incident sparked a march and protest by African-American students which resulted in demands being made to the president on behalf of these students. The demands were diligently responded to by the administration, but the tensions remained. It was our expectation that our residence halls, like others throughout America, were the most likely places on our campus for racial harassment to occur. It was our intent to target the residence halls as primary sites for the Institutes for the Healing of Racism on our campus.

As a student affairs practitioner, I have worked in the areas of student life for fifteen years. I became committed to the concept of the institutes after hearing Nathan Rutstein speak to a community group in Louisville, and describe the success of the institutes throughout the country. From his speech, I embarked on an effort to communicate these benefits to my colleagues so that we could provide these institutes to our students. For those readers who are also practitioners, I will attempt to cover the "nuts and bolts" of our efforts to successfully implement the institutes at the University of Louisville, and also share some of the positives and negatives of the experience. Your campus organizational structure or governance may not be exactly the same, but hopefully some of our efforts will be transferable to your campus.

The Division of Student Affairs, of which the Residence Administration and Life Office was a part, had provided or participated in campus-wide diversity programming for two years prior to the implementation of the institutes. The Celebration of Diversity projects were successful large-scale efforts to bring attention to issues of diversity and multiculturalism. Both years, the diversity programming had brought in nationally known speakers and provided workshops and other settings for students and faculty to listen to experts in this area. Through the success of these efforts, we saw a need for students, often away from home for the first time, to think about and evaluate issues of race on a personal and more intimate level. This need to bring students together to provide an opportunity for personal reflection and evaluation, and our desire to provide a sounding board for racial tensions among students melded in a plan for an ambitious campus-wide effort to establish a number of Institutes for the Healing of Racism on our campus. It proved to be an exhausting but exhilarating process which consumed many hours of preparation, but has had a long lasting impact.

As of today, almost one year after their initiation on campus, there have been seven successful institutes which have met regularly for at least five weeks each. Some have met in residence halls and others, composed of both resident and commuter students, have met during the day in classroom buildings. A summer residence hall institute was successful, and a resident assistant training program based on the concepts of the institute was later provided to staff. Another institute composed of faculty and staff trained as facilitators meet regularly to review the progress of the institutes across campus and to discuss issues of race on a personal level with others who have been through the facilitator training program.

The Proposal

The first step in the planning process was to develop a proposal and seek university financial support. Certainly, the topic of race relations was timely, and the name "Institutes for the Healing of Racism" serves to sell the concept on campus. Most campuses have had incidents of racial harassment or unrest in the past few years, and the healing metaphor denotes a positive effort, a cleansing process, that, although difficult, may provide a healthier campus community.

The proposal included, (1) the organization of a planning committee, (2) publication efforts, (3) the introduction of the institute concept to freshmen through orientation and their required orientation class, and (4) the institute kickoff unity picnic, and Nathan Rutstein's visit to campus. Costs for speakers' fees, publicity, the picnic and other planning were included in the budget proposal. Descriptive information about the focus and intent of the institutes was also included, along with a proposal of its application to our campus.

Due to the strong commitment to diversity and multiculturalism in the Division of Student Affairs, the proposal was readily accepted and funded. If it had not been so readily accepted I would have proposed a similar version to Student Government in an effort to seek funding. In retrospect, the acquisition of funds was the easiest part of the process. So many campuses, even with financial constraints, are feeling the negative effects of racial tensions on campus. Certainly an effort to "heal racism" provides an opportunity to move one step forward in an effort to create a more positive campus climate.

Steering Committee

The next step was creation of a campus-wide steering committee, which began meeting four months before the first institute started. The steering committee was composed of faculty, student affairs staff and students. I selected persons based on their role on campus and commitment to issues of racism and diversity. Certainly these folks, the "cheerleaders" of the institute concept, had to have a strong commitment to impacting change regarding issues of race on our campus. I also sought out those persons who I knew would work hard to implement the project, not just give advice. Members of the committee included staff from many areas on campus including the Multicultural Center, the Residence Administration and Life Office, Office of Minority Affairs, and faculty from diverse areas. Special efforts were made to solicit student input, and the president of the Association of Black Students and the Student Government Association represented students on the committee. This is one instance in which a personal invitation from me to those on the committee seemed to encourage participation from campus community leaders who were already extremely busy.

The steering committee reviewed my proposal and drafted a more specific schedule of planning deadlines as well as served as an excellent resource in advertising and publicity methods for all aspects of the program. The steering committee also attended each of the events surrounding Nathan Rutstein's visit and encouraged others on campus to do so. Certainly this broad-based campus-wide steering committee, which met six times to plan the implementation of the institutes, was an influential aspect in the success of the project.

Advertising

All campus mediums were used to advertise Nathan Rutstein's upcoming visit and those events surrounding it. The first method was the distribution at freshman orientation of approximately 1,500 wallet-size plastic cards which had printed on one side the "Cardinal Creed", which includes a code of civilized behavior described in six separate statements. One of those statements, "I will not condone bigotry, I will strive to learn from differences in people, ideas and opinions", provided a springboard for the statement on the back of the card inviting all students to participate in an Institute for the Healing of Racism. Students were urged to contact our office if they were willing to do so. These cards were passed out during the first morning of each orientation session, and administrators who spoke to the students referred to both the Cardinal Creed and the information about the institutes during their introductory remarks.

Other efforts to provide extensive advertising of the upcoming visit to campus by Nathan Rutstein and the surrounding events included advertisements in the student newspaper, and articles in the city newspaper, and the university-wide staff and faculty publication. We found that the articles, describing the institutes and the events surrounding them, were much more effective than an advertisement. Members of the steering committee were quoted in the articles, and the diversity of this group helped "sell" the concept to the campus community. Although the institutes were sponsored by the Division of Student Affairs, the support of this broad-based committee was much more effective than single departmental sponsorship could have been. In total, over twelve separate articles and advertisements came out in the university media prior to the inception of the institutes.

In addition to the above efforts, presentations were made to faculty, staff and Student Government in an effort to garner support. It was at a staff senate presentation that many staff members asked if they could participate as members of an institute. Although our initial concept had included only student participants, this outpouring of interest from staff encouraged us to modify our initial proposal so that both staff and faculty as well as students could participate as members of institutes.

"Table tents", little cardboard tents placed on dining hall tables, also advertised the presentations and institutes, as did a large banner draped at the Student Activities Center. It was also our intent that the unity picnic, scheduled for lunch time of the day of Nathan's major evening presentation to the campus community, would serve as an opportunity to advertise the institutes. Two days prior to the picnic, handbills advertising the unity picnic were dispersed during the busy lunch time at the Student Activities Center in the heart of campus. We know that free food brings in students, and the free food at the picnic was highlighted in the ads, as well as encouragement to attend the evening presentation.

Handbills advertising the unity picnic and the upcoming presentations were also distributed heavily in the residence halls and student lounge areas. As those of us in program planning know, 50 percent of the planning time and budget for an event need to be devoted to advertising. Many excellent programs are not successful due to too little time and effort expended on advertising. In this project, it is my estimate that at least 50 percent of our effort and time was dedicated to the promotion and advertising of the upcoming institutes and surrounding events. As the concept was new, and possibly intimidating or scary to some, we felt that intense advertising was a necessary vehicle to success.

Facilitator Training

At the same time that the steering committee was working hard on advertising and promotional efforts, a subgroup of the committee was meeting to plan and provide some structure for the facilitators who would be leading the groups. Although structuring the planning of the institutes is not a concept that had been used in other institutes nationwide, we were concerned that our facilitators, composed of persons who may never have led a group of any kind before, may need a structured format to refer to. Our intent was not to structure the meeting of the institute so carefully as to throttle creativity, but to provide some simple exercises or "lesson plans" for facilitators to use as a basis for group discussion if they desired.

We were especially pleased when we found a volume by Judith Katz entitled *White Awareness*. It is Katz's contention that whites are especially in need of personal evaluation regarding issues of race and racism, and that sometimes this can be done in a more honest manner without fear of reprisal if done in an all-white group. Her book, filled with exercises to promote racial awareness and applicable to both multiracial and white groups was just what we needed to devise our own "lesson plans".

While we hoped that our groups would be multiracial in composition, we had no means to assure that, and liked the idea that, if a group was composed of all white members, the group could proceed. After much review and discussion, we decided on seven topics for the sessions:

1. Establishing Goals and Objectives
2. Attitude Survey/Definition of Racism

3. African-American: Historical Overview
4. Fears of Dealing with Racism
5. The Web of Institutional Racism
6. Personal Racial Experience
7. Commitment to Combat Racism / Assessments

We also compiled these seven "lesson plans" in a notebook for the facilitators, which was reviewed with them at their facilitator training. The back section also included film and video resources available on campus for institute facilitators who wanted to use a video or film for part of an institute session.

Throughout the planning process, volunteer facilitators were being sought from throughout the campus community to lead an institute for seven weeks. The advertisements for the upcoming presentations and events always included a "Call for Facilitators," and two separate quarter-page ads were put in our campus newspaper to find interested persons. Facilitators were sent a form and asked to attend the one-day training program led by Mr. Rutstein, and to indicate both day and evening times they were free to lead an institute.

The response from persons volunteering to lead or co-lead institutes astounded us, and finally totalled thirty-two in all. Most were staff or administrators, or students personally committed to impacting issues of race. All persons were scheduled to attend the all-day facilitator training led by Nathan Rutstein during his visit to campus.

Unity Picnic and Presentations

The actual week of the unity picnic, presentations, and facilitator training was a whirlwind of activity. The steering committee met one final time to coordinate plans and efforts, and our office staff worked feverishly on compiling the facilitator notebooks to be ready for the training.

In his three days on campus, Nathan Rutstein gave three separate presentations, met with the president of the university, led an all-day facilitator training and attended the unity picnic. His presentations to the campus community were made to approximately four-hundred persons, with one held during the day and another in the evening. The third presentation was made to approximately fifty student affairs staff as an in-service training session. They responded extremely positively to his message. Many staff and faculty attended the campus-wide lectures (a result, probably, of our extensive publicity) as well as students. After the presentations, tables were set up outside with sign-up sheets for institutes to be held at different dates and times on campus. Nathan Rutstein briefly described the concept of the institutes, and invited listeners to sign up to make a seven-week commitment to a group. Many persons signed up for an institute as they exited the auditorium where the presentation was held. A confirmation card with the date and time of their first institute meeting was given to each person who signed up for an institute.

The unity picnic, held at lunch on the day of the large evening presentation, brought approximately four-hundred students, faculty and staff to the grassy programming area next to the student center on a bright sunny autumn day. Students signed a "diversity pledge", received a free T-shirt with a diversity symbol on it, and ate food while listening to music from different countries. Although the meal was free, cards were given out that had to be completed before an ice cream sundae for dessert was available. The card, advertising the evening presentation, required that each person ask questions of another person at the picnic and write down the answer. "What is your cultural background, your native language, your favorite color, food?" were examples of the questions. Although this concept was a new one on our campus, students seemed to enjoy the interaction that it fostered and enthusiastically participated. Over four-hundred ice cream sundaes were served when "Meet a Friend" cards were returned.

During the picnic, members of the steering committee moved throughout the crowd talking with students and inviting them to that evening's lecture by Nathan Rutstein, entitled "Racism: The

Disease." Students responded warmly (or maybe they were just surprised that an administrator or faculty person was making a personal invitation to them), and the personal oral invitation seemed to touch students in addition to the signs and posters already displayed.

The last day of Nathan's visit on campus was devoted to the training of thirty-two facilitators for the Institutes for the Healing of Racism. He used role-playing and personal experience to illustrate the focus and impact of the institutes. During the lunch period, the self-selected group of faculty, staff and students got to know one another on a personal level. The discussion throughout the day was often emotional and heated as people recounted how racism had touched their lives. Late in the day, the notebook for facilitators was reviewed and the optional structure for institute sessions was introduced. As expected, the optional structure was warmly received as some facilitators were apprehensive of holding open sessions without some structure to use if necessary. A written assessment of the training was done at the end of the day, and the combined evaluations were extremely high and showed strong appreciation for the facilitator training.

Institutes Begin

Four institutes filled up immediately with persons who attended the presentations and began their first meeting the following week. Two of these groups were held in the residence halls, and the other two in classroom buildings. Some logistical details had to be worked out, but all institutes began as planned. Three of the four groups completed the semester's meetings. The fourth group had trouble getting enough members together at the predetermined time, but regrouped for the following semester.

Future Plans

After the institutes had been ongoing for some weeks, the

facilitators who had been trained together met to discuss future plans. All felt that being involved with the institutes had been beneficial to them and wanted to see them continue. In the following semester one group continued and added new members, two previous groups combined, and a new residence hall group formed. Future plans to make a promotional video were made, and community projects in which the Institutes could participate were discussed.

The medical school, after hearing Mr. Rutstein, decided to offer a class on race and multicultural issues for its students. Later, a neuroscientist, Dr. Paul Herron, was brought in to lecture to the School of Medicine on the effects of oppression on the brain.

Impact

Although it is hard to clearly define the impact of the institutes on our campus, I believe that personal and individual growth has occurred on the part of the participants as a result of the honest, open dialogue that the safety of the institute format provides. As a member of an institute group, I can attest to the influence the institutes had on me. As for campus impact, I am aware that the institutes have had an influence on activities on campus. For example, one institute wrote a letter of support to an administrator for one of its members who was being legally brought up on disciplinary charges. The letter diplomatically asked that the possible influence of racial prejudice be considered in the case and factored into the disciplinary case decision process.

In another situation, an institute member was called into a residence hall to provide racial sensitivity training after an incident with racial overtones occurred there. In a third instance, an institute member was asked to provide diversity training for off-campus groups who had heard of the success of the Institutes.

Final Assessment

Not all campus response to the concept of the institutes has been positive. While I originally thought that few would publicly disagree with any program designed to "heal racism", I was surprised and hurt when a particularly critical editorial was printed in a faculty newsletter designed to promote curriculum changes to include issues of diversity and multiculturalism. The editorial criticized the concept of personal change espoused by the institutes and encouraged legislative change instead. Another article in our city newspaper quoted persons critical of the concept of the institutes, but spoke to few who had actually participated in one. The writer, who attended two different sessions of two separate institutes, asked me to describe the "other side", or the negative side of the institutes, after she sat through two especially effective groups. It was clear she was interested in digging up negative feelings about the project. She was searching hard for those who disagreed with or disliked the concept, and was able to find them in the university community, especially among those who had had no contact with the institutes. Even though those she spoke to had not attended an institute, she didn't clarify that in her article and it appeared extremely negative to the reader. It is clear to me that the issues of race are still extremely volatile, and that persons who make efforts to confront racism, regardless of their content or approach, can anticipate negative feedback. Certainly, a university, the "marketplace of ideas", sets the perfect stage for such discussions and criticisms. I have learned we must be prepared for this criticism, even if it is not based on the facts, due to the continued volatility of issues of race.

Suggestions

My personal evaluation of our efforts has resulted in a number of positive suggestions for others who may seek to establish Institutes for the Healing of Racism on their campus. Although we did many things well and experienced a strong response from the campus community, the following suggestions may help another institution avoid some of our pitfalls and highlight some special areas of success.

1. Residence hall involvement needs to be pivotal. Our presentations were attended more by faculty, staff and commuters than residence hall students. We should have held one presentation in a residence hall, and done a better job of advertising in the halls. Actually, we did less advertising in the residence halls because we ran out of people power the last few days. Stronger advertising and presence in the residence halls would have yielded more resident participants.

2. We are now at work on preparing a promotional video based on the institutes to be used next fall for orientation, orientation classes and in residence halls. This would have been a great help the first time, as videos are such effective promotional tools.

3. The campus-wide steering committee was an integral part of the success of our efforts. Their help in providing input, researching information for the facilitator's manual, and providing a broad base of campus support was essential.

4. Flexibility in the structure of each institute was important. One older woman, who originally signed up and attended a primarily student-composed group, was unhappy, but when asked to join another institute which was less "confrontational" and comprised older students, faculty and staff, was extremely happy and completed the sessions with the second group.

5. The planners of the institutes have to be able to emotionally "let them go." After weeks of planning and work it is essential that the institutes fly or fail on their own efforts. My experience shows that most will fly, but a few may not. We must understand that we can only provide the training and the format, and then the institute group must embark on its own journey.

It is necessary to distance oneself from this process after giving it wings in order to move on to the other projects which need your attention. We cannot hope to erase centuries of racism on our campus through the institutes. However, we can provide a forum for individual change and transformation.

After the success of the large scale diversity efforts at the University of Louisville, we saw a need for students to have a safe forum where they could meet and discuss issues of race on a more intimate and personal level. After implementing the institutes, we have seen students, faculty and staff enthusiastically participate in this process. Participants have had very positive experiences, and although the format or structure may change from semester to semester, we feel it has improved the communication and quality of life on our campus and look forward to the continuation of the institutes.

Personal Testimonies

"I felt like the institutes offered me a safe place to come and talk about my feelings," one eighteen-year-old African-American student remarked. "The university is so big, and impersonal, that I wonder if anyone really cares about how I feel."

"The institute I attended became a refuge for me, and I began to feel that I had made some dear friends when I saw the members of my group out on campus. We continued to keep in touch by phone even after our institute finished," a male student said.

Many students described the institutes as "safe havens" on campus, where they could freely voice their deepest feelings about the pain of racism, or discuss for the first time issues relating to race and prejudice. One graduate student from Somalia expressed his confusion about the important role that race plays in American society. Discussions on the history of racism served to describe the role of racism as a part of our country's history.

Some African-American students were able to share, for the first time in a mixed group, the anger and pain of racism in their lives. "This is my chance to describe how it feels to be black in America today. You all (the group) need to understand this now. Future generations will be too angry to explain it to you and will use different methods to get their point across. . . much less peaceful methods", one said.

The pervasiveness of racism throughout society was a common thread throughout many of the groups. Its constant presence, and its part in the powerful hierarchy of our society was discussed throughout the sessions. "The institute I attended discussed the integral part that race plays in our society, in our lives, in every step that we take. I never understood how big of a role it played in our society," said one young white female student. "This was a real education for me to hear black students talk about their everyday experiences . . . I had no idea race was such a prominent issue in our society. It touches everything."

Students of all races who attended the institutes discussed their feelings openly after attending their institute sessions. All felt that they had gained new insights into the issue of racism and had grown personally from the process. Some groups were much more "confrontational" than others, and others were much more concentrated on sharing personal experiences. Each group had a flavor and personal make up that was distinctive and different. Each institute approached the discussion topics from the perspective of the members, which varied in each group. Therefore, the resultant response from the groups was distinctively different, although similarity of experiences were noted.

"The institute I attended helped me deal with my freshman year, and in my institute I learned about other students on campus, and racism's impact on their lives," said another student. "It opened my eyes. I'd recommend it to other freshman students."

Personal Impact of Institute Planner

I personally have been transformed by the process. After months of preparation for the "birth" of the institutes, I had much difficulty separating myself from the project, and I have taken the successes and failures of the project much too personally at times. Compassion fatigue often accompanies such emotion-laden work, and has also taken its toll on me. The experience of working with an issue as deeply painful as racism and discussing the issues, listening carefully to the personal experiences of members, and hearing the anger or pain of the individuals involved has humbled me, and has made it hard for me to leave my emotions at work. I have had to work strenuously at times to continue to put additional energies into the project of promoting the institutes.

As I talk with people who are interested in beginning institutes on their campus I try to warn them about the intense personal involvement that occurs and the resultant "compassion fatigue" that results. I also still am amazed at the anger and resentment revealed by people who don't feel that issues of racism should be discussed at all, and sometimes cloak that perception in critical analysis of the process of the institutes.

After our first year of experience, we have learned much about what works most effectively in running multiple institutes. Our experiences have been painful, but rich, and compassion fatigue is alleviated after talking with a student who has participated in an institute and learned and developed from the experience. My semi-regular meetings with the facilitators that were trained to run Institutes has served to invigorate me. Although I approach each of the meetings with trepidation, sure that no progress has been made, I am continually uplifted by the personal efforts of the facilitators as the institutes begin to work under their own "steam".

Presentations on the institutes at professional conferences also help recharge my batteries. It is these indications of progress on a problem that is so encompassing and entrenched in our society that encourage us to continue our efforts.

References

Lewontin, Richard C. (1982). *Human Diversity.* New York: Scientific American Books.

King, James C. (1981). *The Biology of Race.* Berkeley: University of California Press.

Gould, Stephen Jay (1981). *The Mismeasure of Man*. New York: Norton.

Leakey, Richard and Roger Lewin (1977). *Origins: What New Discoveries Reveal About The Emergence of Our Species and Its Possible Future*. New York: Dutton.

Chapter 14

May This Circle Be Unbroken: Race and the Teaching of English

by Michael Morgan

In this chapter, the writer, a college English professor, discusses how he has come to believe that the English classroom is a place where the issue of race can become a powerful learning tool. He gives specific examples of how teachers and professors can create lessons which are pertinent to both blacks and whites. It is the belief of the author that students need to grapple with the issue of race as it is confronted in the literature they read, and in their own writing and classroom experiences. Ed.

In a recent visit to an intern high school teacher, I observed a Shakespeare lesson in an eleventh grade classroom. In the class were two black students, twenty-five white students and the white woman teacher, a recent university graduate with a degree in English education. The two black students (both male), much to my despair, sat with their chairs pushed against the back wall, while all the other students sat in a semicircle. The young men had disconnected from the circle by their own volition, according to the intern teacher. She had gotten used to their separation by this point in the year (it was almost Thanksgiving), so that the habit of the boys entering the room, and pushing their chairs to the back had become part of the classroom routine.

When I asked the teacher about the students, the teacher told me that at times, when she had asked the boys to join the circle, they had been disruptive, so she just allowed them to have their own space. "That's where they want to be," she said. What was surprising to her and to the vice principal was that, despite the students' apparent disinterest, they were earning "Bs" in this course–an upper level English class.

It wasn't until I drove the hour and a half back to my university, where I work as an English professor, that I truly pondered the situation. It seemed so utterly symbolic as to what happens in this nation: African-American students placing themselves outside the circle, and white persons in positions of power ignoring the issue, or worse, blaming blacks for failing.

As I drove home, I became emotional. Too often in my own short teaching career I had encountered black students not making it in college. I had for a long time been working actively to heal racism, yet I barely even confronted this intern teacher about the racism I observed. Had I accepted it as well? What should I have said to her? I really didn't know, except that I might have chastised her, and that would serve no practical purpose. I needed concrete things to tell her and to tell any teacher or professor about teaching English and healing racism. I decided I would endeavor to gather all my experiences and ideas, together with concepts I had learned from others, and attempt to have a working and growing strategy to offer for promoting multiracial understanding in my field of English at predominantly white schools and universities. This chapter is my attempt to articulate such a strategy and my attempt to suggest ways that we might confront racism more actively in our everyday teaching life.

A RACIAL ROLE REVERSAL

In reality, as a white person, I can only imagine what it feels like to walk into a classroom and find myself surrounded by people who have often been unsympathetic towards me, or ignorant about me. I can only observe what it is like being an African-American student sitting in a white classroom, being taught by a white teacher. However, any observations that I make about multiracial learning, are firmly founded in two experiences which have made me care deeply, and have led me in my life to pursue racial unity and to fight against racism. I must briefly relate these experiences so that the reader knows the filter through which my eyes view the world. My experiences may suggest why the issue of race is an important one, about which white educators and teachers must become more passionate.

When I graduated from Penn State in 1980, I moved to Norfolk, Virginia, where my aunt and her family had moved one year previously. I was looking for a job, and to a young man from central Pennsylvania–where there were no jobs–moving seemed appropriate. I had never lived in a big city before, and I brought with me the naive stereotypes about black people that so many of us acquire unconsciously; that is, that all blacks are dangerous in the inner city and will try to harm whites if given the opportunity to do so. Yet, I didn't think of myself as "prejudiced" against blacks.

I lived in Norfolk for six months before I was finally interviewed and was hired to help set up and open a bookstore at a new shopping mall. I had no idea how defining this experience would be.

Prior to taking this job, I had made no friends in Norfolk. I had also developed a new stereotype – that white southerners were cold and unfriendly towards "Yankees". Much to my surprise, however, I had generally found the blacks I had encountered in stores or on the streets to be friendly, and I was becoming curious. Black folks were beginning to look far more diverse than my old stereotypes had previously indicated.

Funny the way things work. Of all the people I worked with in setting up the bookstore, there was only one person whom I found interesting. He happened to be the only black person working in the place. After a week of working and talking together, I realized that Ted Liles and I had a lot in common; we shared interests in international politics and in the arts. Beyond that, I could not help but realize that we shared a spiritual bond. Ted Liles would be a spiritual teacher to me in ways that he and I probably knew, but could not articulate.

When Ted invited me to his home for the first time, my aunt warned my about going to the "bad neighborhood". I thought about that as I drove over the Campostella Bridge and through downtown Norfolk to Hampton Boulevard, and into what many would call the ghetto, to where Ted lived on 28th Street. It was scary for me to see that one left turn put me in a different world. I didn't see any white persons and I became tense. Unlike, in the neighborhoods in other parts of this city, the people here were very visible on the streets and I felt they were all watching me. I learned immediately how uncomfortable it must be as "a minority".

As I parked my car and began looking for Ted's house, I thought sure that the people were thinking, "What's that white guy doing here?" I must admit that I wondered that myself. Once I found Ted's house and he greeted me at the door, my guard dropped. In a short time, friends of Ted began dropping by, and before too long I was sitting in the living room as the only white guy among ten black folks. Again, I felt the intimidation of being a "minority," even though everyone was friendly and engaging. I kept wondering what they all really thought of me, and if there was anything I could do or say to let them know that all white people were not bigots and racists.

Little did I know that Ted's house and neighborhood would become my hangout in Norfolk, and that I would often be the only white person among a crowd of African-Americans. Not every black person I met wanted to be my friend, and many black people mistrusted me because of my skin color (and I them). But I became accepted at Ted Liles' house and on his street, and I will never forget how I was treated. When I was told by Ted's sister one evening after dinner, "Mike, you're one of us," my heart was changed forever. Although I was (and still am) battling the racism that is thrust upon us in this society, I had come a long way, to a place many people never get.

I didn't ask for the experience I gained in Norfolk; it really happened on its own, almost by accident. But I now firmly believe that white people need to spend time in places where black culture defines life. More of us need to know what it feels like to be "a minority". More of us need to remember that the minority experience for African-Americans, because of history and because of white domination in the United States, is ten times more intense and threatening than anything that I could experience in inner city Norfolk. The laws and the norms of society always protect us white folks. Nonetheless, I am defined in part as a human being because of what I learned and experienced in Norfolk, and also by a second experience that most whites do not have: living in Africa.

For almost two years, I lived and worked in the Republic of Botswana in Southern Africa. One hardly needs to be reminded that Africa is a continent populated by people of color; pale skinned people like me are "a minority". My time in Africa has changed my life in many ways, and I could not possibly write in these pages what it had done for me. However, what is relevant to the topic here is similar to what I experienced in Norfolk.

In the United States, we live in a world where white folks comfortably make up the majority population. In Africa, black and brown faces are everywhere, doing everything. In the United States, most whites are not in the habit of being a minority, but in Africa and in the larger world (very quickly becoming the American world as well), it is most certainly the case. This realization was for me a very powerful recognition. It was also only the beginning for me in recognizing the reality of race in the world. But it did start me along the path of asking questions that continue to guide me as an educator.

Not everyone can travel to Africa and live amongst non-whites as part of their preparation to teach in high school and college. Perhaps not every white person can even make their way into black neighborhoods of this country for any meaningful length of time. Nor could those experiences be enough to make every teacher and professor healed from the disease of racism. My own racism is still lingering somewhere inside of me, and it tends to worsen when I am in the midst of teaching in a white institution where black people are not often valued.

I confront what many other professors confront. I walk into my English classes each semester, and I see mostly white faces, and I am reminded of the statistics on retention for African-American students, and I wonder why anyone non-white would want to come to a large regional university like this one. I wonder why African-Americans wouldn't want to go to traditionally black schools. But I also know that most African-Americans are like me in Norfolk, or in Africa, looking for a neighborhood and a place to call home, and that there is something I can do to try to create an environment that promotes the inclusion that I experienced.

In this chapter I will discuss race and the English classroom, with a focus on the college setting. However, it is my belief that many of the specific ideas I discuss in a later section of the chapter are applicable to almost any setting. Throughout this chapter, I will use anecdotal information and stories to help illumine the racial situation as I understand it in the college environment. It is my hope that the stories will remind other teachers of situations they may have encountered in their own schools or universities. I wish to remind readers that the issue of race is a very powerful one, and that once one takes on the responsibility of dealing with it there is likely to be an inertia that will begin to energize you. Race and the teaching of English are very compatible, and you will find that learning about racism and addressing it as a teacher inspires the learning of writing, literature and language.

BACKGROUND: COLLEGE ENGLISH DEPARTMENTS

While many African-American students persist and succeed in school, more do not, because white teachers and administrators deny that racism still exists. The history of segregation, busing, separate but equal education, and of hurtful stereotypes continue to scar African-American students and infect many white teachers and administrators. African-American students carry a huge weight on their shoulders in trying to succeed, when historically their talents have been ignored and marginalized. By the time many blacks get to college they are outside the circle, learning from a disadvantaged position, with their seats up against the back wall.

What we must remember is that 70 percent of all black students who enroll in four-year colleges drop out at some point, as compared to 45 percent of all white students (Steele 1992). Many thoughtful ideas and theoretical assumptions are being debated, not only to assist African-American students in college, but also to raise the consciousness and the learning of all students as they relate to race, gender and culture.

These ideas and theories are controversial, and are imbedded in political agendas. For the most part, scholarly ideas concerning race, gender and culture in schools and colleges have done little to address the real problems that we face as professors and teachers in so-called "trenches". As an English professor, I hear and read the arguments of the times, and I wonder how we will ever move forward to help the students. I call a lot of what we do in higher education "trickle down" theorizing. We spend much of our time writing and thinking and debating, and, if we are lucky, a tiny bit of what matters trickles down to the learners. Much of the debate, in fact, has been so controversial that it inhibits any real progress towards eliminating racism and prejudice in universities and schools. Following are some of the issues that help to define departments of English.

1. MULTICULTURALISM: Most of us were schooled in the texts and the ideas of Western Civilization, and our schooling was generally dominated by the men who wrote the stories, the theories and the concepts with which every learned person must be acquainted. Multiculturalism, then, has been an attempt to broaden perspectives so as to include writers and thinkers whose heritage is, for example, African-American. The so-called "multicultural movement" has been eagerly embraced by some who are politically compatible with the idea of "inclusion," and has been opposed by those who feel that multiculturalism imposes a potentially reverse

marginalization of traditional texts.

2. AFFIRMATIVE ACTION: Traditionally, colleges have been populated by a white male faculty, and by a predominance of white students. As in the nation in general, laws have been passed which seek to balance, for example, the number of students of color who teach or study in certain departments. Proponents of affirmative action consider the practice as one that focuses necessary attention on non-white applicants whose credentials might otherwise be overlooked. Opponents of affirmative action regard the process as discriminatory, and suggest that the nature of affirmative action causes an increase in animosity between whites and blacks.

3. BASIC WRITING AND READING (DEVELOPMENTAL ENGLISH): This is a subject that is less known to those outside of English departments. Developmental English exists for students whose skills have been tested and assessed as below average for college. In some universities, developmental English consists of graded courses, and contribute to a student's overall graduation credits. In other universities, developmental English is ungraded and does not contribute to graduation credits. In either case, developmental English tends to be a continuation of "marginalization" for many black students (a shove outside the circle). Many suggest, however, that black students would have no chance to succeed in college without assistance from such courses.

4. "BLACK" ENGLISH: William Labov (1972) began the discussion of "black" English long ago, and his research revealed that "black" English is a legitimate linguistic system, and "not merely a collection of verbal aberrations arrived at by reckless violation of the rules of a so-called superior variety of English." (Gilyard 1991, p. 27) Dialects, whether they be international versions of English, or black English (or west Kentucky English), are unacceptable by the conventional standards of college English departments. Period. Many African-Americans do not, in fact,

speak black English, and resent the stereotyping which occurs because of such labeling. Others consider the recognition of black English as a useful way to acknowledge a specific vernacular, and to assist students who speak it.

5. THE LITERARY CANON: Traditionally, this has been the novels, poem, stories and essays considered most historically meritorious from a literary perspective. In American schools, the cannon is almost exclusively writers from Great Britain and the United States. Despite the arrival of people from Africa, mainland Europe, Asia and places in between, the canon has remained much the same. Some wish to "revise" the canon so as to make sure that students of literature study works of greater ethnic variety (as well as gender). Others believe that the canon should remain mostly as it is–reflecting literary works of traditional artistic merit–and passing along to students the best texts available for the study of the English language and literature.

As a generalist in the field of English, I feel somewhat unqualified to discuss in more detail any of the issues above. As a college professor, I must confess that the debates and scholarly inquiry into the issues of our times in my field intrigue me. But I must also confess that the climate in departments of English, because of these debates, is mostly contentious, which makes it very difficult to promote socio-spiritual ideals like the oneness of humankind, which ought to be our focus for the healing of racism (Rutstein 1991).

It is not difficult to see which of the positions within the above issues are "politically correct," and, because they are such, they are "winning" the battles in English departments and in universities in general. Because the arguments take place without any mention of racism in the lives of the individual professors or students, these theoretical issues end up being divisive. That is not to say that the arguments are not important ones in which to engage, and that the outcomes are not relevant to addressing the issue of race. What is overwhelming, unfortunately, is that the hearts of students and professors are missing from these debates. There are no forums in departments of English for discussing one's own racial healing, and the curriculums often leave no space or create no pedagogy for dealing with real issues of racism in classrooms.

I recall one of our most talented professors asking a question at a symposium last year. The university had devoted an entire semester to a program entitled, "Focus on Africa." It was a good program, composed of writers, scholars and playwrights of color from throughout the world. Our own faculty served on panels for discussion. Students were excused from class to attend and participate. One must, most assuredly, gather such academic knowledge. But when this professor asked her question, I realized that our agenda must also be personal and in academia we have a hard time getting beyond our minds.

The professor, who is a white woman, asked a simple question at one of the panels, on which I happened to be serving. She asked, "Whenever I discuss issues of race in my classroom, I feel, because of the low number of African-American students in my class, that I am putting undue pressure on the students of color to respond and to represent the issue. I feel a bit uncomfortable; how can I deal with that?" It was arguably the most important question asked during the semester-long symposium, and our answers, including my own, were weak and not worth repeating. We did not give her an adequate answer, and I could see the frustration on her face.

I felt frustrated as well. I knew that racism was the reason that discussions were difficult in classrooms. We fear what will happen and who will be uncomfortable when we talk about racism, because we have no history of sharing our feelings in a safe forum. Academic discussions about revising the canon, for example, or about any of the issues outlined above masturbate our minds, but never reach our hearts. There is never room for discussions of questions such as the one brought up by my colleague. My call in this chapter is for a balance of heart and mind.

Since my experiences in Norfolk and in Africa, I knew that I cared about these issues deeply, yet I am only now seeking answers to questions like those raised by my colleague. I've come a long way since the symposium, and since my observation of the intern teacher mentioned at the beginning of this chapter. I know, however, that there will always be new questions.

LEARNING IN A MULTI-RACIAL CLASSROOM

It is a tense time for racial understanding on campuses across the nation. Is it any wonder? We live in a nation in which at any given moment in Los Angeles, or in any other large city, a black man driving in his car, obeying the law, is subject to being pulled over by the police just because he is black. It is a nation in which students in my classes who have been labeled "white" can't understand what the blacks want; they think all is well and that racism is a thing of the past.

In the classes that I teach, I try to counteract the superficial belief systems concerning racism by endeavoring to encourage an open dialogue. I encourage all my students to write about racism, and I try to allow classroom discussions to be safe places for such dialogue to ensue.

Recently, in my advanced composition class, one of the African-American students wrote a personal narrative essay describing her reactions to the Rodney King beating. When I read the essay in a one-on-one conference with her, I asked if she would use it for our large group workshop. She was somewhat hesitant but trusted me enough to share her piece with the class. The student, Alacia Bigham, had not often encountered white professors whom she trusted. It is hard work to establish trust between a white professor and black students, but I believe this is one of the powerful roles that we must undertake as white educators. To establish trust we must empower and amplify voices that are often not heard in traditionally "white" classrooms.

On workshop night in the class, several people had written powerful pieces about issues ranging from AIDS to mid-life crises.

All students bring copies of their work to class, and they are read aloud and discussed. We discuss ways the piece might be revised, and we also react to the piece as one might react to any forum of public discourse; that is, we talk about the content and respond. I try to teach students that they have a voice, and that the classroom is their forum for that voice.

When it came time for Alacia to read her essay, I watched the reactions of the other students and I could see the discomfort exhibited in the body language of many of them. It was the first time they had heard "in person" an African-American make such personal statements about the issue of race. Many of them, in their own circles of friends, had probably discussed race before, but most of them had never addressed the issue in a public forum with both blacks and whites present. When Alacia finished reading, I asked everybody to write down on the back of the paper their reactions, and I told them they would be asked to share those reactions, or that they could "pass" if they chose.

Here is a short excerpt from Alacia's essay.

> We live in a nation that sent an entire army halfway around the world to fight for the human rights of a nation whose population is less than the black population in this country. Yet, we cannot generate enough interest to go across town and stand up for civil rights of fellow Americans. We have campaigns to save the whales, the rain forest, but we have not saved ourselves. It is no longer enough to say, "I don't mistreat anyone, so I'm not part of the problem." Everyone who is not actively a part of the solution is part of the problem.

The discussions that followed were, to my surprise, mostly unrestrained. A few of the younger students "passed," and one young woman (who I will discuss in more detail later) actually left the room in the midst of the discussion. Alacia's essay and each individual's personal reaction to it had liberated everyone so that they could tell stories of their own racial battles. Most of the white students spoke very passionately about confrontations they had had with blacks, or about prejudices they had. It was not neat and clean stuff, but I reminded the students that it was OK to feel uncomfortable.

The real breakthrough reaction came from Otis, one of the older white students. His reaction to Alacia's piece was extremely personal, and it was painfully honest. His job as a wildlife educator at a state park was in jeopardy because of affirmative action, and he was "sick and tired of reverse discrimination, and of blacks complaining of their lot in life." In the time that remained in the class, honest words were spoken from honest hearts, and we felt the liberating nature of our discourse. It set the tone for the remainder of the semester, and, although we still have a long way to go, there was healing begun in that classroom and in that course. Oddly enough, Otis and Alacia, because of their honesty, and because of their personalities, got along very well during the rest of the course, as if they had reached an understanding that they would try to learn from one another.

College classrooms, and most especially English classrooms, must become communities where voices like those of Alacia and Otis are heard and are responded to. Any number of scholars (e.g. Bruffee 1984; Elbow 1981) from the field of rhetoric and composition have written about the role of community in the process of learning to write. Within that theory is the notion that school writing should become part of the public domain, much like a newspaper, so that audience and writer become almost as one. When this happens, the act of writing is shared, so that the community learns from its communicative successes and failures. Hence, learning to write becomes shared, and topics, such as racism, become the "property" of the classroom discourse community.

The community we build in our classrooms must be one that encourages and inspires participation by all its members. Too often, classrooms have unwittingly reflected a cultural bias that excludes blacks and other minorities. By not writing about racism and other topics central to the black experience, we fail to hear voices like Alacia's. Most of the time, it would be far too risky for blacks to write about such topics unless encouraged by their professors or teachers. Yet long ago, W.E.B. DuBois reminded us what college should be for black people:

> Herein the longing of black men must have respect; the rich and bitter depth of their experience, the unknown treasures of their inner life, the strange rendings of nature they have seen, may give the world new points of view and make their loving, living and doing precious to all human hearts. And to themselves in these days that try their souls, the chance to soar in the dim blue air above the smoke is to their finer spirits boon and guerdon for what they lose on earth by being black. (p. 82)

Do we yet know the "unknown treasures of their inner lives?" Are we creating a space to hear those experiences? DuBois wrote in a time when black students attended segregated schools. He wrote in an attempt to establish and maintain those schools. In the present times, predominantly white universities must be reminded of his words, because we do not know the richness and the fullness of what students of color think and know about the world, especially regarding being black in the United States.

Perhaps we have been, as English teachers, too uptight about what we regard as appropriate for the English classroom. We are too interested in training our students to write traditional academic essays. I believe we need to see our purpose as teachers of English as reflecting a broader view of writing, learning and literacy.

Literacy is power and for far too long this power has been denied to African-Americans (and working class whites). So-called academic, or "school" writing (e.g. essays and research papers), must "offer our knowledge not as a means to conformity or submission but as a way to uplift, a way to change society for the better, a way to power." (Holt 1990, p.102) Do we see ourselves, as teachers, aiming to "conform" our students (both black and white) to what we believe is a higher and better literacy? To the exclusion of reading and writing about subjects such as racism that may uplift or educate in a different way?

The well-known Brazilian educator, Paulo Friere, calls the historically literate social class the "namers of the world," and warns us that those namers must not "rob others of their words." (Friere, 1990, p.76) In essence, he is telling teachers to engage in a dialogue with their students, and it is within that dialogue that the world evolves and is "renamed." Freire reminds us that the world is constantly being re-created by us through naming it and renaming it, and he warns us to remember to whose benefit the naming aspires. Creating a dialogue and a discourse on issues of importance to black students renames the world. Omitting such literacy activities constitutes the reinforcement of traditionally naming the world in an exclusive way, which has often meant a racist way.

Teachers, educators, and academics must share a dialogue with their students, most especially with their students of color. The namers of the world have also been obsessed with "correctness" and this focus on correct grammar and spelling has held us back from hearing what students have to say about such topics as racism. Geneva Smitherman, an expert on the question of correctness, writes:

> Language conventions and the English grammar handbooks–which anyone who passes through the American educational system is exposed to–are based on a preoccupation with the all-engrossing question, "What is correct English?" Not: What is dynamic and vivid language? Not: What is contextually appropriate language? Not even: What is truthful language? But simply: What is "correct" language? Such uptight language attitudes, which are fostered in the schools, are grounded in the "doctrine of correctness" that emerged during the eighteenth century. The correctness obsession was a logical consequence of the

coming to power of the "primitive" middle classes and the decline of the "refined" aristocracy in post-Middle Ages Europe. (1977, p. 1886)

Smitherman's insights remind us of our still "uptightedness" in teaching writing, literature and other facets of English and other subjects. Eventually, because of our uptightedness about "correctness" as it relates to grammar, style and genre, we exclude truthfulness. Then, the students, like the African-American boys alluded to in the beginning of this chapter, find themselves outside the circle and turned off by what they find inside of it.

SUGGESTIONS FOR PRACTICE: RACE AND THE TEACHING OF ENGLISH

In my advanced composition course, which I mentioned earlier, I discovered that one young woman could hardly bear the discussion of race in the classroom. She is the person to whom I alluded who left the room during the midst of a difficult deliberation about racial prejudices. She is also a person who, later in the semester, sat at her desk unable to look at an African-American woman doing an oral report about encounters with racism. During the talk, the young white woman sat and flipped through the pages of her datebook with a disgusted look on her face.

I learned a lesson from this student in my struggle to make classrooms places where we can work on healing the many strains of the disease of racism. I learned that many white students have deep-seated prejudices that are not easily overcome. That statement is no surprise, but what I learned is that no matter what I am undertaking in the classroom I must not be so wrapped up in my own beliefs that I do not recognize even the most obvious of problems. I must recognize that students have their own correctness about which they become uptight.

I should have been alerted to the fact that this student was troubled on the night she left the room during our first discussion of racism in advanced composition class. But, as teachers, we (I, in this case) too often do not take time to discuss individual concerns with individual persons. This is, in fact, the first rule of creating a multi-racial classroom; teachers must develop a one-on-one dialogue with every student. The one-on-one contact must be continuous throughout the year, even if it is for just one or two minutes every few weeks. This contact also requires that the teacher be observant.

After the evening that my student fidgeted with her datebook during the oral presentation, I asked to see her. Although I had met with her at least two times during the semester to talk about her writing, I had not once addressed her as a real human being and as a person who was struggling with her own racism. I realized that although I had dealt extensively with the topic of racism in that classroom, I had spoken only to the black students individually about it, and not to the white students.

When I met her in my office I spoke almost immediately to her about her actions during discussions about racism. I believe that I did so in a non-confrontational and soft-spoken manner, but still the tears rolled down her cheeks and she cried for the rest of our time together. She told me that her sister had been dating a black man, and that the man beat her sister, and that she and her family were terribly damaged. That family's view of their personal crisis was one of racial hatred via stereotyping. They are bitter.

As the woman sobbed, she also told me that she knew her beliefs were wrong, but that she couldn't help it. Why hadn't I asked her about this earlier in the semester, I wondered? Maybe her healing needed to begin in just the way it had. But maybe if I had been more personal with her earlier she could have learned more from our classroom discussions, rather than shutting them down. I ended up asking her if she would take time to write about her anger and to put all of her feelings into words, and to not hold back, and I told her that she should include this writing in her end-of-the-semester portfolio to be turned into me in a few days. I also told her that I would only skim the piece (she was very worried that her grade would be affected). I told her I would not read it or make any comments (I might do this differently for other students, depending on the nature of the situation and the timing).

She turned in a piece of writing that was six pages long, handwritten on notebook paper. It was inserted as the last paper in her portfolio, and, as I promised, I did not read it. I did skim the paper, which she entitled, "It'll Take Time to Heal," enough to see the hate that had developed in her heart. She and her entire family had dredged up attitudes about African-Americans which one might think disappeared long ago.

When one teaches one hundred-eighty students per semester, getting to know them is a difficult task, but I wish I had gotten to know this one student better, at an earlier time in the semester. It can be done; good teachers know how to schedule one-on-one conferences effectively, utilizing the time available. Within those conferences with students, especially in the writing classroom, teachers need to ask students how they feel about the topics about which they are writing. Teachers should also be certain to ask white students how they feel about undertaking such assignments as writing about racism. Are they comfortable? Why or why not?

WRITING ABOUT RACISM AND OTHER SUGGESTIONS FOR CLOSING THE CIRCLE

With the above strategy in mind, I offer in the following paragraphs ideas about dealing with racism in the classroom. Some of the suggestions seem especially suited for the English composition classroom, but others are easily adapted to other classrooms. My major emphasis is a somewhat lengthy description of a way to get students writing and thinking about racism. Later, I discuss other strategies and ideas for shaping classroom environments, and for creating classroom assignments, which help foster racism awareness and racial healing.

One Writing Assignment

1. *Writing and Discussing Racism in the Classroom.* There are many ways to think about racism as a topic in the writing classroom. No matter what your idea, the simple suggestion is simply to *do it*. You may find it difficult to initiate a unit on racism, for reasons which have been discussed already; it *is* an uncomfortable topic, but once the dialogue is started it gets easier. Tell the students that it will be uncomfortable, and that you are not totally at ease with it yourself.

Then proceed as follows. On the first day of the "racism unit" get the students to "free write" for a sustained time about their own experiences with racism, or on their opinions about racism in their own university, or in the country generally. You may want to put a couple more specific topics on the board, like, "The Rodney King Incident." Tell the students to write, without worrying about form and content, spelling or grammar. Just write.

Give them at least 15-20 minutes, then break the class into small groups and ask them to share with one another what they wrote about; they can read verbatim if they want, or just relate what they said. Be prepared for some students to feel uncomfortable. It's OK for them to feel that way as long as you are there to help them along. It may be the first time that white students have talked about the subject with black students. Tell the groups to engage in discussion and to disagree with one another if they are so inclined, but to do so with respect for one another's opinions.

During small group sessions get all the students to take notes of their group meeting. Tell them to appoint one student to be the oral reporter who will be called upon to tell the class a summary of topics and discussions pursued by the group. Give the group time to prepare for their report. They should use the collective notes of all the group participants. Judge for yourself how much time you think all of this will take. When you feel it's time–when everybody in the small group has had a chance to talk and that one person from each group is ready to report–call the class together.

You then call on each group to make its report; help the

reporter along if he struggles. As the reporter from each group speaks, no cross talking between groups or between persons is allowed. You act as a recorder and put lists of all the items from each group on the blackboard. Be creative and allow each group to generate what you will soon call "topics". For example, someone might say, "We discussed 'reverse discrimination' and we all had strong feelings that blacks get too much priority these days." You write on the board: Validity of Reverse Discrimination. After the last group has reported, get students to write down all the "topics" listed on the board.

Then ask the students to make a written response to any one of the newly generated topics (many of the students will be very ready to respond in writing because they were permitted only to listen previously). Tell them they should try to respond to any *one* of the topics from the board. They may do it right in class if there is time, or the students may do it at home. Remind them that they are to respond freely (as with their first writing); this isn't yet a formal essay. All the writing they will be doing so far is just free writing; no one except them will yet see the writing. They can respond in anger or in agreement or in any other way they choose. The response should be a "free" writing of at least 25-30 minutes.

By now, you should be into another class period (although you could just take a break if you are teaching a longer class period), and students will have generated a good deal of "raw" material, that being their own personal racism writing and the response assignment. This writing is the basis for an essay which will eventually communicate to an audience beyond the individual writer. Assign the students the task of writing a first draft. When they've completed their drafts, collect all the work and plan to meet with them individually and discuss. As mentioned earlier, I have not always been sensitive enough to know how white students view this type of assignment, but I will start addressing this more carefully. Mostly, however, the conferences are for talking about their draft, and suggesting ways to revise them.

After students revise, I have them bring their papers to class to share in small groups. After small-group critiquing, we have a whole-class discussion. I solicit some of the topics about which students read in the writing of their classmates, and we discuss them. This becomes a time when great learning takes place; when students' positions on these issues begin to evolve. It is, for example, a time when the subject of "reverse discrimination" will begin to look differently to students. It is a time when you, as instructor, can subtly add some of your own thoughts to encourage the evolution of thinking.

The students then revise once more. They should have received some suggestions from their small groups, and should be influenced also by the large-group discussion. After the second revision, I ask permission from several of the students to make copies of their work to use for the whole class. I call this, "Large Group Workshop." At this point, students engage in lengthy discussions of student writing, where we attempt to understand the issue of racism by using *student* texts. I advise you to use as many of the student texts in this unit on racism as time allows you. Encourage students to keep revising as they get responses from the class.

This is my "recipe" for one writing assignment and, in fact, for a whole unit on racism. The assignment serves as a means to improve writing skills and writing processes, while also challenging students to confront race. The recipe can be altered any way you like, but the important part is to get students writing, thinking, and discussing. Remember that this is a "hot" topic, so you'll need to remind students that the unit will require everyone to be gentle with one another. Everyone needs to feel "safe" writing whatever he wants.

Suggestions for Creating the Right Environment

2. *Using Music in the Classroom.* Music in the classroom? Yes, begin every class with a song. Play tapes or CDs while students are composing. One of the purposes of using music is to allow the classroom to become a model of diversity–a place where many different kinds of music will be played. The study of writing and

English generally intimidates students, including many of the African-American students. Using contemporary music and encouraging students to bring in their own tapes and disks helps make the classroom safe for students. I usually adopt a "theme" song every semester, and I choose songs by the reggae artist Bob Marley, or songs by popular artists from Africa. There are also many contemporary songs which focus on the issue of race which you may want to use for class discussions, and for informal writing assignments.

3. *The Handshake.* I have learned to make shaking hands a part of my classroom routine; it helps in welcoming all students into the day's events. On the first day of class, I go around the room and shake hands with every student and remind them that I will do this at each and every class meeting. It helps make the classroom a community in which all members feel more comfortable. It may take you a few minutes every day to do this, but it will allow you to make contact in a personal way with every student. This process is especially important when teaching so-called low achieving or at risk students, many of whom are black, because it gives them a sense that you care about them and about their success in the class.

4. *Creating Mentor Relationships.* I try to undertake individual relationships with black students whenever possible. I am upfront with African-American students in my classes, and explain in a one-on-one conference that I have an interest in seeing African-American students succeed. I tell them that I want to know throughout the semester how they are doing in all of their classes. Black students need to know that at predominately white universities, white professors care. At the same time, one must be careful and thoughtful so as not to condescend; many black students have been stereotyped in their secondary schools by white teachers who assume that the students don't care about school. This has damaged the students. I must add that many good people who have liberal beliefs fail to challenge black students. Being a mentor means

getting to know a student's capabilities and then challenging him to achieve.

5. *Home Field Advantage.* I tell all the students in my English classes that "the home crowd" is on their side. We all pull for each other to succeed, and we seek to work as a team to that end. That's why we play music and shake hands and address issues, such as race, that might not be addressed anywhere else. This class is home field and while we might not always win, the odds are in our favor.

Other Ideas for Teaching

6. *Race Awareness Reading Project.* Assigning short stories is not new to English teachers. Perhaps assigning two or three specifically to deal with racism is somewhat unusual. The objective of this assignment can be to help students learn to write "literary" essays, but a second and equally important agenda can be to use the literature to write and think about racial issues. There are many stories to consider. A few are: James Baldwin's "Sonny's Blues," Flannery O'Connor's "Everything That Rises Must Converge," Reginald McNight's "The Kind of Light That Shines on Texas," John Edgar Wideman's "Little Brother," and Langston Hughes' "Professor". They invite students to empathize with black characters and to think critically about what racial identity means in the United States. One can also assign African literature–you don't need to be an "expert" on it. A few good choices are *The Collection of Treasures* (short stories from Botswana), by Bessie Head, *Kaffir Boy* (autobiography of a South African black), by Mark Mathabane, and *Bones* (a novel about the struggle for liberation in Zimbabwe).

7. *Writing About Films.* Viewing films such as *Do the Right Thing,* or *Boyz 'n the Hood* work similarly to short stories. Remember, the objective is to expand consciousness of white students while at the same time making African-American students feel more empowered in the classroom. Films, being contemporary visual artifacts, work

well to accomplish both things. As with the short stories, students can write responses, or essays, which explain cinematic and thematic aspects of the films.

8. *African American Topics*. Black students will succeed when topic choices in writing classes include ones which are relevant to them. This has been covered to some degree in this chapter. If we give students choices of topics that include things such as "Malcolm X's Contribution to the Civil Right's Movement," "The Significance of Churches in Black Communities and Neighborhoods," or "The Artistic Merit of Rap Music" we will see potentially dramatic upward assessment of blacks. Be conscious of topics, and have suggestions ready to give students who seem to be struggling trying to decide what to write.

9. *Cross Cultural Interview Project*. This is a racial/ethnic "journalism" project I've used in writing classes. I assign students the task of interviewing someone of a different racial or ethnic background, and then ask them to write up their discoveries. It's remarkable that students think they know everything about other races, and then come away from this assignment realizing there was a lot they didn't know. The first step in this project is to get students to come up with good questions–a balance of questions which will make them realize that there are differences in cultural aspects of life, but also that there are many things which they didn't realize were *the same*. Have the class brainstorm questions together in class then have them go "out into the field" and do some research; they can use tape recorders if they want. Give them a day off from class to do their interviews, and then have them bring their "raw data" back to class and discuss some of the things that were discovered. They should then work toward a finished piece. They may want to include some autobiographical information in order to compare and contrast.

10. *Encountering Racism Through Writing*. This is an informal writing

assignment, meant only to give people a forum for talking about racism. While you may use this assignment to inspire longer, more formalized writing assignments, it can be used independently, just as a way to use writing to explore feelings and experiences. Students are asked to anonymously write short responses to the following questions: (1) recount a time when you have acted in a racist way; (2) recount a time when you saw someone else act in a racist way and did nothing about it; (3) recount a time that you experienced racial unity. Collect all responses, type them, and then make copies for everyone. Pass out the responses so that each student gets a copy of all of them. This exercise does two things remarkably well: it reminds us that racism is alive and well in the actions of people all around us, and it shows how emotionally satisfying it is to read the stories of racial unity.

To summarize, I would remind the reader of two things: (1) strive to make every English course devoted in some way to the discussion and the ongoing healing of racism, and (2) go out of your way to be sensitive to the needs of black students in your classes. To do the latter, some of the ideas discussed above will be helpful but some may not; black students *need to be asked* what their needs are.

As for the healing of racism, it is so powerful an issue that it will most assuredly enhance whatever else it is that you want to teach. The best writing in my composition class occurs when students delve into the racism issue. Students often get so wrapped up in their work on this topic that, by measure of shear *involvement*, they learn more than if they were writing a traditional freshman theme.

As for literature, a recent class I taught is indicative of what can happen. Of all the short stories and philosophical essays we read during the semester, none were remembered more lucidly by students than the stories that dealt with racism (see suggestion 6 above). How do I know? When it came time to write the final exam and I asked students to explain the one thing they felt they had learned about the most in the class, an overwhelming number of them talked about race and about the unity of humankind. Those stories that dealt directly with that issue were the ones they could explain and detail with the most lucidity. I realize that the teacher's emphasis may have had something to do with that. However, it is not difficult for me to conclude that, because of that emphasis, the students enhanced their abilities as critical readers and thinkers while, at the same time, addressing the most crucial social issue of our time.

CONCLUSION

One of my colleagues recently said to me, "Don't you think the blacks would be better off if they would integrate more with the white students?" She had observed that most of the African-American students in our university attend classes and socialize with one another exclusively. I responded, "No, it's a pretty unsafe world out there."

I believe this is still very much the case for black students. Our schools and classrooms often must seem to them uncomfortable, and even threatening, especially when there are so few black teachers and so little concern for issues of relevance to black people. In fact, this anecdote from a black friend of mine may sum it up well. She told me that she and a friend were invited to a party which would be attended by both blacks and whites. Her friend said she didn't feel up to it. "It's too much like work to be with white folk," she said.

Yes, in some ways we are living only the myth of segregation in education and in our nation, mostly because we have never seriously addressed and confronted the issues of race and culture that will allow us to practice being one people. If we can't do that in school and college, then where will we do it?

Our students are in many ways far ahead of us, if we only help them along a little. Unlike those of us who are one or two generations removed from college age, our students live in a world in which true equality has more potential than ever before to become a reality, and I believe that our students sense it. They sense how different it is than when their parents were their age, and they know in their hearts that old stereotypes are no longer relevant.

But they need our encouragement as teachers to give them the will to complete the change. They need to read and write about this issue and grapple with it so that their generation will be the one that ushers in a new vision of understanding. Many of our white students have black friends and black acquaintances, yet know nothing of the disease of racism in either its historical or present day manifestations. These friendships and acquaintances often fail because our white and black students do not have the opportunity to think, write and talk together. Composition and literature courses are the perfect forum for this sharing.

In closing, I will share something personal, something not directly related to teaching English, but something that represents for me the potential for racial unity. Last semester, a message was left on my answering machine. It was from one of my former students, a black man. His message was that the brothers of Alpha Phi Alpha, a black fraternity, would like me to serve as their faculty advisor. The message brought tears to my eyes. Although I never much cared for fraternities, I was overwhelmed by the gesture of unity expressed by these young men. I pray each day that I can make a difference, and this gesture on the part of Alpha Phi Alpha represented an opportunity for me to model unity.

I mention all of this as a conclusion, because, sooner or later, realities occur out of what we believe, and, most importantly, out of what we do as teachers. As college professors, we can reach out and set examples in our teaching and elsewhere that will become a positive confirmation for our students–the next generation. They need to see us doing what they hope they can do, and they need to trust us enough, to be able to believe that something better is possible.

References

Baldwin, J. (1957). "Sonny's Blues." In J. Baldwin, *Going to Meet the Man*. New York: Doubleday.

Bruffee, K. (1984). "Collaborative Learning and the 'Conversation of Mankind'." *College English*, 46, 635-652.

Du Bois, W.E.B. (1990). *The Souls of Black Folks*. New York: Vintage Books.

Elbow, P. (1981). *Writing with Power*. New York: Oxford University Press.

Friere, P. (1990). *Pedagogy of the Oppressed* (M. Bergman Ramos, translator). New York: Continuum.

Gilyard, K. (1991). *Voices of the Self: A Study of Language Competence*. Detroit: Wayne State University Press.

Head, B. (1977). *The Collectors of Treasures*. Portsmouth, N.H.: Heinemann Educational Books.

Holt, T. (1990). "Knowledge is Power" The Black Struggle for Literacy. In A. A. Lunsford, H. Moglen, J. Slevin (Eds.), *The Right to Literacy*. New York: Modern Language Association.

Hove, C. (1988). *Bones*. Portsmouth, N.H.: Heniemann Educational Books.

Hughes, L. (1971). "Professor." In L. Hughes, *The Ways of White Folks*. New York: Random House.

Labov, W. (1970). *The Study of Nonstandard English*. Urbana, Ill.; National Council of Teachers of English.

McNight, R. (1992). "The Kind of Light That Shines in Texas." In R. McKnight, *The Kind of Light That Shines in Texas*. Boston: Little, Brown & Co.

Mathabane, M. (1987). *Kaffir Boy: The True Story of a Black Youth's Coming of Age in Apartheid South Africa*. New York: Penguin Books.

O'Connor, F. (1964). "Everything That Rises Must Converge." In F. O'Connor, *Everything That Rises Must Converge*. New York: Farrar, Straus & Girouz.

Rutstein, N. (1992). *Education on Trial*. Oxford: One World Publications Ltd.

Smitherman, G. (1977). *Talkin' and Testifyin'; The Language of Black Americans*. Detroit: Wayne State University Press.

Steele, C. M. (1992). "Race and the Schooling of Black Americans." *The Atlantic Monthly*, March 68-78.

Wideman, J. E. (1989). "Little Brother." In J. E. Wideman, *Fever*. New York: Viking Penguin.

Chapter 15

Cooperative Learning and Racial Harmony: Working Together with a Difference

by Lynn Kirk

The writer, an adult education instructor, describes how "cooperative learning" can be used to allow persons of different races to work and learn together within the context of a college course. She explains how cooperative learning mimics situations in life in which a person has to work creatively with other people for the collective good. She discusses a theory of using cooperative learning which provides students with the opportunity, and the necessity, of working with people who are different from themselves. Ed.

I suspect that if Helen and Mark had met in any other way, they would have spent the remainder of their lives trying to avoid each other. But Helen and Mark, by my choosing, ended up in the same cooperative learning team in my writing class two years ago, and they had to work with one other person in a three-person team to produce a piece of writing. They collided from the first moment that they met.

To say that Mark and Helen were different would be an understatement. Helen, now a graduate of the Cambridge College master's program in the college where I teach, is an African-American woman, about forty years old, and a single parent. She does AIDS training for the local division of the state funded Family Planning Council. She is bright, witty, articulate, and speaks her mind freely.

Mark is a Anglo-American man about thirty-five. He is married and has two children; his wife is a full-time mother and homemaker. Mark is a religious man; he is a faithful church-goer and mentions his religious commitment often, both in writing and in his comments in class. He is a sales manager for a large marketing firm, and has made his way to a position of significance in a relatively short period of time.

Soon after the semester began two years ago, Helen's team lost one member, who dropped the class, and I moved Mark over from his four-person team to restore the threesome. Helen's team had only met once to work on the writing project; I assumed they were not so far along that they couldn't adjust to a new member. Inadvertently, I created a disaster.

Now, with two years worth of hindsight, Helen shares her perceptions about Mark's arrival the team. "It was frustrating, very frustrating," she said. "I saw Mark as a white, male chauvinist. He was used to control, and he just jumped right in and wanted to impose himself... without waiting to see what the direction the team had already taken."

Helen says that she made a conscious decision not to go into "head to head" combat with him. "I can be pretty controlling myself," she said. She reports that she deferred when he spoke, despite her inclination to do differently.

Mark speaks of his arrival on the team. "They wanted it to run their way; they didn't want an outsider." And he thinks that he backed off and deferred to Helen and Yvette's already established direction for the work. "Almost immediately Helen and I went like this" (he rams his two fists into one another to illustrate the collision); so I backed off. I think that Helen backed off a little, but then she started taking control again... Helen and I are very much alike; we both like to facilitate. I just wanted to get the work done."

Despite the interpersonal snags, the work moved forward. Helen, Mark and Yvette faxed drafts back and forth on a daily basis, but, by their own admission, were far from satisfied with the quality of the piece they were composing. Helen talks about the two-fold frustration of not being able to reconcile personal differences, and not being able to produce a satisfying piece of writing, either. She has since pondered the cause and effect of those two factors, but has come to no conclusion.

The team called me in to help when the semester was almost over. I worked with their interactive styles briefly, but by that time they were exhausted and just wanted to get the essay written and handed in. I helped them focus on the writing, and they eventually submitted an essay that we all found minimally acceptable. Helen and Mark ended the semester with an unspoken understanding that they would try to avoid each other in the future.

If the story ended here, I would consider the team effort a relative failure, and I would conclude that I had erred in not intervening sooner. But the story does not end here. Three months went by and, in the fall of that same calendar year, Mark and Helen found themselves in another class together. Helen describes their reunion. "All of a sudden he was very happy to see me; I was one of his friends. As painful as it had been, he felt a kinship with me. We had struggled through something together and made it. I don't know whether he really got it that I had been totally frustrated... but he told me a little about himself, about his background, his family, his religious commitment... We were OK. Mark was a man I didn't want to have anything to do with, and never be in a team with. I wanted to turn my back on him. But I didn't do that. We worked in that last class and we wound up appreciating each other in the end. It felt like a positive experience... When I think about the last time I saw Mark, he gave me a hug and I remember thinking, 'Oh God, have we come a long way.'"

Mark tells a similar story about their reunion that fall, and adds, "We have a friendship now. There's a mutual respect. We know that we have very strong temperaments and we clash a little. But it's a friendly clash. I have a lot of respect for Helen."

The Context: Cambridge College

A major factor in the success of the Mark and Helen story has to do with the context in which it all happens. Cambridge College is an institution dedicated to bringing together people who are different. I consider myself fortunate to be teaching there.

Cambridge College is a small, (1200 students) private, nonprofit school which serves professional adults who are returning to school mid-life, mid-career. The main campus is located in Cambridge, Massachusetts (hence the name), and a smaller campus is located in Springfield, Massachusetts. Only twenty years old, Cambridge College was founded on principles of access and diversity. The mission statement reads, "By design, Cambridge College attracts a student body diverse in ethnicity, race, economic status and educational and personal experiences. . . and provides an adult learning model in which. . . personal and professional life experiences (are brought) into the classroom."

Current demographics at the college make the point. Sixty percent of the student body are women; 40 percent are people of color. Three of the four department chairs are people of color; the president is a woman, and 50 percent of the higher level administrators are black and Hispanic. Almost 80 percent of the admissions representatives are black, and the chairman of the Board of Trustees is a African-American man. I don't know many schools like that.

The commitment to diversity shows in other ways, as well. Several years ago our staff and faculty underwent two full days of intensive training. So that everyone could participate, the college hired substitutes to cover the phones and front desk. There's more. A course on diversity is a *requirement* for the graduate management degree, and the college offers an elective course entitled "Diversity in the Classroom Promoting the Oneness of the Human Family" in the graduate level teachers' education program.

What is significant about the school's commitment, however, is the Diversity Committee on the Springfield campus. This committee's primary responsibility is to support faculty in its on-going efforts to address issues of diversity in the classroom. The committee comprises three faculty members, who plan and execute training sessions specifically for the faculty.

What is particularly striking is that these training sessions are on-going. Some of the most well-intentioned efforts to address diversity make the mistake of producing one-time or sporadic events. I believe that the problem of race in this country warrants continuous effort. It's relatively easy to respond to a dramatic event with dramatic efforts. When the Los Angeles riots broke out in the spring of 1992, there was a public outcry, and much attention was paid to the problem of racial injustice in this country. But once the drama of the moment died down, so did the enthusiasm to do something about it. Race problems need to be addressed on a day-to-day basis; it's the day-to-day nature of oppression that wears out the soul and wearies the heart.

The Cambridge College Diversity Committee, designed to address issues of race on an on-going basis, is key to growth and development in the college. As the teacher in the classroom, it would have been easy for me to be discouraged about Mark and Helen. I watched them in their struggle and worried about what would happen. The uncertainty is understandable; we're working on a social frontier.

Several months ago the Diversity Committee conducted an in-house workshop to address specific issues of race. Faculty were given three scenarios which illustrated different kinds of encounters; faculty were asked how they might handle each situation. One scenario was about several African-American students pointing out that the text book was culturally biased. Another was a situation where an Anglo woman tells the instructor that she feels uncomfortable working with an African-American male. The third was a situation where several students of color tell their white instructor that some of her language is racist.

Faculty read the three scenarios and broke into small groups for discussion. I don't know that anyone at this stage of the game came up with answers. What was valuable was that faculty had a forum to put the dilemmas on the table, and begin to examine ways of handling specific situations.

Teaching "Diversity in the Classroom": Some Real Life Experiences

I am one-third of the team that teaches the "Diversity in the Classroom" course mentioned earlier. The single most consistent theme among all of the teachers who take the course is that they are afraid to address issues of race because they are worried that they won't be able to manage the situation. They fear that it will somehow blow up in their faces. (And it can.) They ask, "What do you do when your students bring up race?" "Do you encourage it?" "How can you say what you think is right and not offend people?" "What do you do if the situation gets out of hand?" "And what do you do if you make a mistake?"

Last semester I had a class that was about half black, half white. The group had been together for two successive semesters, and there was a high level of trust among them. At the last meeting of the course, students were making presentations on individual learning experiences that they had contracted for and carried out individually. One student had written a book for children and conducted research on children's reactions to her book. As she began her presentation, she passed out copies of her manuscript, fully illustrated, to her fellow students and myself.

Her work was well organized, carefully executed and the presentation was excellent. As I sat there with my copy of her manuscript in front of me, however, I was thinking fast and furiously about what I should do. All of the illustrations in her book were white people. The presentation was coming to an end, and I was paying far more attention to my internal dialogue about how to handle the situation than I was to what she was saying. I ran through my options.

I could pull her aside privately after class and mention it to her. Or, I could do nothing (that was easiest). I could pray that one of the African-American students would mention it, and then I could support his comment. A thousand thoughts ran through my head. Maybe the African-American students don't notice. Will the white students say to themselves, "Oh no, here we go again with this race stuff?" Will I create a disruption that undermines the supportive atmosphere of this last night of class? And what message will I send if I say nothing? In the end, what pushed me to decide to say something was a commitment to role model, for white people, a more proactive position. I rehearsed a few decent possible comments; my heart was pounding.

Timing mattered. If she finished her presentation and we moved on to the next person, my decision would be made for me. Cathy finished and walked to her chair; her classmates were still applauding her work and none of the African-American students had noted the illustrations. She sat down and the words, almost involuntarily, came out of my mouth.

"This is fine work, Cathy," I said and offered a few specific, positive comments about the story and the research. "I have one thought about the illustrations, however," I said "I assume children of many different races will read your book and I wonder if they will get the wrong impression. Will they look at the illustrations and think that this story is only about white people? I doubt that that was your intention."

It worked. Cathy said that she wanted to make the book appropriate for all children and that she had overlooked that aspect. One of the African-American students added his comment, and another classmate thanked Cathy for her willingness to see the situation differently.

Opportunities like that present themselves frequently in the classroom, but faculty need a certain level of clarity and confidence to address them. That doesn't come easy; I sweated a good three minutes before I made my comment, knowing that the situation could have gone wrong in several different directions.

The other night in my writing class I was setting up a mock situation for a case study exercise, and I made a statement that was grossly Eurocentric. I was in essence asking everyone to put themselves in the shoes of a white person. At the time I didn't hear it. The exercise I was using was new to me, and I was concentrating on whether I had given the students enough information to do the assignment properly. That, by the way, is when my ingrained Eurocentrism is most likely to slip out – when my mind is not paying attention to its Eurocentric training.

Ruth, an African-American woman, raised her hand. "I'm sorry, Lynn," she said, "I just can't pretend to be Anglo; I just can't do that." I felt terror in my heart. I suspect it showed on my face. I apologized, thanked her for making the comment, and quickly reconstructed the case study so that the writer could choose to be of any ethnicity.

At the break, I went over to her. "Ruth," I said, "Thank you so much for saying something. I hope you will always let me know when something I say makes you uncomfortable. I'm terribly sorry for my error, and I appreciate your calling it to my attention. Please don't hesitate to do it again".

I felt terrible; in fact, the bad feelings lingered over into the next day. But I think that discomfort comes with the territory. I think it's about taking risks, making mistakes sometimes, and trusting that we will work the misunderstandings out together. It would be easier to never mention race, and let the students cluster in small racially homogeneous teams, and teach them writing. But I think that classrooms, because they reflect so much of what is real in life, provide us with an opportunity to help students figure out how to get along better in the world. I think we would be remiss if we let that opportunity pass us by. It is in this context that I use "cooperative learning" as a way to promote racial harmony.

Learning is the Focus

Cooperative learning is not a classroom strategy that has as its major purpose the promotion of racial harmony. Cooperative learning's major purpose is to promote learning. It does; and that's why I use it. My most important obligation as a classroom teacher is to teach my students to learn to write. Cooperative learning helps me to do that.

Cooperative learning's ability to promote racial harmony and probably works best *because* it is a secondary gain. Its effectiveness, I suspect, is due in large part to the fact that it works indirectly. In the process of seeking information, looking for answers, and solving problems, students suspend momentarily their preconceived notions about racial superiority, and attend to the business at hand. In the interests of getting the work done, they use each other as resources; skin color, socioeconomic background, and gender fade as criteria for meaningful interaction. What takes over is a desire to do the work well together. Eventually, over time, attitudes change for the better.

The story of Rod and Denise provides an example. Rod is a African-American male about thirty-five years of age; Denise is a white female, also about thirty-five. I had formed eight teams of two in the classroom this particular night to do a "pass-a-problem" exercise which I will explain in detail in a later section of this chapter. Rod and Denise were one of the eight dyads.

For this pass-a-problem exercise, each dyad was given an essay that needed some editing. The team was to decide how they would change the essay to improve it. Rod and Denise were working on an essay about classism, and were trying to decide how to change the thesis statement so that it better reflected the main point of the piece. This is the essay's first paragraph:

"Recently, there has been renewed focus in the media of the growing gap between the upper and lower income groups in the United States. With the election of a new president, there is hope that the disparity between these 'classes' can be diminished. It is unlikely one person will be able to accomplish such an enormous task. (Thesis statement:) Unfortunately, classism has been an inevitable course in American history."

As I traveled around the room eavesdropping on the teams, I

could feel that there was "heat" in Rod and Denise's corner. A discussion was underway as they tried to rewrite the thesis statement. I watched carefully without appearing to watch carefully. The conversation was animated, but each seemed to be respectful of what the other was saying. I decided not to interfere, but to check it out later.

The next time that the class met, I asked Rod and Denise to talk to me during the break. I asked them what had happened, what they were talking about, and how and if they had resolved the matter. They were happy to explain.

They said that they had been working on the last sentence of the paragraph, trying to find the right words. They considered replacing it with, "Classism has been and continues to be a part of the American tradition." But Rod had called the word "tradition" into question, and thought "culture" would work better. Rod said that at the time he had some trouble articulating why he objected to the word tradition, but he did. In retrospect, he said, it it had to do with race prejudice. Tradition, for him, was tied to old ways of doing things, and that included racial injustice. He didn't want to use the word "tradition", because it seemed to sanction a way of life that has been painful. He was interested in change, not tradition.

Denise, on the other hand, explained that "tradition" to her meant Christmas packages and Fourth of July celebrations, and that she liked those aspects of American life. Race prejudice had never entered her mind.

What was important in both discussions was that Rod and Denise could understand each other's opinion. In the previous class and in conversations with me, each was making a sincere effort to understand the other. Denise had never had her concept of "tradition" challenged, and it is to her credit that she never became defensive. "We got along well," said Rod, speaking of the incident. "We both tried to see what the other meant. In the end, we simply agreed to disagree. I think we needed more time."

They did need more time. It takes time. They made a beginning. And each heard the other's perspective. That they could even agree to disagree is a far cry from never having the chance to explain what the word "tradition" means for different people.

Contact Theory

> . . . blacks and whites share responsibility for (undoing racism). Whites must guarantee a free and fair society. But blacks must be responsible for actualizing their own lives." (Steele, 1990, p. 34)

Creating a situation that will enable students who are different from one another to work cooperatively is not necessarily an easy thing to do. I know lots of teachers who put students together in groups, and give them a problem to solve or a project to work on, but I seldom see legitimate cooperation under those circumstances. In fact, what I often see is group members moving themselves into familiar positions of leaders and followers – much like what already happens in the larger society. That situation I think is problematic. While some people do have natural tendencies toward leadership positions, and some simply prefer to be followers, in today's culture too much of who does what is a factor of race and gender, not ability and talent.

Cooperative learning structures, by their very nature, work against what, for our students, is largely learned behavior about leading and following. Cooperative learning structures promote new behaviors based on shared responsibility and working together in harmony.

The reason that cooperative learning structures are successful in this way is that cooperative learning rests on a theoretical foundation called "contact theory." Contact theory was developed by Gordon Allport, author of *The Nature of Prejudice.* (1954), a book that played a key role in the hearings for Brown vs. the Board of Education. *The Nature of Prejudice* describes what race prejudice is, explains how it is a learned phenomena and prescribes an antidote for "unlearning."

Contact theory evolved from Allport's observations of racially mixed groups. Allport concluded that when racially mixed groups interact successfully, three conditions are consistently present: (1) the members of the group perceive each other as being equally valuable, (2) there is support for the group from some larger authority outside of the group, and (3) group members have a common focus. Allport further noted that when any one of these three conditions is absent, racially mixed groups of people become competitive, or worse, hostile.

In a classroom setting, these three conditions work this way:

1. **Perceived equal status.** All team members regard every other team member as equally important in their efforts to successfully do the work. It is more difficult for "perceived equal status" to be put into practice than either of the other two conditions. Initially, prejudice keeps team members from regarding each other as equals. Time, however, makes a difference and team members' perceptions of each other become equal as the work goes on (Slavin 1977; Slavin and Oickle 1981).

2. **Institutionally sanction.** The teacher and the institution show obvious signs of support for racially mixed teams. When I sat down with Rod and Denise to ask about their discussion of the word "tradition," I was mostly interested in understanding what had happened. But inviting our conversation sent an important signal from teacher to students: this is good; these conversations are important.

3. **Common Interests/Common Humanity.** The cooperative learning exercise exploits those things that team members have in common. With Mark and Helen, both highly motivated students, the writing exercise exploited their common interest in producing a quality piece of writing. The work progressed when they decided to put aside their dislikes for each other and get the essay done.

It is important to note two things. First, that these three conditions of contact theory are not necessarily pre-conditions. They are really emerging conditions and a cooperative learning team begins with some measure of each of those. As the team matures, however, these conditions augment. They are actually recursive and success begets success.

Second, that contact alone, lacking the three conditions that promote racial harmony, has the potential of doing more harm than good (Allport 1954, Amir 1969). If a team of students, for example, never regarded each other as equals, never valued equally what each person brought to the process, the results would be neutral at best and divisive at worst. Allport (1954) himself says, "Contact, as a situational variable, cannot always overcome the personal variable in prejudice" (p. 280), and, referencing Williams (1942), that "when segregation is the custom, contacts are casual, or else firmly frozen into superordinate-subordinate relationships. . . such contact does not dispel prejudice; it seems more likely to increase it." (p. 263)

Cooperative Learning Defined

Clearly, cooperative learning is something beyond mere contact.

Definition: cooperative learning is structured teamwork, with a "we all sink or we all swim" philosophy, in which the acquisition of social skills is as important as the mastery of the subject matter.

In other words, students are put into teams. Team members work together to achieve a very specific goal. Roles are assigned and rotate among team members. The ideal cooperative learning lesson is followed by team processing, where students examine their behaviors and assess their interactive patterns. Cooperative learning is not what many educators call "group work." Cooperative learning is much more carefully crafted, much more structured.

Nor is cooperative learning synonymous with "collaborative learning", a term that educators use frequently today. Collaborative learning, as I make the distinction, is an umbrella term for a variety of educational approaches involving "joint, intellectual effort" by students with other students, or students and teachers together (Smith and MacGregor 1992, p. 10). Cooperative learning is the most structured of the many approaches that fall under the collaborative learning umbrella. I like all of the collaborative learning approaches, and use most of them from time to time. I have a particular affinity for cooperative learning for reasons that I will elaborate upon shortly.

Two critical features of cooperative learning are what practitioners refer to as "positive interdependence" and "individual accountability." Together, they create the philosophical balancing-act between "we are all in this together," and "ultimately I am accountable for myself." "Positive interdependence" describes the relationship between members of the team; it means that team members care about each other and need each other to succeed. Positive interdependence is built into the cooperative learning lesson by, for example, having students drill each other on the material, or limiting paper and pencils so that they must be shared. "Individual accountability" refers to the fact that ultimately every student is responsible for his own work. Cooperative learning builds individual accountability into lessons by having students take tests by themselves, and giving individual grades.

Appealing Features of Cooperative Learning

There are several features of cooperative learning that I find particularly appealing because they provide students with an opportunity to practice important social skills. Cooperative learning exercises, carefully executed and adequately processed, help students (1) to figure out how to manage the balancing act between self and other, (2) how to share influence, rather than grapple for power, and (3) how to use each other as resources in an open, honest fashion. Cooperative learning, for me, is about "doing life." I will elaborate on each of these three.

1. Managing the Balancing Act Between Self and Other

Cooperative learning structures mimic those situations in life where a person has to work creatively with other people, but ultimately be responsible for his own choices. I believe that most of us in this society, which has preached rugged individualism for so many years and spurned signs of "giving in" to the collective good, don't know how to do the balancing act between self and other.

I am reminded of the American reaction to Maksaka Owada's decision to set aside her professional aspirations and marry the crown prince of Japan a few years ago. Americans rather consistently saw her as having "succumbed" to tradition. On the contrary, I saw her as having masterminded the balancing act between her personal ambitions and a desire to serve the collective good.

As educators, I think that we owe it to our students to help them discover how to do that balancing act. If not in the classroom, where else can students, young and adult, get practice at working with people who are different from themselves while discovering what they personally need and want.

The story of Helen and Mark comes to mind once again. Each of them struggled with how to balance his own need for leadership with the other person's need to do the same. In Mark's words, "The problem was that we were alike; we both like to be in charge." In the context of wanting to get the work done, Helen and Mark decided, independently of each other, how much to give and how much to take.

2. Encouraging Shared Influence

A second appealing feature of cooperative learning is that it encourages shared influence and undermines the temptation to create stars. It does this by assigning, and then rotating roles. There are usually four cooperative learning role designations in a team: facilitator, timekeeper, materials person and note taker. Different roles require different skills and abilities and team members eventually get a chance to do it all. The role assignments and role rotation are not necessarily comfortable for everyone at first, but students eventually get better at doing all of them, and develop a broader repertoire of participation skills. Role assignment and role rotation create a situation where no one bears an undue burden, and no one is stuck in a less influential position.

In some of the cooperative learning exercises that I use, I insure shared influence by timing each person's participation. When my students freewrite, for example, in a write, pair, share, move exercise (which I will explain later), I often have them take two minutes each to share their thinking. I keep a stopwatch and let them know when it's time to start and stop. Student 1 begins and at the end of two minutes, I say, "Number 2, please." and Student 2 starts to talk. No one interrupts the speaker, whose responsibility it is to fill the two minutes with thinking out loud. It is simply not possible for any one person to take over or anyone to fade into the background.

This feature of shared influence and shared participation is what attracted me to cooperative learning in the first place. As a woman, I had grown weary of being in groups where men took over. I was tired of having to spend a disproportionate amount of time either listening to what they said, or bulldozing my way into the heart of the discussion. Cooperative learning spares me that discomfort, thereby freeing my mind to think thoughts of substance, rather than planning my strategy for participation.

Deliberate structure makes the difference. I've watched groups of students work together without structure, and I've seen what happens "naturally." Those who are comfortable with leadership roles begin to take over; those less sure of themselves fade into the background. It doesn't take long before the group reflects what is a problem in the larger society: some people making decisions for everybody, and some resources going unused. Groups left to their own "natural" inclinations too often do the same old thing, and no one learns anything different. As educators, I believe, it is our responsibility to offer a model that supports equity and regards every voice as important.

Two years ago I asked students to write down at the end of the semester what the cooperative learning experience had been like for them. Below, an Hispanic student comments not only on his pleasure with his cooperative learning team in our writing class, but compares it to "group work" that he has experienced in other classes.

"I enjoy doing group work in our writing class, the group that we have is the best one out of all of my classes here at Cambridge. Everyone participates in the group equally, everyone has good things to add to the group, different background, good feedback, In my other group people don't always participate equally, there's not much talking. We go into strong debates, and don't get things accomplished, we do this in our group here, in other outside groups it has been the same. I have gotten a lot out of this group and look forward in working with the group, In the past I have not been talkative as I have been in this group. I at times surprise myself in how much I talk and participate."

3. Using Each Other As Resources

The third appealing feature of cooperative learning is getting students to use each other as resources. This may be the one feature that is most difficult for students to adjust to. My adult students have come through an educational system which taught them to use the teacher as the only human resource in the classroom. When they have a question, they ask the teacher. When they miss an assignment, they ask the teacher. When they want to know if what they have done is "right", they ask the teacher. Cooperative learning changes all this by encouraging students to ask each other their questions.

In my classes, for example, students routinely ask each other about their homework and help each other to solve problems. They also "cover" for each other when someone is absent. One designated member of the team collects handouts, takes legible notes, contacts the absent student the next day. I stay out of the way. In fact, if an absent student calls me to ask what he missed, I refer him to his teammates for assistance.

Three Strategies I Use and Like

I have chosen three cooperative learning strategies that I use frequently, even routinely, hoping that they will paint a picture of the kind of activity that goes on in my classroom.

Strategy 1: Write, Pair, Share, Move

"Write, Pair, Share, Move" is my variation of "Think, Pair, Share", which was developed by Kagan (1992). In Think, Pair, Share (which I also use from time to time), the teacher poses a question, students take a minute to think about the answer, then they turn to their neighbor and share their thinking. One of the most frequently used cooperative learning strategies, Think, Pair, Share "primes the pump," in each student's mind and makes for much richer class discussions.

In a Write, Pair, Share, Move exercise, instead of having students think in their heads, I have them freewrite for five minutes. Then they share with the other three members of their team. At the end of the round, they move on to the next team. We share as a class usually after rounds 2 and 4 – or whatever makes sense, given the material.

I often use a quote and some related questions for the exercise. The overhead projector works well with this exercise.

The quote might be, "Like many people, you may feel that the activity of discovering ideas to write about is the most mysterious part of the writing process. Where do these ideas come from? How can you draw a blank one minute, and suddenly know just the right way to support your argument or describe your experience the next? Is it possible to increase your ability to think and write creatively?" (Ede, 1992, p. 92).

I would then follow up with these questions in separate and

subsequent rounds of writing and sharing:

1. What do you currently do to get yourself started with a writing assignment?

2. What kinds of things do you think about, and what do you do?

3. How does what you do compare with what our writing text book suggests?

4. Which of the (textbook) author's suggestions have you tried?

5. Which appeal to you; which do not?

6. Of all that you have said and heard in the last fifteen minutes, what one new strategy might you try some time?

7. Why have you chosen this one?

8. What appeals to you about it?

Strategy 2: Check-in Routine

The "Check-in Routine" is a cooperative learning strategy that accomplishes two important goals. First, it gets students in the habit of relying on each other for information and support. Secondly, it is a record keeping system that takes an enormous amount of clerical work off my shoulders.

The Check-in Routine was developed by Dee Dishon of Cooperation Unlimited. I was reluctant to try the Check-in Routine at first; it is designed for young children and I wasn't sure whether adults would take to it. The results have been astounding, however, and I now consider it an essential aspect of my teaching. The procedure takes a little getting used to, but once students get the hang of it, it works.

In brief, it works like this: I put students into heterogeneous groups of four. At the beginning of each class, I pass out each team's folder, which contains the previous week's assignments, read and graded by me. Students retrieve these papers and check them. Then they insert the current assignment. They have approximately twenty minutes to compare notes, help each other with any unfinished homework and decide if there is anything that they need to ask me. At the end of twenty minutes, we talk as a class about the assignments and I respond to any unresolved dilemmas. The Check-in Routine teaches students to use each other as resources.

Another benefit of the Check-in Routine comes from the personal sharing that team members do. In between the conversations about homework, students talk about their lives. They discuss their professional work, their spouses and children, and whatever else is on their minds. In this way they get to know one another, learn to care about one another, and to make connections on a more than superficial level. This fairly typical story will help to illustrate the way in which this happens.

Felicia and Catherine were two members of a four-person Check-in team three years ago in one of my writing classes. Felicia was an African-American woman from a lower socioeconomic group who came to Cambridge College with only a high school education. She was at the beginning of her professional career, and anxious about starting so late in life. In contrast, Catherine was an Anglo-American, middle class woman, and a vice president of a large bank in the region. Catherine's formal academic background was weak, but she had been trained and groomed by her bank to a level of relative sophistication. Felicia and Catherine were strangers when they were first placed in the same Check-in team.

It didn't take long for them to discover what they had in common, both personally and academically. They had both been through a divorce recently, both had teenage girls, and neither had immediate family nearby. They shared their struggles frequently and seemed to enjoy each other's support. Academically, they discovered that they had complementary skills. Felicia had the ability to pull from Catherine what she was really thinking. She could detect when Catherine's thought processes weren't clear, and she had a talent for asking just the right questions. Catherine, on the other hand, was strong in the technical aspects of writing and would work with Felicia on the final drafts of her papers. I knew we had broken through a barrier the day that I heard Catherine offer to take Felicia's youngest child for the weekend – and Felicia accepted the offer.

Strategy 3: Pass a Problem

"Pass a Problem" is an adaptation of Spencer Kagan's strategy, "Send A Problem." I like it mostly because it requires students to use higher level thinking skills. In Pass a Problem exercises, students not only solve several problems, they compare and contrast more than one right answer, and defend their choices. In the diverse setting where I teach, Pass a Problem works nicely in getting people who are different to work together in a non-pressured situation.

I've used Pass a Problem in my writing class in a variety of ways: we worked with mechanics on one occasion, the development of thesis statements another time, and, at still another, an editing exercise, which works particularly well.

In brief, Pass a Problem works like this: Students are assigned to teams of two; I do the assigning most of the time so that the gender and race of each team member is different. "Problems" are in a manila folder and remain at stations around the room. The dyads move from problem to problem, solving each, and submitting a written solution that they place inside the manila folder. When the next dyad arrives at that station, they solve the same problem without looking at the previous dyad' s solution.

The dyads spend thirty minutes on each problem; I keep track of time. At the end of two hours, each dyad has worked at solving four problems. In the final round, the dyad takes all of the answers out of the manila folder and decides which answer is best and why.

Pass a Problem has yielded some fascinating discussions. When the last round has been completed and we talk as a class, there is ample opportunity to examine why one solution is preferable to another, and to consider how many different solutions might be equally effective, given a certain set of goals and circumstances.

Freedom Within Structure

Cooperative learning strategies can appear to be overly structured, and therefore limiting. Over time and with practice, however, just the opposite is true. Once a teacher has mastered the basics, cooperative learning structures offer freedom, choice and flexibility .

On a very practical level, I exploit cooperative learning strategies for their ability to suit the particular needs of my students. As working adults, my students come to school at 6 o'clock in the evening, tired from a long day at work, and stressed out from the traffic and parking problems that they probably encountered. They are also hungry; many have not had time to eat dinner. Class goes on until 9:30; that's a long haul.

I begin class with the twenty-minute Check-in Routine that allows them to get connected with each other. It also provides them with a forum to blow off steam from a frustrating day, or the bumper to bumper traffic on Route 91.

About halfway through the evening they need a pick me up. It is then that I insert a cooperative learning exercise that gets them physically active. For example, I might ask students to shove all of the desks to the outside and do a "Three-Step Interview" (Kagan, 1992), which keeps people on their feet, moving around the room, and exchanging ideas with new and different classmates.

The most important way in which I use the freedom, choice and flexibility that cooperative learning offers is in enabling students to air and honor different perspectives. What Rod and Denise did as a pair in the Pass a Problem Exercise, can happen for the whole class as well. For example, if I am trying to teach a particular concept about writing and a student asks a question that tells me that he is coming to the material from a different set of assumptions, I stop the process. We do a Write, Pair, Share, for example, and students, some for the very first time, get to sort out their assumptions and identify their own perspectives. We share them as a class and we get practice at hearing other points of view. A norm for respecting differences is established.

When this happens in a racially mixed classroom, students have a chance to understand how points of view are often rooted in the different kinds of experiences that racial groups have. When students feel free to bring their assumptions and perspectives to the learning, and those assumptions and perspectives get aired and honored, barriers come down and bridges get built.

Not long ago, my writing class was discussing an article on diversity that they had read for a writing assignment. I had pointed out one line in the article that said, in essence, that the white men who created the U.S. Constitution could not have adequately represented the interests of all of the people that they claimed to represent. Willie was saying that it is impossible for a white man to have the perspective of anyone other than a white man.

Scott, a white male student, in the class suggested that that was an unfair statement. He said that what Willie was doing was applying a 1994 idea to a 1776 event, and that people then couldn't have known what we know now about the desirability of a diverse group. A black man in the class responded; the notion that Willie's idea was a modern day invention was a bit offensive to him. The white man's comment also seemed to deflect responsibility for having let a group of white men make decisions for a diverse population. Mike, the black man, was apparently irritated. "You should see what I see every day," he said directly to Scott. "I get ignored every day of my life; I get excluded from decisions, and my opinion gets considered only when it's convenient for the white bosses. What Willie says is true now, and it was in 1776." The room was charged with feelings.

Ten exchanges later, Scott was still not fully convinced that the statement was fair, but he was able to acknowledge the struggle of Mike's day-to-day life. They also found some common ground; both Mike and Scott agreed that a homogeneous group cannot fairly represent a heterogeneous population.

A Final Note

What both black and white Americans fear are the sacrifices and risks that true racial harmony demands. This fear is the measure of our racial chasm (Steele 1990, p. 20).

I use cooperative learning mainly because it enhances learning. It changes the student from a passive recipient to an active seeker of knowledge. It stimulates interaction, and it opens up the process of learning so that a variety of perspectives and styles come into play.

But its ability to promote racial harmony is its special gift to humanity. For a student of any subject at any age, cooperative learning provides what I believe to be one of the most effective methods for helping people to learn how to work together with people who are different from themselves.

I do not think that it is easy, but I am willing to make the effort. I am willing to accept those moments of discomfort; I don't mind failing periodically. In the interest of working toward victory over a social phenomena that has kept us all in pain for so long, it doesn't seem like much of a price to pay.

In *The Content of Our Character*, Shelby Steele talks about the importance of making *the effort*. In the beginning of the book, he tells the story of having gone to a dinner party where there were six whites and two blacks. The party had preceded smoothly, and after dinner, as everyone was sipping wine and relaxing, one of the black guests made a comment about his daughter going off to a school where she is one of three black students. His concern was that she would "lose touch" with her blackness.

The comment shut the dinner party down. People tuned out, left the room or stared into space. But no one wanted to talk about what the guest's comment meant. No one asked; no one answered. Awkward as it might have been, no one made the effort.

Our classrooms must be places where we make the effort, where we work with our students so that racial harmony becomes something that we can all talk about. Cooperative learning provides structures which enable students of different races to work together, and then provides mechanisms for helping them to understand what happened. There are awkward moments, moments when it would have been easier never to have asked the question. But the effort is what matters right now, and cooperative learning is one effective way to help teachers make that effort.

References

Allport, G. (1954). *The Nature of Prejudice.* Reading, Mass: Addison Wesley Publishing Co.

Amir, Y. (May, 1969) . "Contact Hypothesis in Ethnic Relations." *Psychological Bulletin.* Vol. 71, no 5, 319-343.

Ede, L. (1992). *Work in Progress* (2nd edition). New York: St. Martin's Press.

Kagan, S. (1992). *Cooperative Learning.* San Juan Capistrano, Calif: Resources for Teachers, Inc.

Slavin, R.E. & Oickle, E. (1981). "Effects of Cooperative Learning Teams on Student Achievement and Race Relations: Treatment by Race Interactions." *Sociology of Education*, vol. 54, 174-180.

Slavin, R.E. (1985). "Cooperative Learning: Applying Contact Theory in Desegregated Schools." *Journal of Social Issues*, vol, 41, no 3, 45-62.

Smith, B. L. MacGregor, J.T. (1992). "What is Cooperative Learning?" In A. Goodsell, M. Mather, V. Tinto, B. L. Smith, J. MacGregor (Eds.) *Cooperative Learning: A Sourcebook for Higher Education.* University Park, Pa: National Center on Post Secondary Teaching, Learning, and Assessment.

Steele, S. (1990). *The Content of Our Character.* New York: St. Martin's Press.

Williams, R. M., & Harlan, H. H. (1942). "Some Factors Affecting Attitudes Toward Jews," *American Sociological Review*, vol 7, 816-833.

Chapter 16

The School of Education's Role in Healing Racism

by Nathan Rutstein

Schools of education have a special responsibility for healing racism. They need to know and assess objectively whether their programs are effective in helping teachers and schools overcome racism in America. The author, one of the co-editors of this book, feels that an organic change in curriculum and attitude is necessary. The author's recommendations may seem radical, but, through his work across the country, he sees what's happening when teachers don't understand the true nature of the race problem. Ed.

Many teachers and principals groan every time they hear a politician, clergyman or parent call for schools to play a more meaningful role in solving society's mounting social problems.

They point out – rightfully – that it is unfair to expect a teacher to function as a psychotherapist, a race relations counselor or a policeman. For one thing, they are not trained or paid to do that kind of work. And when, they are forced by circumstances to do it, some mistakes are made. And that usually compounds education's present-day crisis, often widening the chasm between parents and schools, and further depressing education's already sagging reputation.

So it seems that our school systems are faced with a choice: Continue with what is being done now; or seriously restructure learning environments, teaching approaches and the training of prospective and practicing educators to meet the new demands of the teaching profession. Personally, I don't think it is much of a choice, because the former can only lead to doom, and the latter to hope.

If we expect our schools to play a significant role in healing the disease of racism, our university schools of education need to prepare all prospective teachers and educational administrators on how to become effective healers of a social disease that is eroding the soul of America.

Practicing teachers and administrators should receive similar training from schools of education. Funding for such efforts could come from state departments of education or local school systems, or a combination of both. Financial aid could also come from private foundations and federal agencies.

It is essential that the school of education help all of its students understand the nature of the American race problem: That we are confronted with a disease, certainly not a bacterial or viral infection, but rather an emotional disorder as described by Harvard's Dr. John Woodall in an earlier chapter. The students must also be exposed to the impact the disease of racism has on all of us, especially people of color. Without that knowledge, the teacher will be unable to help heal the wound that most African-American, American Indian and Latino children bring with them every time they enter a classroom. Not only that! When teachers are unaware of the wound, they unwittingly deepen it — of course never intending to. It is important to note, that all the good intentions in the world of a teacher will not prevent that from happening. Later in this chapter you will be exposed to a method (the Institute for the Healing of Racism), which is designed to help the participant gain an understanding of the pathology of racism and how it impacts on people.

To train prospective teachers to create and maintain a racially harmonious classroom, where all pupils feel comfortable in a stimulating learning environment, the school of education needs to offer the following core courses:

1. Discovering , Releasing and Developing Human Potential.

It is important to keep in mind that the word education stems from the Latin word "educare", which means to draw out. What is to be drawn out from our students? Human potentialities. Unfortunately, in most of our schools today a lot more effort is put forth in pushing in than in drawing out.

When some of a child's potentialities are discovered and released and he recognizes them, he is usually impressed and develops self-respect and self-worth, a condition that is often missing in students of color. He begins to understand who he really is. With self-knowledge, a child starts to feel good about himself – which generates internal strength and security. Instead of directing his energy and attention to his ineptness and insecurities, he's enthusiastically focused on the world outside of himself, exploring it and experiencing a sense of fulfillment through his discoveries. He is motivated to want to learn more, and often develops a passion for learning. When this happens, he seeks guidance from reliable sources on how to develop those potentialities that have been released. By engaging in such a process, a "minority" student usually overcomes his low self-esteem, believes he's a member of the human race, and acts accordingly. I witnessed this transformation take place while I was teaching at Springfield Technical Community College.

2. The Oneness of Knowledge.

As nations grow more interdependent and gravitate toward planetary unity, there is a growing awareness that knowledge is interrelated, actually one, which scholars in the past, even great ones, divided and multiplied — and today's educational systems usually reflect. Schools still compartmentalize knowledge by teaching reading for an hour, then turning to mathematics; an hour later teaching history, followed by writing, then science. School curricula should reflect the oneness of knowledge.

For example, a curriculum could be based on exploring the essence and meaning of life. From this approach, students would gain a meaningful understanding of the purpose of life, something most students don't have today, causing deep uncertainty and insecurity. They would also gain a better sense of their relevance to the rest of creation; and through that ongoing effort they would gain a better understanding of themselves, which would stimulate an appreciation for the need to grow spiritually and intellectually, and acquire the ability to sustain the growth.

Of course, basic cognitive skills would not be neglected. But they would be taught differently from the way they are presently being taught. Mathematics, science, language development, social science won't be viewed as separate subjects, but as aspects of a dynamic reality. And every attempt will be made to relate learning to the real world, something I have learned most "minority" students find attractive.

A whole unit could be devoted to studying trees because they are an important aspect of life. For most of us, trees are common objects; yet they must have some purpose other than being a solace to the eyes. Before doing anything else, the teacher would make students aware of how trees contribute to human survival. The point would be made in such a way that students would gain an appreciation of how trees impact on them personally. With that understanding, students would be more likely to want to know more about trees and be more attentive in class.

The seventh grader would gain a mathematical experience by measuring the circumferences of the biggest and smallest trees on a lawn, and trying to determine the exact difference in size. Armed with the knowledge that all of the trees were planted on the same day ten years earlier, the student would be faced with a challenging science problem; why aren't all the trees the same size? Another science challenge would be — why do leaves turn brilliant color in the fall in New England, why are trees used to combat smog. Comparing human digestion and growth with the process of photosynthesis would also be a challenge. Learning what role wood plays in our economy, and having students list all of the products made from trees that are essential to their lives would offer meaningful social studies lessons. Having students prepare a ten-minute speech on how they would have to reorganize their lives if wood were no longer available would stimulate deep analytical thinking. And having students write essays on how trees affect their physical well-being would not only be an English composition lesson, but it would also reinforce the linkage between humans and trees, a reality that would have been introduced at the outset of the unit. Tapping syrup from maple trees, processing it, and selling the finished product could be a rich learning experience, encompassing science, economics and marketing. Writing poems, composing songs and painting pictures of trees could generate creative energy in students.

When he is taught this way, I discovered, the "minority" student finds himself on the same level of the playing field as the European-American student, who usually does well in the more traditional learning systems. No longer in an environment that evokes fear of failure, the "minority" student finds himself in a situation where his European-American counterpart is struggling to make adjustments to a new learning system. In the end, both will benefit a lot more from the "Oneness of Knowledge" approach, because they will be better prepared to relate what they have learned to the real world.

3. Integrating the Principle of the Oneness of Humankind into the School Curriculum.

This is an essential step beyond multi-culturalism, which at best creates a state of toleration, which is a fragile condition. A rumor or an irrational remark can dash that condition, and men and women revert to their old anti-social ways. Also, the way multi-culturalism is taught in North America, it can only lead to sophisticated apartheid. Check most "integrated" schools and colleges and you'll see what I mean. Blacks stay with blacks, and whites with whites.

Though an appreciation of diversity is necessary, just emphasizing the differences can lead to both overt and covert feelings of cultural superiority. Actually, all human beings have a lot more in common than they have differences. Most of the differences are superficial. The fact is that we all belong to the same species, the same family.

Our differences are trival in a biological sense. In fact, genetists estimate that the variations of genetic makeup regarding racial differences occupy only about 0.01 percent of our genes. Genetically, every human being is 97 percent similar. School of education students should learn how to integrate the oneness of humankind principle into the school curricula, not only because it is a vaccine against the disease of racism, but because it is an aspect of reality — the truth. Isn't one of the main objectives of education to expose students to the truth?

A review of the previous chapters dealing with teaching the principle of the oneness of humankind will give you a good idea of some of the different approaches that can be used. What I have observed is that those teachers who have gained an understanding of the realities underlying the principle of the oneness of humankind have been able to overcome their subconscious belief that European-American students are superior to students of color. As a consequence, they find themselves able to reach students they once viewed as beyond reach.

4. Identifying and Healing the Wound that Afflicts the Student of Color

This course is absolutely essential if present-day school systems want to end the unintentional psychological murder of students of color in our classrooms. To be able to identify the wound, the school of education student must undergo a serious review of the studies that have been done as to how schooling has affected black, Latino and American Indian children. The psychological and physiological impact should be stressed. With such knowledge, the prospective teacher will not only have an accurate understanding of why many students of color do poorly in school, but they will be motivated to want to create learning environments and teaching approaches that will put an end to a wounded student's desire to flee or fight in the classroom.

Keep in mind – to create such environments and approaches will require supplanting traditional educational principles with new ones. These principles are a must: Discovering and releasing and developing the potential of students; the oneness of knowledge;

integrating the principle of the oneness of humankind into the curricula; relating learning to the real world; and cooperative learning.

5. On Becoming a Loving Teacher

Should a school of education student master all of his courses and yet lack love, he'll fall far short of becoming a successful teacher, for love is an irreplaceable bonding agent. "Minority" students in particular respond positively to the genuine expression of love. If a teacher fails to bond with his students, there is usually distrust between the two, and the student's cerebral cortex is affected. When unqualified love is expressed in the classroom, both teacher and students are caught up in a wavelength that transcends material differences and barriers. In that kind of atmosphere, students are more than attentive, they are involved in a process that is enriching them, and they like the feeling — and can't wait until the class meets again. Love is such an important quality in teaching that schools of education should provide programs designed to help students become more loving. To do this effectively, it is important to point out that the force of love is manifested in all levels of nature: the mineral, plant, animal and human levels. Love's origin and anatomy should be explored.

6. Parental Involvement in Their Children's Education

Because parents are a child's first teachers, special courses should be offered to help prospective teachers work effectively with parents in educating their children. Ideally, parents should identify their child's potentialities and talents and share their findings with a school teacher. With that information, the teacher's effort to discover, release and develop his students' potentialities will be enhanced. But the relationship shouldn't end there. Whatever the teacher discovers should be shared with the parents, establishing an ongoing interchange of information and suggestions designed to aid in the intellectual and social development of the student. If done properly, this teacher-parent alliance can only help the teacher carry out his responsibilities in a more thorough manner.

Of course, realistically, most of today's parents aren't equipped intellectually or psychologically to participate in such an alliance. This condition presents another challenge to the school of education: And that is to establish a special program that will produce certified teachers who will train parents on how to become educational partners with their children's school teachers.

7. The Institute for the Healing of Racism

To assure that educators become a positive force in helping to eliminate racism, a mechanism must be established in their workplace where they can confront and heal their own race infection or wounds in a non-threatening atmosphere. No one can be excluded from this responsibility, because we are all affected by racism, even those of us with the best intentions.

Such a mechanism has been developed, now operating in about two-hundred places, in churches, corporations, neighborhood centers, schools and colleges in North America and Britain. It is called the Institute for the Healing of Racism.

Every school of education should have one. With the institute functioning as a laboratory, everyone at the school, all of the students, faculty, administrators and staff members should participate for a minimum of two semesters. Why that long? Because there is no quick-fix to changing attitudes, especially attitudes as deep-rooted as race prejudice.

Participants will find themselves involved in a process where they are able to identify their racial infections or wounds, find the means to heal them and replace them with a genuine belief in the principle of the oneness of the human family.

The Institute for the Healing of Racism has two major goals: (1) For the participant to become a healer of racism in his or her community. For that to happen one must become involved in the healing process herself or himself. (2) For the participant to become a force for unity in his or her community.

There are five steps to achieving those two goals: (1) Internalizing and putting into practice the principle of the oneness of humankind. (2) Gaining an understanding of how racism developed in America. This means being exposed to a propaganda-free account of American history. (3) Gaining an understanding of the pathology of the disease of racism, and how it impacts on us. (4) Establishing an ongoing forum where the racially infected and wounded come together to help heal each other on an equal basis, and in a non-threatening atmosphere. It is an experience where we learn to listen more with the heart than the ear. In reality, it is more than engaging in ongoing dialogue; it is a form of group therapy. (5) Social action. Social action is the final step. By social action, I mean helping to establish institutes in other institutions. For example, every school and college should have an institute where faculty, administrators and staff members are involved in racial healing. Through this process, the participants will become equipped to create and maintain schools that no longer psychologically cripple students of color, but, instead, create learning environments and teaching approaches that help students discover, release and develop their potentialities; and develop within them a deep appreciation for the principle of the oneness of humankind. The latter is the vaccine for the disease of racism. If every school in America integrated the principle of the oneness of humankind into its curriculum, racism would be wiped out in two generations.

Those college students who undergo an Institute for the Healing of Racism experience will be motivated to start an institute wherever they teach. A school of education can offer a two-semester course on the Institute for the Healing of Racism, open to both undergraduate and graduate students.

The first semester would be an ongoing workshop where students became well grounded as institute facilitators and participants; and spend the second semester establishing an institute in local schools, headstart programs or youth centers.

To avoid bureaucratic stumbling blocks, this community-service type course could be offered as an independent study.

I know that some of the suggestions I have made seem radical. But these are difficult times; and racism is one of the difficulties that our society has not come to terms with in a meaningful way. Because what is being done in our schools to combat racism is failing, something different must be done; something that gets to the root of the problem.

I am convinced that without providing the kind of courses proposed in this chapter, schools of education will continue to produce educators who will, at best, unwittingly damage students of color in their classes. Not only that, the teachers will not be equipped to prevent other students from being infected by the virus of racism.

Appendix. Establishing an Institute for the Healing of Racism*

Mission

An *Institute tor the Healing of Racism* is founded in the belief that racism is the most powerful and persistent obstacle to the attainment of a just and peaceful society. An *Institute* recognizes the essential oneness of the human race; that all human beings share common ancestors; and that all of us share the responsibility to realize in our personal and social lives the oneness of humanity.

An *Institute* seeks to create an environment in which men and women of all races can address each other in a spirit of open and honest discussion, free of blame and victimization. The principle of trusting consultation, grounded in the belief that truth lies not in the individual perspective, but in the unity of diverse souls, is fundamental to every aspect of an *Institute.*

An *Institute* recognizes that racism is, above all else, a social and spiritual disease, a disease woven into the moral and spiritual fiber of society. It is born of ignorance and fear, which feed upon each other in a monstrous cycle. That of which we are ignorant becomes a source of fear. Fear itself breeds greater ignorance, which further magnifies fear, and so on.

The hope of breaking this cycle lies in the recognition that racism is a disease which takes little account of laws and statutes, but which

**This material was first published in "Healing Racism in America: A Prescription for the Disease" (1993).*

reaches deep into the individual heart and mind. It is felt that only through addressing racism in our own hearts can men and women of all races generate a compelling power to eradicate this pernicious disease which so cripples our nation and retards its progress toward true peace and justice.

Purpose

To accomplish its mission, an *Institute* must foster an understanding of how it affects all people. An *Institute* is based on the notion that whites suffer from an inherent and at times subconscious feeling of superiority, and that ceaseless exertions are required to overcome this attitude. In turn, the suspicion harbored by people of color, resulting from a legacy of oppression, must also be addressed. An *Institute* faces these challenges in a sensitive and non-threatening manner.

Honest and frank dialogue involving all races must occur so that individuals may help heal each other. In the process, mutual understanding develops, which evolves into genuine and sincere friendship and love.

An *Institute for the Healing of Racism* has two major purposes:

1. To help individuals heal their disease or wound, and

2. To become a center for social action, whose aim is to foster racial unity within the community.

How an *Institute* Functions

The purposes of an *Institute* are ultimately inseparable. Neither can operate as a complete remedy, for the wisdom gained through personal reflection must be coupled with action in order to have useful results. At the same time, becoming involved in social action without embracing the therapeutic process could be irresponsible.

Since denial is a major obstacle, participants in an *Institute* begin with group discussions designed to help identify and understand how racism is manifested and how it impacts all levels of society. With this knowledge, participants become motivated to rid themselves of the main elements responsible for perpetuating the disease and retarding the healing of the wound . They become ready to attack the problem.

In a trusting atmosphere, individuals do not hesitate to share their true feelings. They feel comfortable, as their views are shared, not as a form of confession, but with the realization that they are afflicted with a disease or a wound and want to become better.

In this trusting and helping atmosphere, it is easy to recognize that an *Institute* provides women and men with an opportunity to make a sincere attempt to cure their sickness or heal their wound. The sharing is not only a way to relieve inner pain, it is also an appeal for help. When people of color reveal what it is like to be patronized or rejected because of skin color treatment which in turn fuels deepseated suspicion - whites gain valuable insights into the ugly effects of the disease. Conversely, when whites openly describe their struggle to conquer feelings of superiority, people of color observe a meaningful effort to deal with deeply-ingrained emotions. Members of all races respond to each other with appropriate compassion and support, founded upon unconditional love. In this way, an *Institute* fosters a real attempt to destroy the root of a serious, pernicious social ill.

When genuine friendships are forged in this manner, the group evolves into a dependable force for social action. Armed with the knowledge of how hurtful racism is to a person and a community, members of the *Institute* become highly motivated to work to foster racial unity. Many *Institutes* involve themselves by promoting their principles through working with their local school systems. Others may choose another means of action for promoting social action. The key is that the *Institute* has galvanized its members into taking concrete action.

Suggested Topics

In order to galvanize the members into a strong and committed body, it is necessary for several sessions to be scheduled, at which time topics relating to racism can be discussed. No minimum or maximum number of sessions is required. Participants will be ready to suggest a plan of action when they have attained a spirit of love and harmony amongst themselves.

The following topics are suggested:

1. Defining prejudice and racism.
2. How racism is perpetuated – early childhood experiences, misinformation and segregation.
3. The pathology of the disease of racism and the nature of the wound.
4. Unaware racism – how we've all been infected.
5. Internalized racism when the anger, hurt and frustration turn inward.
6. Stereotypes and how they affect us.
7. Institutionalized racism – examples of its presence in the systems that affect us daily – media, legal, school, health care, economics.
8. Oneness and humanity – achieving unity and preserving diversity.
9. Ally-building as a way to heal racism – an individual commitment.

Guidelines for Sharing

Sharing is voluntary.

We want to create a safe, loving, and respectful atmosphere.

Sharing is about one's own feelings, experiences and perceptions, etc.

We are not always going to agree, or see everything the same way, and that's OK.

Each person has a right to and responsiblity for his or her own feelings, thoughts and beliefs

It is important to avoid criticism or judgment about another person's sharing and point of view or his or her feelings.

Avoid getting tied up in debate and argument. It rarely changes anything or anyone, and tends to ultimately inhibit the sharing.

We can only change ourselves. Our change and growth may, however, inspire someone else.

Refrain from singling out any individual as "representing" his or her group or issue.

It is important to give full attention to whomever is talking.

Feelings are important.

We will surely make mistakes in our efforts, but mistakes are occasions for learning and forgiving.

We came together to try to learn about the disease of racism and promote a healing process.

We may laugh and cry together, share pain, joy, fear and anger.

Hopefully, we will leave these meetings with a deeper understanding and a renewed hope for the future of humanity.

Role of the Facilitator

Facilitators must be able to present both the purpose and format of the healing circle in a clear, concise and attractive manner.

Facilitators must be careful to set an example of the kind of behavior that they are striving to encourage in the participants.

Facilitators should find themselves being excited about the process of healing racism, and plan actions leading to their own transformation.

Facilitators should act as instructors by helping participants look for key ideas and find implications for action.

Facilitators should carefully guide the group so that it functions within its intended purpose.

Facilitators must help individuals in the group reflect spiritual attributes, such as personal dignity, courtesy and reliability during sessions.

Facilitators should foster honest communication that is both tactful and constructive, and should themselves be good listeners.

Facilitators must accept in a non-judgmental manner the values and feelings of the group participants, and be able to feed back to the group in a positive, loving way what they perceive, hear and see without adding their own attitudes, feelings and prejudices.

Guidelines for Facilitators

Become familiar with exercises/outline before entering the meeting.

– What points do you want to bring out in the discussion?

– What issues do you think the group will bring up?

Arrive early to be abreast of any last-minute instructions.

– Create necessary seating arrangement (if applicable).

State purpose of session and begin with introductions.

– Give general outline of events to take place during the workshop.

– Be concise in your statements.

– Do some kind of ice-breaker activity to make group feel comfortable, at ease with you. (They will be somewhat familiar with each other.)

– Show enthusiasm.

Use listening skills.

– Listen for content and context of statements as well as effective level.

– Ask questions to check accuracy of what you're hearing: *"Do you mean?"*

– Paraphrase the person's comments in non-judgmental terms: *"Are you saying you never thought about white privilege?"*

Feedback is descriptive rather than evaluative. By describing one's own reaction, you leave the individual free to use the feedback as he or she sees fit. By avoiding evaluative language, you reduce the likelihood of a defensive reaction.

Be flexible and maintain some control of the group.

– Do not let one person monopolize conversation.

– Do not let one person get ganged up on, or allow a two-way debate between participants.

– Draw the quiet or passive participants into the discussion.

– Be assertive without intimidating.

– Roadblocks may arise in the discussion. Use feedback at times like this. Highlight a group dynamic you see active; be open (yet selective) to sharing from your own experience. You may also want to circle back to a previous comment. People may still need/want to talk, but do not know where to go. In these cases relate their last comment with an inflection that makes it into a question.

– Do not be afraid of silence. Do not put words into participants' mouths or succumb to the urge to steer them to what you feel is a right answer. Try and be comfortable with a participant's inability to be articulate about the point, recognizing, however, what the person has tried to say. Be affirming, supportive and directive where possible.

Leave time for closure.

– Try to leave people feeling empowered to change rather than depressed.

– Stress that this is only a beginning. Encourage them to seek other resources and continue working on these issues.

Some close-out questions.

– What have you learned today?

– What have you thought about in a new way this morning/ afternoon?

– What concerns have challenged you? Can we brainstorm about potential things to do?

– How can we stay in touch to discuss future developments involving the diverse issues we explored today?

Material for this guide was assembled from various Institute sources by Dr. Mark Rossman, director of graduate studies at Ottawa University, Phoenix, Arizona, and a member of the Executive Advisory Board for the Institute for the Celebration of Cultural Diversity in Scottsdale, Arizona.

For assistance in establishing an Institute for the Healing of Racism, please contact Whitcomb Publishing, 32 Hampden Street, Springfield, MA 01103 - Tel: 1-800-354-1789.

ABOUT THE CONTRIBUTORS

Robert Atkinson

Robert Atkinson is associate professor of human development and director of the Center for the Study of Lives in the College of Education at the University of Southern Maine. He graduated from Long Island University, Southampton Campus, and has master's degrees in American folk culture from the State University of New York (Cooperstown), and in counseling from the University of New Hampshire. His Ph.D. is in cross-cultural human development from the University of Pennsylvania. He has taught at Chicago, Pennsylvania, and Harvard Universities, has co-authored *The Teenage World: Adolescent Self-Image in Ten Countries* (Plenum, 1988) edited *Songs of the Open Road: The Poetry of Folk-Rock and the Journey of the Hero* (New American Library, 1974), and written for many magazines and journals, including *Psychology Today, Encyclopedia Britannica,* and *Audubon.* He is also the author of *The Power of Stories: Autobiography, Personal Mythmaking, and Life Stories as Tools for Transformation.*

Brian Aull

Brian Aull earned his Ph.D. in electrical engineering at MIT in 1985, and works as a staff scientist there. He has been active in the Coalition for a Strong UN. He was chairperson of the Cambridge Peace Commission for two years, a founder of the Alliance for Our Common Future, and is a co-author of "Healing Racism: Education's Role" in this book. He spent a year in Taiwan as a visiting professor.

Denise Gifford

Dr. Denise Dickerson Gifford is vice president of student affairs at the University of Louisville, an urban institution with a student population of 21,500.

Dr. Gifford holds an Ed.D. degree in higher education administration from the University of Kentucky, an M.Ed. in student personnel administration from Ohio University, and a B.S. in hearing and speech science, also from Ohio University.

As vice president for student affairs, Dr. Gifford is responsible for the administration of three divisions of the University of Louisville that serve and affect all students: Student Life, Student Development, and Student Services.

Barbara Hacker

Barbara Hacker teaches a Montessori primary class of three- to seven-year-old children at the Post Oak School in Houston, Texas. She has training and certification by the Association of Montessori Internationals at both the primary and infant levels, and has been practicing Montessori education for over twenty years. Additionally, she has a B.A. in sociology/urban studies from the College of Wooster, and an M.Ed. degree and Certificate of Advanced Study from Harvard Graduate School of Education, where her concentration was in human development.

She is a founding member of the Center for the Healing of Racism, a Houston area nonprofit organization, and currently serves as co-executive director as well as workshop facilitator and speaker for the organization.

Paul Herron

Paul Herron is a neuroscientist and an assistant professor of anatomy and neurobiology at the University of Tennessee, Memphis. He studies how alterations in experience and brain chemistry affect brain functioning. He received his B.S. in chemistry, M.S. in psychology, and Ph.D. in psychology and neuroscience from Michigan State University. His study and work have given him the opportunity to live in several different parts of the United States, and in Australia, and Canada. He has taught and lectured on a variety of subjects in the classroom and the laboratory for undergraduate, graduate, medical and dental students, and in mentoring programs for local high school students.

He has experienced firsthand the virulent effects of racism in schools from his own childhood. He grew up in Mississippi at a time when state law mandated that primary and secondary schools, colleges, and universities be racially segregated.

LeNise Jackson-Gaertner

LeNise Jackson-Gaertner is a community activist and founder of MOTHERS FOR RACE UNITY AND EQUALITY, a non-profit organization to "dismantle racist attitudes, socio-economic prejudice, and cultural intolerance through promoting multicultural awareness." Her expertise as an adjunct lecturer and consultant/ facilitator in race relations and multicultural issues has been recognized by school districts, universities, community organizations, and parent groups for whom she holds workshops, seminars, and public speaking engagements. Mrs. Gaertner is the co-instructor for a class called "Racism and the Role of Education" with Dr. Esteban Diaz, the associate dean for the School of Education at California State University, San Bernardino.

Mrs. Gaertner was commended in 1991 by Congressman George Brown, the Alternative to Gangs Unit program for the City of Paramount, and in 1992-1994 by the County of Los Angeles for her work on diversity with educators, parents and the community. She began her organization for the sake of her five African-European-American children, and ultimately all children and adults hurt by racism and cultural intolerance.

Lynn Kirk

Lynn Kirk has been teaching and training for thirty years. She has taught on junior high, high school, college, and, currently, adult levels. She is an associate professor at Cambridge College in Springfield, Massachusetts, and is coordinator of the college's writing program. She has a B.A. from Millersville University in Pennsylvania, an M.Ed. from Duke University, and an Ed. D. from the University of Massachusetts in Amherst.

Patricia Locke

Patricia Locke, a Hunkpapa Lakota and Chippewa of the Mississippi Band, lives on the Standing Rock Reservation in South Dakota. A. MacArthur Fellow (1991-1996), she is the 1992-1993 Libra Distinguished Visiting Professor in the College of Education at the University of Southern Maine, and an advocate for the sovereignty of Indian nations in education. She assisted seventeen Indian nations in the establishment of tribally-controlled colleges on their reservations, and is currently helping twelve Indian nations to develop their own codes of education and education departments. At the University of California at Los Angeles her undergraduate and graduate work was in the fields of education and public administration. She taught at UCLA, San Fernado Valley State College, Alaska Methodist University, Denver University, and the University of Colorado at Boulder. She is the author of twenty-eight articles and publications.

Michael Morgan

Michael Morgan is an assistant professor of English at Murray State University in Murray, Kentucky, where he has taught for four years. Besides teaching graduate and undergraduate courses in English, he serves as director of the Murray State University English Language Institute, which specializes in teaching English as a second language to students from all over the world. Dr. Morgan has taught and traveled in Africa, East Asia and the Middle East. He is advisor to the Murray State chapter of Alpha Phi Alpha fraternity, a predominantly African-American fraternity. He earned his doctorate at the University of Massachusetts in Amherst in 1993.

Robert Postlewaite

Robert Postlewaite teaches English at Taiwan's Cheng Chi University. He earned his bachelor's degree at the University of Kansas, and his master's at Harvard University's Graduate School of Education.

Anita Remignanti

Anita Remignanti is a psychologist in private practice in New Hampshire. She received her doctoral degree from Rutgers University in 1980. After teaching psychology for a year, she began to see children and families in psychotherapy. She specialized in psychological testing for children and adolescents with attention deficit disorder and related behavioral problems. Anita and her husband, Drew, have three children, Kirk (14), Ben (12) and Laine (8) and a dog named Max. Anita organizes a youth program and theater.

Nathan Rutstein

Nathan Rutstein has written eleven books, including *To Be One: A Battle Against Racism* and *Healing Racism in America: A Prescription for the Disease.* He is a former network news journalist and a retired professor, having taught at Springfield Community Technical College and at the University of Massachusetts at Amherst. He has lectured at scores of universities and government institutions on the topic of racism, and is one of the founders of the Institutes for the Healing of Racism, of which there are over 150 operating in North America. Rutstein has produced a documentary entitled "Black and White in Springfield" and is a former consultant to the White House Conference on Children.

Tod Rutstein

Tod Rutstein has been active in efforts to improve race relations for a number of years, most recently through his association with the Institute for the Healing of Racism. In 1989, he co-authored a position paper entitled "Healing Racism: Education's Role" which led to the creation of a nationwide network of these institutes. On the local level, he helped found Baltimore's chapter in 1990, and currently serves on its steering committee. Mr. Rutstein has conducted workshops as a member of the AWARENESS TO ACTION consulting team throughout the Middle Atlantic region as well as in New England and the Southwest. In 1989, he served on the steering committee that planned the Baltimore City Summit on Race Relations. For the past ten years he has been a member of the governing body for the Baha'is of Baltimore, a diverse group whose fundamental principles revolve around the concept of the oneness of humanity.

Since 1986, Mr. Rutstein has worked in the middle division of Friends School of Baltimore as a teacher of history and social studies. In this capacity, he has also been active in promoting healthy race relations.

Bernie Streets

Bernie Streets is co-director of the After School Program for New Morning Schools, Inc., at the Peter Woodbury Elementary School in Bedford, New Hampshire. In addition, he is a scientific/technical consultant to the food, beverage, and chemical industries and to governmental agencies. Since 1965, he has been a teacher of black history and actively lectures and presents seminars on this subject, as well as on racism and multi-culturalism, to various groups, schools, and colleges.

Donald Streets

Donald Streets is principal of Lindberg Elementary School in Mesa, Arizona. He has held a number of university appointments, including that of associate dean of graduate studies at Vista Campus of National University in San Diego. He has written several articles on the teaching of mathematics, and is a former special consultant to the Office of Child Development in Washington, D.C.

John Woodall

John Woodall, M.D., is a psychiatrist who specializes in the treatment of trauma and the psychological issues involved in conflict resolution. He is medical director of the post traumatic stress disorder clinical teams at the Brockton Veterans Administration Medical Center, and at the New England Shelter for Homeless Veterans in Boston. He is also on the clinical faculty at Harvard

Medical School's Department of Psychiatry. He was the founder and director of the Program on International Affairs and Conflict Resolution at the School of Medicine at the University of California, Irvine. His work in the field of ethnic conflict led to research, and the conduct of training programs and interventions in a variety of ethnic conflicts in the Middle East, the former Yugoslavia, Central America, Cyprus and in refugee populations in America. He has lectured extensively on the issue of racism in America for over twenty years, and taught a course on healing racism at Harvard University following the Rodney King trial.